Out-of-Body Experiences

PRAISE FOR *OUT-OF-BODY EXPERIENCES*

'Samantha Treasure's groundbreaking book stands as probably the most comprehensive review of the out-of-body experience yet published. The book is precise, refreshing and explores the intersections between personal experience, science and wider culture.' – **Graham Nicholls**, author of *Navigating the Out-of-Body Experience*

'Both wildly fun and informative. This book expertly walks the razor edge between scientist and experiencer. I loved it!' – **Robert Peterson**, author of *Hacking the Out of Body Experience*

'A rare example of the successful integration of original scholarly research and the kind of insight gained only through personal experience. This is a sensitive, nuanced exploration of the phenomenon, written in an engaging style. Out-of-Body Experiences is sure to be a landmark in the narrative anthropology of extraordinary experience, as well as deserving a place at the forefront of the new culturally informed psychical research.' – **Gregory Shushan**, PhD, author of *Near-Death Experience in Ancient Civilizations*

'A very lively exploration of the width, breadth and cultural depth of OBEs! If you're looking to broaden your mind, I highly recommend this book!' – **Robert Waggoner**, author of *Lucid Dreaming: Gateway to the Inner Self*

'Samantha Treasure's book on OBEs compels a dual reflection of her own namesake; the work should be both treasured as a trove of information, as well as a gleaming milestone in our mental maps as we strive to rediscover the jewel that is our own soul. The sheer synchrony of scholarliness and yet never shying from high weirdness is enough to spark in any reader that vivifying vertigo of double consciousness.' – **Pascal Michael**, PhD, Lecturer in Psychology, University of Greenwich

'Samantha's debut book is a refreshing, detailed and comprehensive exploration of out-of-body experiences. Far from being a sober academic tome, it is full of personal anecdotes, observations and experiences as well as fascinating interviews and insights from academics, shamans and experiencers alike. I particularly enjoyed the chapter on the liminal eeriness of OBEs, and the latter chapters that are dedicated to fieldwork with experiencers from around the world, most specifically, the revealing interviews with shamans in the Tuvan Republic of Siberia. Samantha's book is original, engrossing and totally without woo! A fascinating read and highly recommended to anyone interested in this astral phenomenon, either from a spiritual, scientific or anthropological standpoint.' – **Claire Gillman**, author of *Learning to Love the Spaces In Between: Discover the Power of Liminal Spaces*, and former editor of *Kindred Spirit* magazine

'Finally, a book that offers a captivating exploration of out-of-body experiences (OBEs), blending scientific insights, historical and cultural perspectives along with personal stories to make this phenomenon both relatable and fascinating. It's an essential read for anyone curious about the mysteries of consciousness and its implications for understanding the true nature of reality.' – **Tree Carr**, death doula and author of *Conscious Dreamer*

'Written in the first person, this book is easily readable. Samantha Lee Treasure's aim in writing is to demystify the phenomena of out-of-body experiences. Using in-depth case studies to make her point, she gives us clear examples of Eastern and Western traditions, and cultural understandings of the relationship between the dead and the living. It is a wide-ranging book which offers encyclopaedic comprehensive listings of a huge range of experiences including remote viewing, alien contact and astral travel, from all over the world including Europe: I enjoyed reading the chapter on her direct interaction with Tuvan shamanism. Samantha explores a potential connection with shamanic experiences, astral travel, lucid dreaming and out-of-body experiences, and suggests they are human capacities: anyone seeking training might do so within a controlled environment. Samantha notes that formerly people who had these experiences were stigmatized, and acknowledges the old assumed pathologies around those who had them in the West. She explores why out-of-body experiences are important, and addresses New Age narratives around commodification. I hope awareness of material in this book, around benevolent and negative experiences, might beneficially influence mainstream psychology and psychiatry: it should be on educational reading lists.' – **Dr Natalie Tobert**, Medical Anthropologist

'This book is Samantha Lee Treasure's personal journeys, geographic, intellectual and psychic, to understand the out-of-body experience. It is a journal exploring the inner-universes of our mind. This is far more than just a series of "it happened to me" anecdotes. It is the story of one woman's search for understanding of what she was experiencing. Most books look back on the history of the OBE, but this one brings the experience right up to date by focusing on the latest trends to be found in online communities and with modern youth. This is so important as it shows how modern technology is changing how the experience is interpreted. I can honestly state that this is probably the most important book I have ever read, and certainly one of the most enjoyable.' – **Anthony Peake**, author of *The Out-of-Body Experience: The History and Science of Astral Travel*

'In this original and important work, Samantha Lee Treasure presents a comprehensive introduction to the out-of-body Experience (OBE), its shifting phenomenology and cross-cultural significance. The book is an interdisciplinary exercise that draws together insights from ethnography, psychology, neuroscience and transpersonal research to reveal the complexity and diversity of the OBE experience. In combining richly described personal experience with detailed fieldwork – including interviews with numerous experiencers and practitioners – and extensive scholarly research, this book makes an important and engaging contribution to paranthropological and parapsychological research.' – **Jack Hunter**, PhD, author of *Manifesting Spirits: An Anthropological Study of Mediumship and the Paranormal*, and editor of *Deep Weird: The Varieties of High Strangeness Experience*.

Out-of-Body Experiences

Explorations and encounters with the astral plane

Samantha Lee Treasure

This edition published in 2025 by Arcturus Publishing Limited
26/27 Bickels Yard, 151–153 Bermondsey Street,
London SE1 3HA

AD011539UK

Printed in the UK

CONTENTS

Dedicated to Isaac, Freyja, Aoife
& Gran

FOREWORD

In February 2010, I was in the studios of BBC Radio Merseyside doing my regular slot on *The Billy Butler Show*. Each fortnight I select a topic and discuss it with Mr Butler and, if they're interested, members of his studio team. Sometimes we also receive callers who describe their experiences of, or give their opinions on, the subject in question. This particular day, I was discussing the phenomenon popularly known as near-death experiences (NDEs).

Within seconds of discussing this subject we had a caller phone in to the studio. The gentleman in question was keen to discuss with me an event that had taken place many years before, when he was doing his army national service in Malaya (now Malaysia) in the late 1950s. He explained that he had been up all night on watch duties and had just returned to the barracks. As he sat on his bunk, he realized that he had forgotten to wake the next soldier who was due to replace him outside. He got up and began to walk across the room to his fellow soldier's bunk. As he did so, he felt a strange sensation overcome him – so much so that he felt the need to turn around and look back at his bunk. To his shock, he saw himself, still sitting on the bed staring into space. Quite naturally, this scared the hell out of him and he rushed back across the room to jump back into his body. The next thing he knew he was waking up in his bunk, a few hours later.

It was clear from his tone of voice that this event had long been a mystery to him. He simply couldn't understand how he could find himself out of his body, looking at himself from a short distance away, especially as he hadn't been dying at the time (as the term near-death experience would imply); he had simply been exhausted. Yet this strange thing *had* happened to him that sultry night many years ago – something he described as 'totally uncanny' – and to which he was seeking an answer.

His use of the word 'uncanny' here is of great significance. This term, as it has come to be used in the last 150 years, has its origins in the writings of German philosopher Friedrich Wilhelm Schelling, specifically in his book *Philosophie der Mythologie* (1837). In this, he used the German word *unheimlich* to denote the uncanny or the strange. This literally translates into English as 'un-homely'. And a sense of 'un-homeliness' is exactly what the caller had experienced, given that we consider our body to be our 'home', and he had had what is called an 'out-of-body experience' (OBE). All out-of-body experiences are, quite literally, *unheimlich* in that they involve experiencing the world from another uncanny location.

And it is this sense of the uncanny that the author of this book, Samantha Lee Treasure, is willing to explore, going in search of answers to the many questions it poses. Samantha is an anthropologist in terms of academic training, but, just as importantly, she is also a life-long experiencer of out-of-body states. This gives her a unique perspective from both the phenomenological and the personal points of view.

This book is a narrative of Samantha's personal journeys – geographic, intellectual and psychic – in which she tries to *understand* the out-of-body experience. It reminds me of psychologist Benny Shannon's similar adventures regarding altered states engendered by psychedelics, as discussed in his influential book *Antipodes of the Mind: Charting the Phenomenology of the Ayahuasca Experience*

(2003). Like Shannon's work, Samantha's writing offers far more than just a series of 'it happened to me' anecdotes. It is the story of one woman's search for a true understanding of what she has been experiencing.

Samantha's writing style is an absolute treasure. She is continually at your side, as the narrator, as she describes in detail her own experiences, both of the OBE state itself, and also of her travels and encounters investigating this fascinating phenomenon. You will *share* in Samantha's adventures and puzzlement as she seeks answers. Yet, as an anthropologist, she also brings a rigid and considered structure to her text and, in doing so, she contributes a crucial, possibly even seminal, approach to the new academic studies known as paranthropology: the anthropology of the paranormal.

This is, in my opinion, an extraordinarily important book. It will make you think deeply about many subjects, but most of all, it is a fascinating read.

Enjoy...

Anthony Peake

INTRODUCTION

The out-of-body experience (OBE) is defined as the subjective perception of being outside of the physical body. This is often accompanied by diverse features including a sense of floating, viewing the body from the outside, travelling to other locations and wake-like cognition that allows reflection while it is happening.[1] OBEs can occur from wakefulness, sleep, dreaming or unconsciousness, and can be caused by a number of triggers, such as sensory deprivation, drug use, trauma and meditation.[2]

In recent years, the stigma of these experiences as dissociative, eerie, uncanny, mystical, 'weird' or 'woo woo' has been partially relaxed by scientific acknowledgement, with laboratories from Belgium to Argentina studying what happens in the brain during this state. OBEs have become a topic of scientific, medical and anthropological interest for what they can tell us about the mind–body connection and its impact on beliefs,[3] while also becoming a hot topic in the media and spiritual marketplace. Films and television often depict them as a superpower, a way to spy on others, or a witchcraft practice to communicate with supernatural entities and other living beings. At the same time, some social media influencers tout OBEs as a spiritual practice and a wellness tool, while often profiting from a niche but growing area of interest.

However, not *all* OBEs, or beliefs resulting from them, are welcome by either scientists or by marketeers wanting to sell courses, who may label certain aspects – often seen as meaningful in indigenous cultures – as pathological or less spiritually 'evolved' than others. In his book

Crazy Like Us: The Globalization of the American Psyche (2011), medical anthropologist Ethan Watters decried the impingement of Western frameworks onto other mental health narratives, which meant losing important knowledge about the human experience along the way. And as far back as 1989, anthropologist Franz Boas had urged researchers to respect all cultural practices and their cultural meanings in their *own* right, rather than forcing Western pathologies onto them.[4] Attempts to both destigmatize and commodify OBEs have resulted in the sanitizing of some of the stranger claims related to them, which in practice often lead to beliefs in telepathy, time travel, astral surveillance and astral attacks ('astral' simply meaning related to the non-physical plane of existence to which various psychic and paranormal activity are ascribed).

Although my initial plan in writing this book was to create a rational, sober and academically conservative account of OBEs that would help to destigmatize this phenomenon, it became more crucial to avoid any such sanitization, as well as any of the fear-mongering or sensational depictions that we so often see in the mainstream media. Instead, I hope to demystify – without disenchanting – some parts of the OBE phenomenon, and present both spiritual and scientific ideas which can be equally useful and comforting to experiencers and non-experiencers alike. Having had hundreds of OBEs myself, and also having spoken to hundreds of experiencers from a variety of backgrounds, I understand that OBEs are not necessarily spiritual, although they can lead to spiritual *ideas*. Accordingly, in this book I attempt to give voice to the broad range of differing practices, experiences and opinions that fall within a wider definition of the out-of-body experience than Western frameworks often allow for. Although this might come across as focusing on the negative side of things sometimes, this is only because it doesn't get talked about much, and I wanted to explore these areas in an unbiased way.

In places, I have used pseudonyms to protect the privacy of experiencers; where this is the case, the name is marked with an asterisk.

In Chapter 1, I recount my first experiences with OBEs in childhood and as an adult, which were triggered by astral projection practices. Chapter 2 reviews the approaches to OBEs within the realms of parapsychology (the study of alleged paranormal and psychic phenomena), which take into account a seeming connection with apparitions of the dead and living. In Chapter 3, the liminal eeriness of OBEs is described, alongside the role of both the temporoparietal junction (in the brain) and memory in shaping the nature of the experience, both in the immediate environment and when travelling further. This sets the foundation for Chapter 4, which delves deeper into the factors that make some people more cross-culturally susceptible to OBEs, including what is called 'cultural kindling', while Chapter 5 explores deliberate OBE induction practices and why they work.

The next four chapters then focus on what can happen once an out-of-body experience is achieved. This starts in Chapter 6 by discussing the 'transition' phenomena into OBEs, including vibration sensations and sounds that are often reported before the onset of the experience. Chapter 7 is dedicated to the curious experience of 'invisibility' to others within the OB environment; Chapter 8 then describes navigation, including the feeling of being pulled to certain locations, and the existence of the controversial 'cord', and, in Chapter 9, I recount the strange, recurring experiences that I had once my personal OBE practice was 'kindled', and my struggle fitting these 'Future Tokyo' experiences into my view of the world.

Chapters 10 to 14 are dedicated to fieldwork with experiencers, starting with people who report alien or interdimensional contact, before moving on to the members of a new religious movement called Eckankar, whose practice of 'Soul Travel' is at the core of their beliefs. Next, we review claims of witches who use astral travel for nefarious purposes, before interviewing Jane, a modern 'hedge witch' whose out-of-body experiences have been a tremendous source of comfort to her. Chapter 13 is part cultural criticism and part personal account of the 'astral' aisle in today's spiritual marketplace, and how New Age narratives can affect experiencers. Chapter 14 then features interviews with shamans in the Tuvan Republic in Siberia, as well as some of the strange encounters we had while conducting these interviews.

Finally, then, Chapters 15 to 17 explore the nature of the OBE phenomenon, and the factors that can shape our beliefs and approaches to it. Chapter 15 reviews the types of changes that can happen in OBEs over time; this includes various ways to transmute negative experiences. Chapter 16 challenges the assumption that the physical world can be accurately viewed during an OBE, which, in reality, seems to involve a spectrum of 'veridical' experiences – that is, experiences that coincide with reality. Chapter 17 explores the OBE-like 'shifting' phenomenon popularized by teenagers during the COVID-19 pandemic – a Generation Z iteration of astral travel that combines fiction, the multiverse and a strong sense of agency.

In the Epilogue, I discuss my last 'Future Tokyo' experience with simulation expert Rizwan Virk of Arizona State University, and reflect on what this might mean. Whether my OBEs are glitches in the Matrix, messages from another dimension, or just wild projections of my brain, they've added a layer of richness to my life that I wouldn't trade for anything.

I touch only briefly here and there on topics like sleep paralysis and near-death experiences in this book, so hope to be able to give them their proper due in future writing projects. Nonetheless, I hope that this book demonstrates that, just as there are many ways of being human, there are also many ways of both experiencing and interpreting OBEs. For some, the OBE is a perfectly scientifically explainable journey into a coded spatial memory – a 'backup' model of the immediate environment – while for others it's a way to stay connected with loved ones after death, to fly without wings, or even to watch TV if the power is out. Viewed in this way, the OBE is like a ghost of civilization, saved in a kind of cache file on the astral cloud.

There can be many snags along the path for out-of-body experiencers (OBErs), but it is in the hands of each individual whether to turn back or keep going at any given point, and neither decision is more valuable than the other. The lessons learned along the way – whether the experiences are seen as negative or positive – can be powerful enough to change a person's life.

So let's now dive into an exploration of this world of astral travel together, starting with my initial experiences of OBEs as a child...

1.

BEGINNINGS

As a child, I would sometimes feel as though my body was becoming denser while lying in bed at night. It felt almost as if my skin was becoming thick like a worm, or as if I was made of slowly drying cement. Sometimes the feeling was unpleasant and I would want it to end, but when I was feeling braver, I could observe it, as long as I kept my emotions under control. The first time it happened, my mum assumed that I must have had a fever and said that I was 'delirious'. According to the thermometer, I was fine, but the association with delirium stuck.

'Mum, I'm delirious again,' I said, as I made my way downstairs crying when it next happened. This time was different though – it didn't go away even when I walked around, and it came with another symptom that alarmed me. I plopped onto the sofa, interrupting the programme on TV, to try to explain the feeling.

'I can see that my arm is *there*,' I said, indicating my left arm, 'but it feels like it's up *here*.' I pointed at the air about ten inches above it. I *felt* as if I was moving my arm around, but I could *see* that it wasn't moving.

Recently, my mum and I tried, unsuccessfully, to work out how old I was when I started to have these episodes. I wanted to know if this so-called 'delirium' had started before or after the age of eight, because that's how old I was when I started to suspect that my little brother, Michael* (who was two years younger than me), was a superhero, and I embarked on a plan to follow in his footsteps.

Michael had been taking an afternoon nap on the living room sofa one day when he stood up and excitedly announced, 'I was just outside!' From the kitchen, our mum tried to explain that, wherever he *thought* he had been, he had been here on the sofa the entire time, so it must have only been a dream.

'It *wasn't* a dream!' he protested. 'It was real! I was outside!' He described seeing our elderly neighbour, Betty, walking in the direction of our house, holding a cherry cheesecake. About a minute or two later, there was a knock at the door. Michael and I looked on as our mother disappeared into the entryway and returned with Betty. The moment I saw the cherry cheesecake in her hands, something clicked in my eight-year-old brain, and I could feel my world opening up with new possibilities. If it was possible to somehow go outside while your body stayed in place (surely this must be a superpower!), then I *had* to learn how to do it.

We didn't yet have the Internet in the early 1990s, so my only hope of learning more about my brother's 'superhero' experience lay inside the nearest library, a 20-minute drive across fields of wheat and cattle – a trip that my mum was kindly willing to make. Without any term for this phenomenon, I snaked my way through aisle after aisle of books, looking in sections like history and geography, before coming across an aisle with books on ghosts and magic. I pulled out a large black book called *Psychic Voyages* from the Time-Life Books series 'Mysteries of the Unknown' which introduced me to the term 'astral travel', also known as astral projection, and included tips on how to do it. Astral projection is sometimes defined as a deliberate out-of-body experience, and holds more mystical connotations due to the spiritual motivations of many practitioners. The use of this term is sometimes limited to experiences in remote or fantastical locations, such as other planets or 'astral cities', which can seem like imaginal or non-material realms, while others use the term interchangeably with 'out-of-body experience' and include a wide gamut of features.

From that year onward, I would go through a phase every year or two when I would become obsessed with this phenomenon, and spend weeks at a time practising the techniques I found in library books. Then, six years after the mysterious cherry cheesecake visit, I woke up in the middle of the night to an experience that would change my life.

THE BLUE GHOST

In the eight years that we had lived on the farm between 1989 and 1997, there had been no less than seven apparition sightings – by my brother Michael, our little sister Sarah*, our grandmother, and also two friends of mine, one of whom swears to this day that she saw a disembodied hand float through my bedroom window while I was sleeping one night. (And there have been more such sightings since we moved out.) Besides the fact that they were apparitions, these 'ghosts' were not out of place in their old-fashioned clothing (and in one case, sitting in a phantom rocking chair).

I had been lucky not to have seen anything, and I wanted to keep it that way. So, to make sure that I didn't see anything scary in the middle of the night, I came up with the idea around age nine of what I called a 'blankie forcefield', which involved tucking the covers over my head every night and leaving a small hole near my mouth so I could breathe. Still, waking up in the middle of the night in that house was never any fun. My heart would race in anticipation, and the blankie forcefield couldn't keep out the occasional sound of footsteps coming up the stairs (which, for some reason, would always stop halfway). I would try to make my breathing slow and shallow so that, if there was anything in the room with me, it wouldn't hear me, or see the rise and fall of the duvet.

This worked until, one night when I was 14, I woke up in the middle of the night and my cocoon, with its neat little oxygen hole, was gone. Instead, the covers were folded neatly across my chest, as though somebody had tucked me in. This had never happened before. But although my blankie forcefield had now been neutralized, I felt oddly calm. I was lying on my left side facing the window, and for the first time, I felt unafraid to look around my room in the dark, which was entirely illogical in this creepy house after hours. I also noticed a beautiful blueness cast over the room, as if I was wearing tinted glasses. With my head still curled into my chest, I turned over onto my right side, and saw that someone was sitting next to me, their legs outstretched on the bed. My eyes moved slowly upwards – from the boots, to the blue jeans, to the blue checked shirt, and finally to the face. He was staring straight ahead, as if daydreaming, but then seemed to realize that I was 'awake' as he flinched and looked down at me, smiling. I'm not sure why, but my first instinct was to reach out to touch his arm; when I did so, he disappeared. I will refer to him from here on in as the 'Blue Ghost' since both the room and his clothes were blue.

Unlike the other apparitions in our house, this one was clearly wearing modern clothing. The next day, when I told my best friend what had happened, she suggested that he might have been my guardian angel. I wasn't so sure – did angels wear blue jeans?

THREE INTRUDERS

Years later, in the winter of 2009, I was living in a poorly heated flat in London. My parents were born in England and, with dual citizenship, I had recently relocated there after a couple of years in Japan. One cold night, I had dragged my mattress to the mezzanine above the kitchen where it was warmest. Each night for the past two weeks, I had tried an astral projection technique from Robert Monroe of the Monroe Institute (one of the world's leading centres for the exploration of human consciousness). I lay there with only a few feet between me and the ceiling, relaxing each muscle one by one, before imagining a point behind my closed eyes at ever-increasing distances. Every now and then, I reminded myself that my awareness was in my physical body. The idea was to shut out the external world and trick my mind into taking different perspectives in order to encourage astral travel (keep an eye out for these themes throughout the book). But I hadn't had any success yet, so I decided to give up and go to sleep normally.

The next thing I knew, I was downstairs at the front door, wondering how in the world I had gotten there. I had never sleepwalked before, but there was always a first, right? Then it hit me. *Am I even at home?* It *looked* like my flat, but something felt off that I couldn't put my finger on. I ran my hand along the wall and had a closer look around me. *Had I wandered into a neighbour's place by accident, one with the same floor plan, perhaps?* I realized that this would be impossible, because the doors in our building automatically locked when they closed. I tried to retrace my footsteps – I knew that I hadn't been out drinking or done anything else that might explain the strange experience. It didn't even occur to me that it could've been an out-of-body experience, as it was missing the onset features popularized by the media. Unable to come up with an answer, I decided to go back to bed.

As I made my way down the hall, I noticed that I felt abnormally light, and oddly warm, given that it should have taken all night to dispel the chill from the single-glazed windows. I also noticed that the flat was washed in blue, like the night that I had seen the Blue Ghost. I got to the end of the hall and was about to grab the banister when I was overcome with a sense of foreboding. It reminded me of my first visit to a haunted house attraction when I was five years old. The clerk on the Niagara Falls strip had said that I was too young to enter, so I had summoned my most confident voice and assured him that I wouldn't be scared. Finally, with a laugh, he had waved us in. Holding my dad's hand, I had taken one step inside and immediately knew that I had made a big mistake. It was so dark I couldn't even see my own hands – meanwhile, the hidden actors inside laughed maniacally and rattled chainsaw props at a group of thrill-seeking adults. I quickly retreated into the safety of the bright lobby and we went to get ice cream instead.

I had a similar feeling now, as an adult in my own hallway, as if there were hidden actors waiting for me to trip a wire, but there was nobody there to hold my hand this time.

Unless I could wake up my flatmate, Daisuke. So I headed to his room, ready to apologize for disturbing his sleep. But when I nudged the door open, I saw that he wasn't there. Instead, I was met with three men: two standing at the balcony door and one sitting on the bed facing me. Prompted by my entrance, the two men glanced at me, expressionless, before returning their gaze to the tree-lined street. All three seemed nonplussed by my presence.

A whirlwind of thoughts flooded my mind.

I am in somebody else's flat – I knew it!

Wait – but why are three men sitting quietly in the dark in the middle of the night? That's odd.

That's Daisuke's gym bag on the floor!

Where the hell is he!?

Daisuke worked for a Japanese bank, so I started to assume that he had been kidnapped for ransom or something. 'What have you done with him?' I asked. I was painfully aware that I stood no chance against three intruders, but in the moment, I felt like I had to do something. In response, the man on the bed laughed and stood up, making a move in my direction. I tried to make a move for the door, but before I could flee, he grabbed my arm. I was suddenly hit with a feeling of electricity coursing throughout my body, and my ears felt clogged, similar to aeroplane ear. The more I resisted his grasp, the stronger the electric shaking became, and the more intense the ear sensations. *What is this? A stroke? A seizure? This is* not *the time for a medical emergency!* The electric feeling crescendoed until, in the blink of an eye, I was suddenly back in bed, wondering what the heck had just happened.

As I mentioned, it didn't occur to me at the time that my experience could have been an out-of-body experience, despite having practised the technique from Robert Monroe's book for the past two weeks, because it didn't fit the depictions of them that I'd come across in pop culture. I had learned from books that the experience would begin consciously in the body, followed by symptoms like loud noises or vibrations, before feeling yourself separate away from your physical shell, perhaps to see your body, or a silver cord, trailing behind you. But I hadn't experienced any of this, except for the vibrations, which had only come at the *end* of the experience. Still, it was unlike any dream I had ever had, lucid or not.

I also didn't go through the gradual, groggy waking-up process that was usual for me every other morning after 'normal sleep'; one minute I was in Daisuke's room, struggling with the intruder, and, in the blink of an eye, I was awake in bed.

It was also real enough that I was convinced that I had been awake the entire time. The only indication that I was in a non-ordinary state of consciousness was the temperature anomaly, the blueness and the feeling of lightness – as if I was a car with the engine off, coasting.

2

APPARITIONS

'The belief in ghosts and spirits who travel between worlds is often intertwined with that of astral projection, where the soul of the living may visit the dead, appearing as an apparition, or conversely, as the spirit of the dead may be seen by the living.'
– Sir James Frazer, *The Golden Bough* (1890)

No longer the scared little girl on a farm with no Internet, I set out to find all the resources I could – both in person and online, to try to make sense of experiences like this. Over the next three years, the technique I had used set off over a hundred more OBEs, many of which I recorded in a journal. My first stop on this search, just a week or so after my rather frightening experience with the Three Intruders at age 26, was the Society for Psychical Research (SPR), which was founded in 1882 by a team of Cambridge students and academics, headed by Professor Henry Sidgwick, who taught moral philosophy at Trinity College.

As Scottish folklorist and anthropologist Andrew Lang, who served as the SPR president in 1911, wrote in *The Book of Dreams and Ghosts* (1897), 'the cock-sure common-sense of the years from 1660 to 1850, or so, regarded everyone who had experience of a hallucination as a dupe, a lunatic or a liar.' In this climate, even eminent people kept unusual, unexplainable experiences to themselves, often emphasizing that they must have been merely a dream.

Lang noted that both the science and religion of the time discouraged the study of psychic or paranormal phenomena. The scientists believed that doing so would encourage an indifference to logic and evidence, unravelling the progress of the Enlightenment and perhaps allowing a re-emergence of the kind of religious extremism that had led to the witch trials. On the other hand, religious believers were told not to enquire beyond the boundaries that God had placed us in, so as not to question His power. In Lang's opinion, the scientists had a point, but he argued nonetheless that studies should focus on *truth*, not consequences. And, in response to the religious point of view, he said that we have as much right to explore the phenomena of these minds as to explore the ocean.[1]

Meanwhile, movements such as Theosophy and Spiritualism filled the gap between science and religion, teaching astral projection to their students in Europe and beyond. In 1875, Russian–American mystic Madame Blavatsky (1835–1891), along with Freemason Henry Olcott, co-founded the Theosophical Society in New York City, later opening branches in Europe and India. Blavatsky claimed to have first come across esoteric knowledge after stumbling upon her Freemason great-grandfather's private book collection, which inspired her to travel widely in search of more knowledge.[2] Freemasons often collected ancient knowledge from locations such as Egypt, Ethiopia and India, and from traditions such as Hinduism, Buddhism and the Kabbalah. Adapting ideas from these kinds of sources, Theosophy teaches that the world is made up of multiple levels or 'planes', which we can access with multi-levelled bodies.

Astral travel was important to Theosophists because it was seen as a way to explore the 'astral plane', which was seen as 'simply nothing but the continuation of the physical world in finer matter.' It was also believed that it could be used to explore what are known as the 'Akashic Records', an astral (non-physical) archive of everything that has ever occurred, and to navigate life after death.[3] A number of books were written about astral travel experiences in the following years; of notable mention are H. Durville's *Le Fantôme des Vivants* (1909), M. Gifford Shine's *Little Journeys into the Invisible: A Woman's Actual Experiences in the Fourth Dimension* (1911) and Caroline D. Larsen's *My Travels in the Spirit World* (1927). The general doctrine of the time was that there was a cord between the astral and physical bodies – both vehicles of the soul, which coincided while awake but could hover during sleep. The soul could detach from the physical body spontaneously or with anaesthetic, fainting or deliberate practice.

APPARITIONS OF THE DEAD AND THE DYING

The term 'out-of-body experience' (OBE) was first coined by SPR member G.N.M. Tyrrell in his book *Apparitions* (1943) to avoid the mystical and occult connotations of the terms 'astral travel' and 'astral projection'. Tyrrell aimed to look at OBEs in a sober light, while also refusing to shy away from the stranger aspects of the phenomenon. He proposed that OBEs be investigated in connection with apparitions, due to reports of people subjectively leaving their body when close to death (like a ghost). He illustrated this with the well-known case of Dr Wiltse, which was first published in 1889 and took place in Skiddy, Kansas. Although Dr Wiltse had been declared dead as a result of typhoid, having had no perceptible pulse or heartbeat for four hours, he survived and afterwards reported leaving his body during this time. (Note the bluishness, invisibility to others, and the clarity and stability of the environment – these features will come up again in later chapters.)

Dr Wiltse reported that he felt and heard the snapping of small cords which seemed to be linked to his body, before feeling himself emerge from his skull. As he emerged, his new form appeared to him as 'like a jellyfish' in both shape and colour. He continued, 'I floated up and down and laterally, like a soap-bubble attached to the bowl of a pipe, until I at last broke loose from the body and fell lightly to the floor, where I slowly rose and expanded into the full stature of a man. I seemed to be translucent, of a bluish cast and perfectly naked.' He walked to the door, and noticed that he was now suddenly wearing clothes. He was further shocked when his elbow went right through a man physically standing in the doorway. Dr Wiltse tried to attract the attention of his friends, but realizing that he was invisible to them, he gave up and walked outside into the street. He was surprised by how clear everything looked to him, and remarked on 'the redness of the soil and of the washes the rain had made'. He then noticed a thin cord protruding from his shoulders which he likened to a spider's web, which stretched into the house (and presumably to his physical body). Before he could do anything else, he seemed to be propelled, as if by a pair of invisible hands, to another road with a mountain and forest below it. He wandered around this area for a while, until a 'black cloud' descended onto him and he found himself back in bed.[4]

Although Dr Wiltse was invisible to others during this out-of-body experience, a 'double' of a person *is* reportedly sometimes seen by others at the point of death or illness. This ghost-like figure, or wraith, is generally said to never speak, and to vanish if the witness speaks to them.[5] This is often seen as evidence of life after death, especially when there was no prior knowledge of the person's condition. In his book *Adventurings in the Psychical* (1914), Canadian journalist Henry Addington Bruce noted that in nearly every case received by the Society for Psychical Research, the witness of this type of apparition was alone and in a passive state of mind, usually just before or after sleep or in a period of absent-mindness.[6]

There are also accounts of people seeing their *own* wraith before their death. In 1893, Thiselton-Dyer included the following case in his book *The Ghost World*:

> The beautiful Lady Diana Rich, daughter to the Earl of Holland, as she was walking in her father's garden at Kensington to take the air before dinner, about 11 o'clock, being then very well, met her own apparition, habit and everything, as in a looking-glass. About a month after, she died of small-pox.[7]

Nowadays, this is known as heautoscopy, which is defined as 'a complex psychosensorial hallucinatory perception of one's own body image projected into the external visual space.'[8] It is a well-known but rare medical phenomenon, but the underlying mechanisms are still unknown. In medical literature, it seems to be viewed as being triggered by grief, stress or medical conditions such as epilepsy or schizophrenia, and it does not always signify a person's death.

APPARITIONS OF THE LIVING

In addition to an association with death, early psychical researchers and believers alike also correlated OBEs with sleep or supernatural abilities. Apparitions of the living are found in many cultures, known by the term *doppelgänger* in Germany and *ikiryou* in Japanese. Accounts of bilocation are also found in religious literature, in stories from St Thomas of Aquin to Sister Maria Fernández Coronel. This motif was also written about by authors such as Edgar Allen Poe and Fyodor Dostoyevsky; has been depicted in artworks such as Dante Rossetti's *How They Met Themselves*; and has more recently featured in films like *Annihilation* (2018) and *Us* (2019).

Generally, the person whose double is seen is either asleep or does not report anything unusual at the time, like in the following case reported by US esoterist and author Sylvan Muldoon:

> I am well acquainted with an old occultist, Carl Pfuhl, who told me that, on one occasion, a little girl who was sleeping in a hammock outside the seance room, while a materialization seance was in process inside, materialized in the seance room, and claimed to be the daughter of a member of the circle – who had a spirit daughter about the same age. Yet the form was that of the girl sleeping in the hammock outside, and had not been in any way 'transformed' to represent the girl she claimed to be! The girl who slept in the hammock knew nothing of it, on awaking![9]

Stories like these inspired adventurous minds to try to project their own form to others through astral projection. In 1953, American sociologist Hornell Hart presented a collection of such reports at Utrecht University. He termed this 'ESP Travelling' or 'ESP Projection', which he defined as 'any type of experience in which an observer observes from a point in space-time outside his physical body'. (Just to clarify, ESP stands for 'extrasensory perception'.) After removing cases of probable coincidence and suspected fraud, he was left with 60 examples, some of which either verified information about locations that they could not have otherwise known about, or involved a witness to the experiencer's apparition or 'double'.

Hart concluded that the best evidence had been obtained in cases involving hypnosis and deliberate self-projection, and that more experiments in this vein should take place to learn about veridical experiences; that is, those that correctly reported on the physical environment.[10]

Similarly, Henry Addington Bruce had been told by a Professor James of Harvard (he was likely referring to William James) that he had been experimenting with 'telepathic apparitions'. He had tried to project his astral body to a friend who lived in his neighbourhood without informing her about it beforehand, and received the following letter from her the next day:

Last night, at about ten o'clock, I was in the dining-room, at supper with B. Suddenly I thought I saw you looking in through the crack of the door at the end of the room, toward which I was looking. I said to B.: 'There is Blank, looking through the crack of the door!' B., whose back was toward the door, said: 'He can't be there. He would come right in.' However, I got up and looked in the other room, but there was nobody there. Now, what were you doing last night, at that time?[11]

Another example comes from a friend of parapsychologist Alex Tanous, a member of the American Society for Psychical Research and a well-known participant in OBE experiments. His friend, who was at home in Canada at the time, said that he was visited by Tanous late one night, and they were drinking tea and chatting, while his wife could hear the conversation from upstairs. He didn't suspect anything odd until he realized that there was no sound of a car leaving after Tanous had departed. It turned out that Tanous had been in New York the entire time.[12] These experiences of the double seemed to begin after boiling water was accidentally spilled on Tanous at age five. The doctor found nothing wrong with him and recommended that he just get some rest. This is when his first encounter with his double occurred:

Two medieval lovers meet their doubles in a forest in Dante Rossetti's How They Met Themselves *(1851).*

As I started climbing the stairs, I looked up. I saw myself at the top of the stairs, not clearly, but I knew it was me. I waved and the other self waved back to me. Our friendship grew, and lasted several years. As time went on, the other self became clearer and I saw it was my double. I adopted him as my imaginary playmate.[13]

All of this calls into question what is a phantom. Growing up, I had tried to fit the Blue Ghost into the 'ghost' narratives of the time, and failed. The modern clothes he wore made it unlikely in my mind that he was a previous inhabitant, an ancestor or even a past-life loved one coming to visit. On the other hand, a living doppelganger, whether close to death, ill, sleeping or astral projecting at the time, *might* be a possibility. Of course, this doesn't answer the question as to why he was in my room of all places, which remains a mystery.

THE METACHORIC EXPERIENCE: APPARITIONS AS PART OF A HALLUCINATED PANORAMA

Some of the most compelling cases come from accounts that leave us questioning the reliability of our senses and the boundaries of consciousness. One such story, originally published in the book *Phantasms of the Living* (1886), has stuck in my head for years. After lunch, an officer was speaking outside with his friends and host when a servant approached with a message from the hostess, asking him to speak to her at the house:

> I at once left my friends, and accompanied the man back to the house, following him through the verandah into the room where the luncheon had been laid. There he left me, and I waited for my hostess to come, but no one appeared; so after a few minutes I called her by name, thinking that she might not be aware that I had come in. Receiving no answer, after once again repeating her name, I walked back into the verandah, where, on entering, I had observed a [tailor] at work, and asked him where the man was who came in with me.

The tailor replied that he had not seen anyone come in with him, and that he had seen the officer lift the verandah blind himself, although the officer swore that the servant had done it for him. He returned to his friends outside and told them what had happened, and they all confirmed that they hadn't seen a servant calling for him before. One remarked, 'You were in the midst of saying something about the alterations when you suddenly stopped and walked back to the house; we could not tell why.' The officer claimed to be in perfect health at the time and afterwards.[14]

In sharing the officer's case in their book *Apparitions* (1975), parapsychologists Green and McCreery highlighted how his perception of events diverged from what others saw: while he saw the *servant figure* lift the blind, his colleagues saw the *officer* himself lift it. This discrepancy between what he experienced himself doing and what his physical body was doing, according to witnesses, led the parapsychologists to liken this to an out-of-body experience. In their work, they attempted to collect witness reports without prematurely forcing them into a category, such as 'apparition' or 'out-of-body experience', which led them to noticing significant overlap between the two. This made Green and McCreery wonder whether actions perceived during apparitional experiences – such as speaking or moving – are enacted physically or remain confined to the hallucinatory realm. They asked, 'When a subject speaks to an apparition, or addresses some real person in his environment while perceiving an apparition, is he really speaking out loud, or only hallucinating doing so?' They cite another case, in which onlookers observed a witness's eyes following the movements of an apparition across the room, although the onlookers themselves couldn't see anything.[15] This might again link back to OBEs (as well as dreams), during which the physical eyes can move in sync with imagery, while it is rare for someone to be able to physically *speak* during OBEs and dreams. OBEs in which the body continues to move in other ways – whether driving, typing, walking, drumming or involved in some other activity – are also rare, but not unheard of (see Chapters 4 and 14).

Stories like these invite us to question not only our senses but also the boundaries between states of consciousness. Green and McCreery would later coin the umbrella term 'metachoric experiences' – from the Greek *metachoreo*, meaning 'to go to another place' or 'to withdraw', to describe experiences in which the entire field of vision is hallucinatory. This included dreams, false awakenings, out-of-body experiences and apparition cases. In their view, apparitions were not imposed onto physical space, but were part of this entirely hallucinated panorama.[16] In 2017, then President of the Society for Psychical Research, John Poynton, put it this way: 'an apparition need not be thought of as located in the observer's physical space at the moment; it may be considered as located in a non-physical space that the observer has entered in a slightly dissociated state.'[17]

This leads me again to my Blue Ghost experience. Because of my astral projection practice at the time, and the features it shared with other reported OBEs, such as blueness, calmness and incongruities like the folded sheets, I eventually came to think of this as an OBE. This suggests that the Blue Ghost was located in this non-physical space that I had entered, as Poynton suggests.

It is widely believed by experiencers, including shamans and occult practitioners, that the out-of-body state is conducive to mediumship skills. In addition to the doppelganger, there are many reports of encountering the deceased in the OBE state, and for some, this is the main reason for their practice. Alex Tanous claimed to astral project into haunted locations, and after listening to the spirits' concerns, the haunting was said to cease. He describes this in more detail in his posthumously published book *Conversations with Ghosts* (2013). This aspect of the out-of-body environment – as populated by all manner of beings, living and deceased, will be explored more in later chapters.

The ideas that sprang from parapsychology around this time greatly influenced both mainstream psychology and the scientific approach to OBEs, but the normalization of this topic has been partly achieved by stripping it of the stranger elements mentioned above, like those involving shared experiences, verified information or encounters with the deceased. These elements are critical in understanding the cosmologies that arise from OBEs, as we shall see.

ISOLATION ZONES

'Our normal waking consciousness . . . is but one special
type of consciousness, whilst all about it, parted from
it by the filmiest of screens, there lie potential forms of
consciousness entirely different. We may go through life without
suspecting their existence; but apply the requisite stimulus,
and at a touch they are there in all their completeness.'
– William James, *The Varieties of Religious Experience* (1902)

I am convinced that the out-of-body experience is the closest we
can get to entering *The Twilight Zone*. In the pilot episode of this
TV series, a man finds himself in a small town with no memory of
who he is. He stops into a café, where he finds coffee on the stove
and a jukebox playing, but no sign of any people. The man wanders
downtown and finds only mannequins and a pre-recorded message in
the phone booth.[1] He is completely alone in a liminal space, a normally
populated place of transition and movement, a place best described
as 'eerie' which, according to philosopher Mark Fisher, we find 'more
readily in landscapes partially emptied of the human'.[2] In the real
world, this liminal eeriness is often sensed in empty hotel corridors or
shopping malls after hours. It's as if the space has been removed from
the social dynamic, leaving it a deactivated, static snapshot of the past.

I was struck with the same sense while walking around Tuva
National Museum in Kyzyl, Russia, recently. All other visitors were on

the far side of the museum looking at Scythian gold, leaving me alone with taxidermal elk and Styrofoam snow. For a moment, I felt like the last woman alive. Today, the online concept of 'the Backrooms' similarly elicits the eeriness of liminal spaces. This depiction of large, empty, extradimensional space beyond our everyday reality went viral after high school student Kane Parsons uploaded his video *The Backrooms* (2022) onto YouTube. His protagonist walks through seemingly endless, nearly identical halls of faded yellow wallpaper and harsh fluorescent lighting, all alone – or so it seems.[3] Although isolation is at the heart of this genre, these spaces will occasionally feature a robot, shadow figure or monster, or at least the sense that something either unsettling or alien may be just around the corner.

OBEs are the quintessential eerie, liminal Backrooms and Twilight Zone-esque experience. Like Backrooms, they are often devoid of figures, at least in the beginning. In some Backrooms video games, players can escape to other spaces through walls and objects, an ability known as 'noclipping', which echoes the jump to remote places sometimes (but not always) seen in OBEs. In the OBEs I had after my Three Intruders experience, I would usually leave my room to find the rest of the apartment intact, while at other times, especially when going through a wall, window or doorway, it would be a different time of year or location entirely. Parsons describes the Backrooms as 'a manifestation of a poorly remembered recollection of the late 90s and early 2000s'.[4] Similarly, OBEs, at least in the beginning stages, are usually set in a kind of Backrooms of the immediate environment constructed from spatial memory. OBEs can begin from a childhood bedroom, or some other realistic setting that can be either familiar or unfamiliar to the person, yet maintain that eerie or liminal feeling. (In Chapter 17 on what is called 'shifting', we even see an example of a bedroom at Hogwarts.) As astral projector and High Priestess Witch Tree Carr puts it, 'It's weird, it's just like, you feel like a ghost. It's like you're in this weird "isolation zone", and there's no "spark"... It always feels weird going there. It doesn't feel like, "Ah, awesome, I'm home now." It always feels like *oooo*.'5

In an interview with Joshua Rothman for *The New Yorker*, philosopher of mind Thomas Metzinger reveals that he started experimenting with OBEs after an experience at a ten-day meditation retreat when he was 19. At the time, he was studying philosophy with a focus on the mind–body problem, and believed that the soul was a construction of the brain. After his experience, he wasn't so sure. However, he changed his mind again after having dinner with psychologist Susan Blackmore, who suggested that, rather than floating around his bedroom, he had been floating around in a *mental map* of his bedroom. This idea was influenced by psychologist Philip Johnson-Laird's book *Mental Models* (1983), which suggested that instead of working through problems logically, we visualize them on a 'mental stage set', where we are able to rearrange the actors and props into different scenarios. Metzinger describes the OBE as an 'offline-activated state' which is akin to 'visiting the set at night, when it [isn't] being used.'6 However, unlike lucid dreams – dreams in which you're aware that you're dreaming – you may feel less like a director and more like an actor without a script.

THE ROLE OF THE BRAIN'S TEMPOROPARIETAL JUNCTION

Today, science provides a modern perspective on the 'metachoric experience' of a hallucinated panorama mentioned in the previous chapter, with the view that there is a spectrum of perception based on cues from the senses, and that stored memories and expectation based on pattern recognition 'fills in' reality to reduce mental labour. As neuroscientist Anil Seth concludes, 'We're all hallucinating all the time, including right now. It's just that when we agree about our hallucinations, we call that reality.'[7] An area of the brain known as the temporoparietal junction (TPJ) is responsible for the integration of information which helps to present us with a coherent and accurate reality. It does this by bringing together the physical senses, the vestibular system (which affects the perception of body position and movement) and distinctions between the self and other (such as others' point of view)[8] which allows us to 'be' in the world.

As Anthony Peake notes in his foreword, 'we consider our body to be our "home"'. Central to this experience is our body image, which is about our perception of our own bodily appearance, and our body schema, which tells us about our position and actions in the world. Usually these two things are synchronized, reshaping each other to limit prediction errors and provide us with a correct representation of the self in relation to our environment.[9]

The psychological model proposes that OBEs happen when this information fails to integrate, usually due to contradictory, overwhelming or muted sensory input. During wakefulness, OBEs can be triggered by drug use, macular degeneration, an accident, strong emotions, or meditation (in particular those involving other points of view), all of which can disrupt the usual integration of sensory information. This prompts the mind to cobble together an alternate backup reality from memory, expectation and imagination.[10] Sometimes the body seems to be the only thing that veers from the original, sometimes it's the environment, and at other times there is a shift in both the body *and* the environment, which means we can find ourselves in both second bodies and second worlds. OBE author Robert Peterson aptly calls the alternate model a 'Story of Experience'.[11]

Dreams can *also* be thought of as 'Stories of Experience', but exist further along the imagination side of the spectrum. They are like a private sandbox during the sleep cycle in which to process the past in preparation for the future, ideally helping us to keep a flexible, adaptable mind while regulating our emotions. There is also evidence of an 'intermediate experience' or spectrum *between* OBE states and dream states, with some people reporting that they can 'click' from one into another.[12]

In contrast, OBEs, at least in the beginning of the experience, seem to act as a *stand-in* for the immediate environment until the senses are back online. Sometimes this switch to the backup reality can come to our attention through transition signs centred around the body (like vibrations or a bodily exit) or incongruities in the environment, before the model of reality corrects itself or 'reconnects online'. However, the disconnection from the live sensory model may be so brief, or replaced so accurately, that it goes unnoticed. Both parapsychologist Celia Green and esoterist Sylvan Muldoon have reported that the majority of OBEs are absent of transition signs, which can sometimes make the experiencer think that they are awake as normal. This realism explains why my brother insisted that *his* experiences, like the cheesecake one I shared earlier, weren't dreams, and why I assumed that I had been awake during my Blue Ghost and Three Intruders experiences.

THE ROLE OF MEMORY

There is an interesting theory which argues that OBEs have an evolutionary purpose, allowing us to detach from physical pain in order for us to think clearly about what to do next, like escape or fight.[13] Accordingly, OBEs should be more reliant on accurate copies of physical reality as stored in memory, like a web page made of cache files while the Internet is down, at least in cases geared towards *physical* survival.[14]

Dr Cecilia Forcato, a biologist at Instituto Tecnológico de Buenos Aires, who specializes in OBEs and has experienced them since she was 17 years old, says: 'I think that [they are] completely related to memory.' As an example, she explains that while we are focused on our conversation, a dog might enter the room that we don't consciously notice, but the brain still encodes this into memory. 'I think that in out-of-body experiences, we can have access to this information which would normally be forgotten,' she says. During the sleep cycle, there's a normal reduction in the synaptic strength of memories, so the dog entering the room will eventually be forgotten. The content of out-of-body experiences suggest that at least *some* types of memories are retrievable, at least during this state of consciousness, regardless of the length of time that has passed.

Cecilia wanted to explore memory in OBEs in more depth, so conducted some personal experiments outside of her academic studies. In her next OBE, she decided to go outside to another building and check the colour of the floor, which she couldn't recall consciously either while awake or during the OBE itself. She proceeded to check the floor in detail during the experience, information that seemed completely new to her at the time. Once back in the live, physical world, Cecilia went to the actual physical location that had appeared in the OBE and found that it was exactly the same. This suggests that spatial memories may be retrieved intact in OBEs – importantly, in their *original context*, unlike in dreams in which the floor pattern might have been remixed into a different room or object.

Carrying on the theme of memory, I ask Cecilia about why I sometimes have trouble recalling certain memories during the experience: once 'there', I sometimes forget what I had planned to do. 'For some people,' she says, 'declarative memories can be impaired while out of the body. But I don't think it's because some areas of the brain are compromised when out of body, but because the experiencer is in another situation, another space.'

'Could it be similar to when you go into another room to get something and then you forget what you went in there for?' I ask. She nods and laughs in reply.

This should all convince us that the OBE is a perfectly logical and mundane phenomenon, right? Yet remember, we have also entered the Twilight Zone, an inherently eerie space where anything can happen. As such, the out-of-body environment can occasionally also be populated by weird objects and entities, or those that we feel 'should not exist, or at least [should] not exist here'.[15] This can include strange lighting, mysterious writing on the window, an unfamiliar key on the coffee table, a cord protruding from a second body or an intruder. Hedge witch Jane*, who we will meet again in Chapters 7 and 12, explains: 'In the first OBE I had in this apartment, there was writing on my window – like in the astral, not physically – and there was writing in red, and I couldn't read it.' She went back into her body, and then out again, and saw that the writing was still there. However, much to her frustration, she still couldn't read it. If the OBE is a replica of the physical environment, then what might be the purpose of these weird, out-of-place details?

As mentioned, although the out-of-body environment can match the physical equivalent even beyond the immediate location, sometimes if one exits through a window, door or other space, one can end up somewhere else entirely. The initial location is sometimes referred to among experiencers as the 'waiting room', while the point of passage into a new environment is often called a 'portal'. The experience of going through portals, whatever their form, is like the scenes from the films *The Matrix* or *The Adjustment Bureau*, where a door on street level might lead to a rooftop or a football field. In traditional societies, the portal can be a hollow tree, a hole in the ground or a hot spring, after which one might either exit from the same type of object in another area, or in an unrelated place far away. Indoor portals can include doors, windows, walls or mirrors; astral projector and High Priestess Witch Tree Carr (also mentioned earlier) sleeps in a room of mirrors just so that she can float through them

Tree Carr in her room of mirrors that act as portals during OBEs.

when out of her body. However, it's also possible that there might be no *physical* equivalent to the portal seen during the experience, whether that be swirling water on the ceiling or a small galaxy in the corner of the room. Some experiencers even say that they can create portals ad hoc with their hands or by imagining them.

Just like there can be incongruent elements to the immediate OBE environment, there is always the question of *why* we end up in certain locations. It's not like analyzing the patchwork of a dream: *I dreamt of having lunch with Sally because I saw her yesterday; we were on a Greek island because she's travelling to Ikaria next week; and a zombie invaded the restaurant because I watched a zombie film before bed*. In OBEs, these places can include remote locations which also seem to be stored spatial memories, like a childhood bedroom, a relative's living room or a nearby building. But sometimes they can be more fantastical, with historic, futuristic or space scenes, or we can even skip the out-of-body transition, waiting room or portal stage entirely, and teleport straight to the surprise destination. This makes them more like dreams, but experiencers insist that these experiences feel more realistic, partly because they appear more stable, whereas dreamscapes seem to change more readily.

This might be explained by another theory. In addition to the idea that OBEs allow us to detach from physical pain and work out a survival plan, there is also evidence that they might function to protect our mental health when triggered by a traumatic experience, as mental clarity and calm emotions are a common feature of the experience.[16] Cecilia thinks that a similar mechanism might be at work even in non-trauma-induced OBEs. She says: 'It *could* be because the first part of the OBE is more terrifying, as the experience is very vivid and realistic. We interview a lot of people with lucid dreams and OBEs, and for them, in lucid dreams, you can modify the environment, the entities, but in OBEs, you have to interact, you can't modify the entity, but you can modify what you do in the context, or you can shuttle to another context. For me, the worst part, the most intense part is when I "wake up" in my room. Once I jump to another scene, it's less complicated than the first part. Perhaps, jumping to a different scenery makes your mind relax a bit more, maybe it's a way to control negative emotions.' My hope is that future research will shed more light on the relationship between OBE content, our memories and our emotions.

In the next chapter, we look more deeply at what triggers the OBE, including the role of cultural beliefs and practices.

4.

THE CROSS-CULTURAL OCCURRENCE OF OBEs

There are plenty of techniques that can help us override the normal sensory reality and switch to a backup or alternate reality, and yet it seems to come easier to some people than others. In Western populations, studies have found a prevalence of OBEs ranging from 8 to 15 per cent of the general population and 10 to 25 per cent of college students.[1] The difference in percentages found across studies can be due to different definitions used, a cultural bias against experiencing mystical states, or even the attitudes or reputations of the researchers themselves. However, there may also be something about a specific group that makes them more susceptible to altered states of consciousness. For example, the higher prevalence among university students compared to the general population might be due to sleep disruption or an increased exploration of new ideas and states of consciousness. And this number jumps to 50 per cent for people interested in spiritual topics.[2]

One of the key features of a successful astral projector is what is known as 'absorption', which is most commonly experienced when someone is fully 'absorbed', or engrossed, in something such as a film, a book or a particular task. During periods like this, the outside world seems to disappear, which puts you in what could be described as a trance-like state, and which allows the muting of external sensory input. Absorption can also be developed intentionally through techniques that mute the senses, such as meditation and attention exercises, sensory deprivation and what are known as 'deepening' techniques in hypnosis, which cause the subject to go deeper into a trance (through counting backwards, for instance). Depending on whether one's culture values the capacity for absorption or not, people may be socially conditioned to develop or suppress this ability. And then the experiences that result from this ability can shape, and are in turn shaped, by cultural beliefs, practices and expectations.

Around the world, there are a variety of beliefs about the soul, what it is made up of, and what it can and cannot do. Writing in 1871, anthropologist Edward B. Tylor suggested that the belief in the soul, and the belief that it can exist independent from the body, was a logical conclusion drawn from dreams and visions, including apparitions of the dead or dying.[3] In 2005, Thomas Metzinger argued that the belief in the soul specifically originates from naive realist interpretations of OBEs:[4] *I can subjectively leave the body, hence I – my soul – can exist without it.* The perceived properties of the soul can influence cultural practices, ranging from burial customs to the use of binaural beats to synchronize brain waves. The soul could, for example, be made of materials like blood, breath, eye and shadow, with some cultures using the same word for breath as they do for soul, as both are viewed as animating forces of the body, so can be thought of as one and the same.[5] In modern science, the soul is commonly thought to be made of neurons, which has influenced the development of technology to induce certain brain states that can trigger an OBE.[6]

A 1978 paper by sociologist Dean Shiels is sometimes cited as claiming that 90 per cent of cultures hold beliefs in out-of-body experiences. I couldn't find his paper online and had to order a physical copy of the journal; when it arrived, I was surprised to find that it didn't conclude this at all. Shiels used the Human Relations Area Files (HRAF, pronounced *RAF*) database, a compilation of files such as old missionary notes and anthropology books, scouring them for mention of this phenomenon. One of my lecturers warned me to take these sources with a pinch of salt, as their methodologies and biases were often unclear, but I was nevertheless curious about his findings. Shiels retrieved each microfiche card coded 774, which, according to the current list, is the code assigned to data relating to animism. It is unclear why Shiels would choose the cards labelled for animism rather than, for example, religious experiences (781) or general religious practices (780), but this may have been inspired by anthropologist Edward Tylor's use of this term in relation to beliefs of the soul. Shiels does not mention how many cards he initially found under this code; only that he left out those not pertaining to OBEs, as well as those that only focused on a certain part of a culture (e.g. *rural* Irish), which did not represent the entire culture. The HRAF also did not contain information on industrial societies; only those that could not be easily located.[7]

It's worth pointing out here that although culture is defined as a set of beliefs that people agree on, the views that end up representing 'one culture' in literature do not necessarily reflect the beliefs of the whole group – only those of the informants willing to speak at the time; opinions and experiences can vary from person to person and from generation to generation. Culture is always in the making, which means that the term 'cultures' (*plural*) might seem like a more fitting term.[8] All of this helps to remind us that Shiels' paper should not be taken as a study on the *prevalence* of OBE beliefs in cultures worldwide, but rather just as a comparison of OBE beliefs, *where they exist*, in non-industrial societies in which animist beliefs are found. In other words, he didn't conclude that 90 per cent of world cultures held a belief or opinion on OBEs, but that among those who had records *mentioning* OBEs, 90 per cent believed that they exist, while the rest were ambiguous or believed that OBEs did *not* exist. In the unused records, either the subject did not come up, or the interviewer had not asked related questions.

It is also possible that some interlocutors do not want to disclose certain experiences or beliefs to the anthropologists and missionaries who collected such reports. As anthropologist Roger Ivar Lohmann notes, while Bronisław Malinowski wrote that dreams seemed unimportant to the Trobrianders he lived with in Papua New Guinea, on the next page he mentioned that they used magic spells for dreams to help their *kula* trade during the day (i.e. their system of trade exchange).[9] Lohmann suggests that 'rather than being insignificant, dreams had so great a supernatural power for Trobrianders of Malinowski's day that they may have downplayed their significance to protect themselves.'[10]

Shiels' methodology left him with 67 'cultures' where a mention of OBEs was present: 60 that believed in them, four that believed that the soul only leaves the body at death, and three that believed in OBEs in some way that Shiels was unable to clarify due to insufficient information. Among the 60 cultures that believed in them, 46 per cent stated that most or all people could have these experiences, while 43 per cent believed that only a minority of people could experience them, such as shamans, mediums, initiates or, interestingly, those born on Christmas Eve as in Malta, who were limited to projecting on Christmas Eve alone (while retaining no memory of their journeys). In terms of spontaneous OBEs, where causes were given, sleep was listed as a cause in 34 cultures, illness in nine, emotional states in four, accidents in three, and narcotics in two.

Only 14 of the 67 cultures (21 per cent) had mentioned beliefs in voluntary astral projection. However, in all of these cases, the phenomenon was thought to be restricted to a certain type of person, such as a witch, shaman or other special individual who entered the experience through ritual-induced trance, narcotics or 'at will'. For example, among the Tsonga in southern Mozambique and South Africa, people said that projection was normal, but that only witches could do it voluntarily. However, there were some risks involved: if the *moya* (soul) stayed away from the body for too long, the person could die. This belief is not uncommon. This may be due to the association of illness or near-death with OBEs (OBEs can be seen as the cause of ill health or near-death, rather than the result). It could also be the logical conclusion of people who believe in the soul as the animating force of the body – that if it is away for too long, the body could expire.

In terms of the methods and locations of travel, 32 per cent of cultures for which information was available believed that journeys were limited to the Earth plane only, while 68 per cent believed that they could travel to spirit planes, or both Earth and spirit planes. Among the Winnebago people in Nebraska, a small group of men had learned a peyote ritual to project the soul at will (peyote is a small spineless cactus plant that contains the hallucinogen mescaline). During these experiences, they could travel anywhere on Earth and 'to the heavens'.[11]

I was able to access the now digitized archive through Yale University to see what I could find beyond the parameters that Shiels was using. The database doesn't return any search results for 'out-of-body experience', but the search term 'soul' will advise you to look under 'animism 774', just as Shiels had. When I went back to the main search bar and typed in 'leave the body', check-marking other categories including sorcery, magic and mental therapy, shamans and psychotherapists, medical therapy, bodily injuries, cosmology, religious experience, sacred objects and places, ritual, sleep and animism, there were countless search results. However, a closer look found that some of these pertained to possession and illness rather than out-of-body experiences.

This brings up an important point when it comes to studying OBEs. In order to get anywhere meaningful with research, first you have to be familiar with the local and historical terminology used and be aware of the criteria that include or exclude certain experiences among different categories of people in different places. While doing my master's research in South Korea, for example, I described my project to two acquaintances on separate occasions, using the word *yucheital* (Korean for out-of-body experience). At first, they just nodded casually, recognizing the term from pop culture, but when I described the features of an OBE in more detail, they both exclaimed, 'I had something like that!'

One had fainted and found himself floating in another world, but he didn't think of this as an OBE because it didn't fit the depictions that he'd seen of *yucheital* in superhero films. In his mind, OBEs were self-controlled journeys through what looked like the real physical world, while his experiences occurred from fainting, were set in a world that looked like it was drawn with crayons, and in which he could only move from the neck up as he floated in the sky. Another factor to take into consideration when researching OBEs is that experiencers might make up their *own* terms about what they went through, which are unsearchable online and in the literature. As an eight-year-old, for example, I thought of my brother's experiences as a kind of 'X-ray' travel, while hedge witch Jane, who believes in nature spirits, called her childhood journeys 'fairy flights'. My sister-in-law, Sophie*, told me that since giving birth, she had often found herself floating around her bedroom, watching my brother and their baby as they slept, but she called these 'vivid dreams'.

Besides the issue with terminology, it might also be difficult to come across experiences that aren't considered meaningful or impactful enough to share with strangers. This means that there is likely a bias in many studies towards those deemed extraordinary or socially acceptable. In some cases, the reason for sharing the experience is purely practical, and it might not be seen as anything special, even if it is seen as inherently spiritual. The other acquaintance of mine that I was talking to about my master's research in South Korea told me that she had woken up to find herself floating towards the ceiling and that she believed that she had briefly entered the world of the afterlife that night. Her friends told her that it was because she had been working too hard and advised her to take traditional Korean medicine and get some rest. She listened to their advice and didn't have another experience. She said, however, that this experience did not affect her beliefs; she had already assumed that there would be an afterlife – as far as she was concerned, her physical weakness had simply brought her closer to that realm before her time. Instead of a spiritual experience, she saw it as a wake-up call to strengthen her body so that it would stay in the land of the living.

INDUCED, OR 'KINDLED', OBEs

Usually, OBEs are described as either spontaneous (with no known cause), deliberate (typically brought about by a spiritual practice of some sort) or forced (caused by trauma, drugs or illness). Interestingly, research suggests that the way in which an OBE is induced can shape the nature of the experience. In Shiels' study, reports of non-Earth planes were more common with voluntary projections, with 58 per cent of voluntary reports and only 32 per cent of spontaneous cases thought to involve travel to spirit planes.[12] Psychologist Susan Blackmore found that there were certain traits associated with people who had either spontaneous or intentional OBEs. Participants who had more spontaneous OBEs also tended to be prone to daydreaming, forgetting their surroundings (in other words, high absorption) and other mystical experiences, while those who were more successful in inducing deliberate OBEs reported more lucid dreams and dream control, and more capacity for concentration and seeing with their eyes closed. Blackmore's study also found that deliberate OBEs featured more imaginary content[13], which might line up with the non-Earth planes of Shiels' study.

When I began interviewing experiencers, I quickly found that it wasn't so easy to pinpoint whether an OBE had been spontaneous or deliberate (although it was generally obvious when an OBE was *forced*; for instance, by drugs or an accident). This is partially because OBEs can sometimes happen hours, days or even weeks after the trigger (the trigger often being a deliberate practice). An example of this can be found in Natam, a Korean-born YouTuber based in New Zealand. In a video entitled 'How I finally achieved my first astral projection', Natam recounts that she had been feeling stressed during high school when she came across astral projection while searching for a coping mechanism in books about psychology and dreams. Each night for the next three months, she tried techniques, such as meditation, to try to induce an OBE, but she had no success. However, one day during a nap, she unexpectedly found herself coming out of her body.[14]

In one study, only 8 per cent of experiencers reported having had an OBE *while* meditating,[15] but this does not mean that meditation cannot induce such experiences – it may just take time to see results. During my Three Intruders experience, I had been practising a technique every night for two weeks, but the out-of-body experience only happened on the night that I had given up. It was almost as though I was a wind-up toy that had been fully charged, and only needed the release of the key to spring forward into another world. Similarly, Natam's experiences began during a nap, but she had been committed to a regular meditation practice every night before bed for months. There seems to be a letting go of control that is necessary to initiate the process leading to an OBE.

Out-of-body experiences can also happen when meditating for reasons *not* connected to the desire to have one. For example, Busan native Ji Yeon reported having two spontaneous OBEs three months before we spoke. I asked whether she had meditated around that time. At first she answered no, but about an hour into the interview, she mentioned that she had been taking an extrasensory perception (ESP) course. When I asked what that involved, she told me that it required meditation several times a day, and the visualization of gold being sprinkled onto her body. So she *had* been meditating. I have come to refer to these types of induced experiences as 'kindled OBEs' in light of the theory described below.

THE CULTURAL KINDLING THEORY

In 2014, medical anthropologists Julia Cassaniti and Tanya Luhrmann presented the 'cultural kindling' model of spiritual experiences, which posits that certain practices can 'kindle' certain types of experience through an 'interaction between expectation, cultural invitation, spiritual practice, and bodily responsiveness'. It may take time to have the initial experience, they argue, but once it happens, it has a 'kindling' effect, allowing further experiences to occur with greater ease, like a self-sustaining fire.

The authors suggest that, although experiences like OBEs have universal core features, either the experience as a whole, or certain features of the experience, are recognized as spiritually meaningful ('hypercognized') or ignored as meaningless hallucinations ('hypocognized') in line with the cultural beliefs and attitudes in which they are being considered. This is affected by knowledge production (how knowledge is produced and used in a culture) as well as cultural invitation, or the way in which meaning is given to certain mental or bodily sensations that might otherwise go unnoticed. These sensations are in turn affected by certain practices, like meditation. According to this 'cultural kindling' model, significance given to certain sensations can make people more sensitive to them, lowering the threshold for them to occur.[16]

This kindling effect might explain something strange that happened when I came home one afternoon and sat on the sofa, not tired or stressed but simply to pause for a moment. As soon as my back touched the cushioned surface, I felt vibration sensations course through my body that I, by this time, knew often precede my OBEs. When asked if I can have an OBE at will, I'm never quite sure how to answer, as it doesn't quite work the way that most people imagine. Instead of mentally intending to have one, I seem to have built a kind of 'muscle memory' or association between lying down and having an OBE: *Ah, I'm in the supine position, that means it's OBE TIME* – like one of Pavlov's dogs salivating at the sound of a bell. On the sofa that day, this association had now progressed from lying down to just feeling my back against a surface. This suggests that my spiritual practice of lying down and meditating had programmed an association or 'expectation' that triggered a 'bodily responsiveness', as mentioned in the cultural kindling theory above. In other words, although a practice can start out as deliberate, at some point the sensitivity to physical sensations could set in action an automatic process, leading to an OBE.

This meant that, rather than gaining mastery of my capacity for OBEs, it was as if I had 'kindled' a fire that had grown out of my control. I could have let this continue, but I was afraid that it would continue to snowball until it happened during conversations or, more worryingly, while doing things like crossing the street. At the time, around age 29, I didn't know any other experiencers, and with no one to share these experiences with without sounding crazy, I decided to take a year-long break. After a few weeks of shaking off the onset vibrations by forcing myself to physically move, my muscle memory seemed to 'take the hint' and this process of automatic OBEs stopped. If I wanted to have more OBEs in future, I had to kindle the process all over again – through actions such as meditation, which normally take a couple of weeks. So far, I haven't let my practice continue long enough to snowball again.

THE IMPACT OF EMBODIMENT

A key factor in being able to have OBEs is embodiment, by which I mean the feeling of being connected to or grounded in your physical body, which can include sensory and emotional experiences. In 2009, psychologist Susan Blackmore was addressing a crowd of retired psychologists, psychiatrists and mediums in the dark lecture room of the Society for Psychical Research headquarters. During her talk, she called for a volunteer to take part in an experiment. I raised my hand, and she invited me onto the stage, indicating for me to sit at the table where a rubber hand sat on one side of a dividing screen.

As instructed, I placed my hand on the other side of the screen, out of sight. Next, she stroked my fingers one by one, while simultaneously doing the same on the rubber hand. After a minute or two of this, she stopped stroking my fingers but continued with the rubber hand. At this point, about two-thirds of people will continue to feel their hand being stroked – a sort of phantom touch. The point of the experiment is to prove that the self – or the soul – is an illusion, and that this can be triggered by tricking the brain. I was one of the one-third who did *not* experience the phantom touch. I wondered why that might be until I came across a study of the Rubber Hand Illusion more than a decade later, which was led by Jason J. Braithwaite, a psychology professor at the University of Lancaster.

Braithwaite's team found that people who report spontaneous anomalous bodily experiences, such as OBEs, took longer to notice the Rubber Hand Illusion.[17] A further study focusing specifically on OBErs had similar results, which led the team to conclude that OBErs displayed 'over-embodiment' compared to non-OBErs. Over-embodiment is the heightened awareness of the body or its sensations, which can include anything from breathing and heart rate to the feeling of fabric against one's skin. Their paper, entitled 'Deliberate and spontaneous sensations of disembodiment: capacity or flaw?' proposes that rather than a pathology or flaw (as some people think), the OBE is a (spontaneous) human capacity.[18]

Embodiment, or over-embodiment, can be a learned cultural trait. I always wondered why it was that people swore that mental practices such as mindfulness and visualization, and physical practices like martial arts and yoga seemed to lead to more OBEs (as well as lucid dreams), and now I had my answer: these practices can strengthen embodiment. There is also a biological basis for how some people might experience embodiment differently. For example, over-embodiment is often seen in people with autism spectrum condition (ASC), which can make them especially aware of sensory stimuli. This might explain why, as found in a 2017 study, 93 per cent of adults with ASC reported having had anomalous perceptual experiences, including out-of-body experiences.[19]

Out-of-body experiences are also sometimes triggered by seizures, which are defined by a sudden burst of electrical activity that interrupts the regular communication between neurons. A seizure can be a one-off experience, brought on by triggers such as high fever or flashing lights, but when it happens more than twice, the person can be diagnosed with epilepsy. Susan Leybourne, a Northampton-based psychic and doctoral student, is in the former camp, having had only one seizure in her life, and she suffered with classic migraines as a child. She has had several spontaneous out-of-body experiences throughout her life, the first of which was triggered by her seizure. It occurred when she was 14 years old, while watching the black and white *Monty Python* sketch 'Blackmail'. It was around 9:30 p.m., and her mum was in the kitchen asking her what she wanted on her toast, when the television started to flicker. 'The sketch was flickering at a certain rate, which set off a seizure,' she says. 'I fell to the ground at the door of the living room and could see my body from across the room.'

Curiously, she looked down to see her 'astral' self wearing school clothes, although her physical body had been cloaked in a nightdress. She then experienced a kind of three-way consciousness: aware of her body on the living room floor, her spirit watching her parents carry her body to the settee and discuss what to do, while another part of her was moving rapidly, 'like on rollers'. I had heard of dual consciousness in OBEs before, but this was the first time I had heard of *triple* consciousness. This fast-moving third part of her was wearing an old-fashioned white dress as white-washed Edwardian houses sped by in what looked like London.

After the experience ended, her mother made her favourite comfort food (mashed potatoes), and they all sat down to watch a new thriller that was just starting. This is when they realized that her experience had a bizarre after-effect. Susan's parents watched, baffled, as she began to pre-empt the actors' dialogue as if she had seen it before. She could even point out the villain at their first appearance.

Like me, Susan had been trying to astral project since around eight or nine years old, with techniques she found in a library book. In her case, she had not been specifically looking for this information but came across it by chance (Sylvan Muldoon, she thinks). And just as I experienced, the techniques never worked for her when she was trying, but only once she had given up. She would sometimes watch *The Tomorrow People* on television, which featured characters with telepathy, bilocation and other abilities, and had wondered whether she might be a 'tomorrow person' herself.

SLEEP- AND DREAM-INDUCED OBEs

Although certain practices, traits and medical conditions can make us more susceptible to OBEs from the waking state, it is possible that OBEs occur to all (or most) of us at certain times of the sleep cycle, and that you only need to be consciously aware to catch them. Awareness during sleep and dreams can be achieved by conscious sleep practices such as *yoga nidra*, which involves breath awareness and mentally scanning one's body, lucid dreaming or interrupted sleep, keeping a journal of all nocturnal experiences, and with oneirogens (dream-enhancing substances) like galantamine, which will be discussed in the next chapter. In my own longer OBEs, I sometimes noticed dream-like elements seeping into the otherwise stable environment, like hallucinations or an augmented reality game. It occurred to me that this might indicate that I was changing sleep stages, each of which are associated with certain features, including changes to sensory, vestibular and social information, which as mentioned can propel us into alternate 'Stories of Experience' (see pages 45–7).

We typically have around four to six sleep cycles per night, each lasting about 90 to 120 minutes. We move through the non-REM (NREM) sleep stages N1 (transition to sleep), N2 (light sleep) and N3 (deep sleep), before moving into REM (vivid dreaming). And this then all starts again, repeating on a loop. While REM sleep stages become longer as the night progresses, NREM sleep becomes gradually shorter.

N1 (or 'Stage 1') sleep tends to last for about 1 to 7 minutes, or 5 per cent of our sleep time. In the first cycle this is when hypnagogia can occur – the transitional state of consciousness between wakefulness

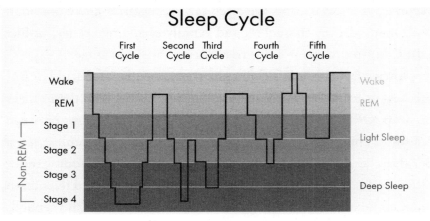

An average sleep cycle as depicted in Western psychology.

and sleep. The images at this stage are referred to as hypnagogic hallucinations, and can range from faint impressions to full-blown colour panoramas similar to passively watching a film on-screen, when you're not quite immersed yet.

Each N2 ('Stage 2') level lasts for 10 to 25 minutes, or about 45 per cent of our sleep time. Reports of N2 dreams say they are generally short and realistic, with fewer characters and places, and with less emotional and perceptual content than REM dreams, but with similar thought processes to wakefulness. N3 ('Stage 3'), the deepest stage of sleep, lasts for 20 to 40 minutes, or 25 per cent of sleep, and is when sleepwalking can occur. Dreams in this stage often show signs of emotions, perceptions and self-imagery.

Finally, REM (rapid eye movement) sleep lasts for 10 to 60 minutes, or 25 per cent of our sleeping time. This is when our most immersive dreams, lucid dreams and nightmares occur. REM dreams are the most recalled dreams as they tend to happen right before waking.[20] When experiencers insist that OBEs are different from dreams, they are referring to REM dreams specifically. This is no surprise, as REM dreams are often bizarre, creative and emotional, with many dream characters and rapidly changing scenes, unlike OBEs. Lucid dreams usually arise during the REM stage.[21]

However, it is possible that at least some OBEs are lucid *NREM* dreams, or have overlapping physiological features with these stages of sleep. OBEs tend to arise from the gaps or transitions between modes of consciousness, such as between waking, dreaming, sleep paralysis (during which the mind is awake but the body cannot move) and unconsciousness.[22] Lucid NREM dreams tend to contain more mundane 'day residue', which may fit with many OBE reports, especially in the beginning of the experience. As British psychologist

Charles McCreery demonstrates, some N1 (Stage 1) dreams can have several qualities in common with OBEs, such as:

- *Externalization*, in which hallucinations appear to be superimposed on the immediate environment (usually the bedroom);
- *Realism*, as the perceptions are closer to waking life than in REM dreams;
- Emotional detachment or composure.[23]

As this 'typical' sleep architecture is based on studies with subjects from W.E.I.R.D. backgrounds – that is, Western, Educated, Industrialized, Rich and Democratic – and as this demographic has been shown to be psychologically quite different from the wider human population, it makes no sense to assume that this would apply to everyone in the world. We also know that sleep architecture (the pattern of sleep stages and cycles that a person experiences during the night) can vary depending on factors such as medical conditions. For example, people with narcolepsy may skip the initial NREM stages and go into REM sleep within 15 minutes, both at night and when napping.[24] They are also more likely to experience vivid dreams or hallucinations upon falling asleep or waking up, as well as sleep paralysis episodes and OBEs. Depression can also lead to earlier and longer REM periods.[25]

Diet can also have an impact on sleep architecture. One study showed that individuals on a high-carb, low-fat diet had an increase in REM dreams and a decrease in deep NREM sleep in the first cycle, while those on a low-carb, high-fat diet had lower REM and higher deep sleep and awakenings. A high-carb, high-sugar diet, with low fibre intake, also seems to increase awakenings during the sleep cycle, as well as a decrease in deep NREM sleep.[26] This might explain why hangovers or junk food can sometimes trigger an eventful night of adventures for experiencers, although many say that vegetarian or keto diets have a better effect in the long term. The old idea that carbohydrates lead to a good night's sleep by increasing tryptophan and melatonin has been debunked by a study that found that this only works when consuming very low protein (the majority of studies gave volunteers a drink that contained 100 per cent carbohydrates and 0 per cent protein).[27] Another study found that low protein intake leads to difficulty getting to sleep, while very high protein intake can lead to difficulty staying asleep.[28] Over the years, some of the people I have interviewed about their OBEs and sleep paralysis episodes said that tweaking their diet altered their nightly experiences. For example, for two women, cutting out gluten stopped their sleep paralysis; for another, cutting out coffee had the same effect (although she had nightmares instead).

OBEs can also be learned *naturally* in response to an undesirable or novel experience of consciousness, such as sleep paralysis or nightmares, or even by accident. For example, an interesting ear-related technique comes from a netizen on Robert Peterson's blog 'The OBE Outlook on Life'. This person claims to be able to control the *tensor tympani*, a muscle in the inner ear, thus triggering a 'humming or roaring-like noise' similar to that often reported during the astral projection transition. Although this 'ear humming' began in this person's childhood just for fun, eventually it became clear that it could trigger an intense astral projection with high awareness. 'I could even come back at will and shoot back out by just tightening the muscles in the inner ear,' they said. Peterson notes that the right temporoparietal junction is close to our vestibular and auditory system, which might explain why sound is sometimes featured in the switch to a new 'Story of Experience' (see pages 45–7).[29]

Another example of someone *naturally* coming to OBEs as a result of an undesirable experience of consciousness comes from occultist and writer Oliver Fox (real name Hugh G. Calloway, 1885–1949), who was ill for a lot of his childhood, and was therefore frequently confined to his bed with nothing to occupy his mind. During this time, he experienced frightening hallucinations, nightmares and trance-like states, but he later became lucid in his dreams, which allowed him to transform his nightmares. He soon found that he could prolong his dreams through willpower, but that after a while this would cause a dull pain in the area around his pineal gland (behind his third eye) during the experience, and a sharp pain at the top of his head. He found that if he ignored these feelings, he would sense a 'click' in his brain, after which he would feel a new kind of experience – free of his body and of fear: an OBE. The first time this happened, he experienced a kind of 'dual consciousness', seeing the shore he had just been dreaming of at the same time that he could see his bedroom. After this 'click', he was able to continue walking along the shore, but now, unlike in his dreams, nobody could see him. (This feature will be explored more in Chapter 7.)

Fox tried to wake himself up from this, much like he had during his lucid dreams, but this time it proved more difficult. After some effort, he felt another 'click' in his brain and found himself in bed, unable to move. By focusing all his willpower on moving his pinkie finger, then his hand, and finally gripping the bedposts, he managed to sit upright, although he wasn't sure if he was actually moving his *physical* body or not. Although ill for the next few days, Fox was determined to repeat his experiments, focusing on exiting through the pineal gland.[30]

As mentioned earlier in this chapter, researchers have noticed differences depending on whether an OBE is intentionally or spontaneously induced. This raised a question in my mind: could the timing of the experience also influence its characteristics? Curious, I asked my biologist friend Cecilia, who we met in the previous chapter, whether she had noticed any differences in biomarkers such as the brain's electrical activity between OBEs starting in Stage 1 sleep versus those triggered by REM lucid dreams.

Cecilia explained that although research on OBEs within the sleep cycle is limited, her studies using EEG monitoring reveal that brain activity fluctuates just before sleep paralysis and OBEs. Accompanying this shift is a brief interruption of breathing, which she calls 'the window to enter that third state of consciousness'. She plans to add respiratory measures in future experiments to explore this phenomenon further. 'I think that the brain interprets [an interruption of breathing] like you're dying, and then there's a transfer of consciousness. It can also happen during an epileptic seizure, for example. But we have to add the sensors [for further tests].'

I then asked, 'What do you think would cause the breathing to stop, especially for someone who has deliberate OBEs?'

'Good question,' Cecilia replied. 'It could be heart arrhythmia,' (interestingly, both of us have this condition), 'or [it could be] something else that we don't understand.'

Although many mysteries remain regarding the mechanisms behind OBEs, we now have a better understanding of the foundations that support and shape these experiences. Reflecting on what we've discussed so far, it will become clearer why certain induction methods are chosen for the job.

PRACTITIONERS AND THEIR INDUCTION TECHNIQUES

The morning of my Three Intruders experience, I phoned my mum to tell her what had happened, but decided to keep it from my flatmate Daisuke, who was preparing breakfast downstairs, safe and sound. My mother's reaction was unexpected. At first, she sounded surprised, but then she said matter-of-factly, 'Well, they might have been Scientologists'. She had recently seen a documentary about them, she explained, which extolled their out-of-body abilities. I was not sure what Scientologists would want with the employee of a Japanese bank, but it was a novel, albeit disturbing idea to consider. So I decided to explore the role of OBEs in the world of Scientology to find out more.

THE EXTERIORIZING THETAN AND PERSPECTIVE-SWITCHING OF SCIENTOLOGY

It turned out that Scientology, like many religions, had started with a journey of the soul. In 1938, during an operation under nitrous oxide, science fiction author L. Ron Hubbard claimed to have had a near-death experience in which he found himself 'sliding helter-skelter down into a vortex of scarlet'. Upon his return he heard a voice say, 'Don't let him know!' These words haunted him – *Don't let me know what!?* – until a word came to him one morning upon waking, which he assumed to be the answer:

SURVIVE.

This word would serve as the foundation for his new self-help organization Dianetics[1], which he founded in 1950. Dianetics focused on the soul's effect on the body, and aimed to liberate the 'superman' within by defeating psychosomatic conditions, fears and insecurities.[2] Two years later, Hubbard founded a new religion, Scientology, to 'study and handl[e] the spirit in relationship to itself, to universes and to other life'.[3] Religious studies scholar Professor Hugh B. Urban describes the religion as a blend of 'eastern religions, alternate spiritualities, and science fiction'. Its space opera cosmology includes reincarnation and the belief that followers are much more than their physical body[4] – they don't *have* a soul, they *are* a soul, or as they call it, a 'thetan' (from the Greek symbol *theta* (Θ) which means thought or life).[5] The thetan can leave the body or, in Scientology terms, 'exteriorize', which is described as 'the state of the thetan being outside his body with or without full perception, [while] still able to control and handle the body'.[6]

For Scientologists, exteriorization could be accomplished by one simple command during what they call 'auditing', which is similar to counselling: *'be three feet back of your head.'* The auditor could then instruct the thetan to travel the Earth and the universe in this out-of-body state, which Hubbard insisted was different from mere visualization or imagination. Interestingly, Hubbard placed exteriorization in a class above astral projection, which he saw as a mere delusion. He argued that some people might believe that they are exteriorizing, when they are instead doing one of two things: remote viewing, or exteriorizing some kind of mock-up of the thetan, which goes somewhere in lieu of it. Interestingly, remote viewing, or the practice of psychically viewing remote locations, people or objects, was largely developed by Scientologists working as parapsychologists and mediums. Scientology placed 'true exteriorization' in a league above these phenomena. During this exalted state, the thetan could leave the body behind to explore the 'MEST' universe – of Matter, Energy, Space and Time – which they could then alter, manifest or dissolve. The thetan was also said to have further paranormal powers as people ascended the Scientology ranks, including the ability to mind-read, heal oneself and others, manifest illusions that can be seen by others, see through walls, remote view and even fix broken appliances by rearranging their molecules.[7] In other words, anything was said to be possible with the powers achieved through Scientology.

In *The Creation of Human Ability: A Handbook for Scientologists* (1954), Hubbard describes a technique to use when a person has just exteriorized, in order to 'get his attention onto the environment':

> *Be outside the Moon*
> *In the centre of the Moon*
> *Outside*
> *Centre*
> *Outside*
> *Centre*
> *Flip back and forth as rapidly as you can*

It continues in this vein for several pages, instructing the student to imagine switching their perspective between space and Earth, and to imagine different temperatures, emotions and colours.[8] He calls this R1-9, the 'Grand Tour' which is to increase the person's confidence that they can 'view anything in the universe'.[9] Urban notes that Hubbard's exteriorization teachings were almost exactly like reports of astral projection in occult publications, in particular from the work of Sylvan Muldoon and Aleister Crowley, which he referenced in a 1952 lecture. Indeed, a decade earlier, Hubbard had been residing with rocket scientist Jack Parsons, a disciple of Aleister Crowley, and they had performed magic rituals together.[10]

ABSORPTION AND VISUALIZATION BY MAGICAL ORDERS

Psychologist Susan Blackmore suggested that the following skills are required to successfully induce an OBE:

1. Absorption ability, or the ability to let go of the external world by disrupting or ignoring sensory input;
2. The ability to mentally construct an alternative reality from imagination and memory;
3. The ability to attend more to the alternative model than the external sensory world.[11]

Techniques to induce OBEs often involve visualizing shifts in perception, similar to the exercise described in the Scientology text above. With sufficient focus and absorption, methods like this can help individuals transition from their usual physical body schema into an alternate one.[12] As mentioned in Chapter 2, astral projection was practised by various movements that gained popularity in the

PRACTITIONERS AND THEIR INDUCTION TECHNIQUES

19th and 20th centuries, such as Theosophy and Spiritualism, many of which employed perspective switching and visualization methods. In 1887, a magical order called the Golden Dawn was founded in London by Freemasons Samuel Liddell Mathers and William Wynn Westcott together with medical doctor William Robert Woodman. The Golden Dawn utilized a wide range of symbolic tools – such as tarot cards, sigils, Enochian squares, the Tree of Life and 'Tattvas' – as gateways into the astral plane. Practitioners would concentrate on an image until it grew and filled their awareness, at which point they could mentally 'leap' through the image and find themselves in an alternate landscape, such as a desert. Once there, they could fly around at will and 'vibrate' sacred words. Within this astral space, they engaged in various spiritual practices: performing magic, communing with deities, nature spirits, angels and beings from other planets, exploring past lives, diagnosing and healing the astral body, and establishing psychic boundaries.[13]

A member of the Golden Dawn since 1889, occultist Aleister Crowley (1875–1947) created a new religion called Thelema, after a voice dictated its teachings to him while on honeymoon in Cairo. This religion also taught astral projection, which was considered a useful tool for practising ritual magick, but only insofar as it contributed to fulfilling one's 'True Will', a core value of the religion. For Crowley, before practising astral projection, the student should first be in good health and sufficiently trained in *asana*, *pranayama* and *dharana* – yogic practices that involve stillness of the body, breathing exercises and visualization. Once ready, the student could use the following technique:

> Let the student be at rest in one of his prescribed positions, having bathed and robed with the proper decorum. Let the place of working be free from all disturbance, and let the preliminary

purifications, banishings and invocations be duly accomplished, and, lastly, let the incense be kindled.

Let him imagine his own figure (preferably robed in the proper magical garments and armed with the proper magical weapons) as enveloping his physical body, or standing near to and in front of him.

Let him then transfer the seat of his consciousness to that imagined figure; so that it may seem to him that he is seeing with its eyes, and hearing with its ears. This will usually be the great difficulty of the operation.[14]

'DREAM-CONTROL' AND EYE-DIRECTION METHODS

One of the most popular esoteric authors in the first half of the 20th century was Sylvan Muldoon (1903–1969), who inspired readers to try astral projection for themselves. In contrast to Oliver Fox's dream-induced experiences described on pages 71–2, Sylvan Muldoon had spontaneous OBEs in which he would either exit his body consciously, or suddenly find himself conscious in a projected state in or near his immediate environment. The first time this happened, he was 12 years old and his mother had taken him and his little brother to stay at a Spiritualist Association camp, where they shared a house with a group of well-known mediums. After a few hours of sleep, he woke up slowly in a silent darkness, unable to remember where he was. When he tried to move, he found himself in 'astral catalepsy' – a state of being unable to move during the out-of-body experience. Suddenly he felt as if he was floating, and felt his body vibrate rapidly up and down.[15]

One of Muldoon's techniques was the 'dream-control' method, whereby you could retain consciousness from waking into the hypnagogic state and then focus on an image such as an elevator or aeroplane, and 'shift' yourself into it just as you feel your consciousness slipping. Muldoon advised the reader to plan the dream they wanted to enter just as they would plan an important task in their daily life. He also suggested other visualization techniques, like imagining 'steaming' through the pores of their body, climbing a rope or whirling around. The following exercise also incorporated eye movements:

> A good exercise for this purpose is to close the eyes, then roll the eyeballs until they are fixed at a point on the forehead, between the eyes – in much the same way as the Yogis do – and make a concentrated effort to gather together your psychic energies at that point. Will, with the whole force of your being, that you are there; and when you have concentrated your full Self at the spot, then will that you shall be projected outwards, in space, from that point of departure. This method is a strain upon the eyes, but is one which has been found very effective – as the result of numerous experiments and experiences.[16]

I think the reason this works is that the eye strain makes the live external visual feed unreliable, while the imaginary dot becomes the point of stability, and thus the better candidate for the chosen 'Story of Experience' (see pages 45–7 for full explanation). At the same time, the eye movements mimic REM (rapid eye movement) sleep, in which immersive visual imagery is more easily generated.

As mentioned in the previous chapter, occultist Oliver Fox wrote that he was able to prolong his lucid dreams with willpower until he felt a 'click' in his head, after which he found himself in an OBE. Psychologist Harvey J. Irwin suggests that lucid dreaming may be an effective launchpad, as it involves the cortical arousal necessary for an OBE – a brain state that increases alertness and heart rate in a somewhat similar way to the stressful conditions that trigger *forced* out-of-body experiences.[17]

DREAM-ENHANCING ROCKET FUEL: GALANTAMINE

As mentioned in the previous chapter, there is the idea that we 'leave' our bodies each night when we sleep, a belief found in many cultures around the world. Besides practices like lucid dreaming or *yoga nidra*, we can also cultivate better recall and awareness in sleep by taking memory-enhancing supplements. In *The Odyssey*, written around 725–675 BCE, the sorceress Circe drugs Odysseus's crew to rob them of their memories of home and turn them into pigs. Hermes tells Odysseus that the antidote to this drug, named 'moly', had black roots, milky white flowers and was difficult to find.[18] Scholars think that these drugs referred to real plants; the memory-robbing drug was likely *datura*, and its antidote the snowdrop flower. Although the snowdrop flower is poisonous as it is, in the 1950s, Bulgarian chemist Dimatar Paskov became the first to isolate galantamine from the plant to use as an acetylcholinesterase inhibitor.[19] This is a chemical that 'inhibits' the breakdown of the neurotransmitter acetylcholine, which is needed for learning, attention and memory, and a deficiency of which is linked with Alzheimer's disease. Although it is unable to significantly *reverse* damage caused by this disease, it can at least potentially lessen the ongoing deterioration.

After psychophysiologist and author Stephen LaBerge suggested that galantamine could also be used to encourage lucid dreaming by enhancing cognition and memory in dreams, it became a popular oneirogen, or dream enhancer. After four or five hours of sleep, the lucid dreamer wakes for around 30 minutes to two hours, during which they should avoid any stimulating activities or bright light. I learned the following cocktail from lucid dreaming instructor Dr Rory Mac Sweeney: wake up after approximately four hours of sleep, and take 8 mg of galantamine, ½ tsp of l-aspartic acid powder, and 150 mg of l-theanine.

When I tried this, it was like rocket fuel, propelling me into an altered state with incredible mental clarity. It was also like playing a game of roulette – sometimes the boule landed on a lucid dream, and other times it landed on an OBE, often switching between the two. Galantamine seems to 'wake up the conscious mind' wherever it is in the sleep cycle, and reunite it with the subconscious, as Muldoon and others have alluded to. Although I have sometimes had hour-long out-of-body experiences *naturally*, taking galantamine seemed to make them more likely to occur. If you are interested in taking galantamine, there are a few things to consider first. It's good to wait at least four nights between uses, as the body can develop a tolerance to it. Also, the increase in acetylcholine can cause stomach pain and nausea in the morning, so it's best to take galantamine with ginger or avoid taking it on an empty stomach. (As I have a sensitive stomach, I only have 4 or 6 mg at a time. I open the capsule and mix the powder in a small glass of water and drink it, then take it *right* before falling back to sleep.) Otherwise, it can kick in too soon and cause annoying mind-chatter that makes it hard to relax!

As with any substances, consult a medical professional before use and be aware of the legality of its use within your region.

USING SOUND TO ENCOURAGE ASTRAL PROJECTION

In the previous chapter, I briefly mentioned the use of sound technologies to induce OBEs. These tools have been around for several decades, and include 'Hemi-Sync', patented by the Monroe Institute, 'Sacred Acoustics', developed by Eben Alexander, and 'Infra-liminal sound', developed by Graham Nicholls. Both Hemi-Sync and Sacred Acoustics use 'binaural beats' – different sounds played in each ear which lead the brain to form a new brain wave pattern in between the two sounds; this is said to create coherence between both hemispheres of the brain.[20] As there are different patterns of brain activity – delta, theta, alpha, beta and gamma – that are associated with different states of consciousness and cognitive functions,[21] the idea is that we can use the binaural beat method to force the brain into the desired frequency band. For example, if we would like to enter theta, one of the most popular brain wave patterns for astral projection, we would need our brain waves to oscillate at between 4 and 7 Hz (or oscillations per second). This can happen during deep relaxation, light sleep and dreaming, but it can also be induced by playing two sounds in each ear that differ by 4 Hz, for example, 40 and 44 Hz, or 15 and 19 Hz. Anthropologist Michael Winkelman's integrative mode of consciousness also posits that certain techniques like drumming and fasting can alter one's brain state towards theta brain waves, inducing a trance or soul journey.[22] In contrast, Infra-liminal sound does *not* use binaural beats, but instead uses complex patterns of sound that Nicholls has found effective in inducing the vibrational state, an easier state to progress to the OBE from.[23]

THE 'ROLL-OUT' TECHNIQUE

One of the most popular current methods of encouraging OBEs is the 'roll-out' technique, which involves relaxing the physical body and imagining yourself rocking an alternate or 'astral' body – in other words, shifting your focus and 'bringing to life' an alternate body schema. My biologist friend Cecilia shares her experience with this technique, which suggests that the method of exiting the physical body may affect the nature of the out-of-body experience. Since her first spontaneous OBE at the age of 17, Cecilia normally focuses her energy between her eyes, projecting herself from that point just through intention, rather than trying to move her second body.

'In the lab,' she says, '[my student] told me, *"No, you have to move, to rotate from one side."* So, I entered the OBE like she told me to, and it was *completely* different. The body was very, very heavy, it was amazing, the change. The way you project yourself from your physical body affects your experience.'

PROLONGING THE EXPERIENCE

Once in the OBE, it can last for what seems like mere seconds, or longer than an hour. Until in-lab studies are conducted on experiencers, we will not know what causes them to extend or end, but self-experimentation has led to some interesting results. In my own experiences, I've found that sometimes kinaesthetic techniques, such as spinning, or grounding techniques used in psychotherapy, such as rubbing your hands together or touching stable objects, can prolong the experience. Hedge witch Jane, who we've heard from several times already, sometimes uses an oneirogen called LucidEsc, which includes Huperzine A and Choline Bitartrate to prolong her experiences.

However, at some point, the experience will end. This may be due to one of the body's needs, like water, food or a toilet break, or due to interruptions like a loud sound or physical touch. If there are no physical interruptions, it can also end due to heightened emotions or through intention. Sometimes, the ending of the experience seems to have nothing to do with either mind or body, at least consciously. On occasion, I have been unable to end an experience even with screaming, pounding and force of mind (I have heard the same about some lucid dreams). In these cases, the experience typically ends with the environment intact, while feelings of drowsiness overtake me, which feels exactly like falling asleep from the *waking* state. This essentially redefined the concept of 'falling asleep' for me; now it seems more like the switch of a channel. Alternatively, the mental state can remain intact but there is a sense of a time limit before the environment either fades or you're pulled back to your body. One astral projector described this as like diving into water and knowing that you have a limited amount of time before you need to come up for air. This suggests to me that there may be a biological shift happening, like the switch between sleep stages or changes in the circadian rhythm.

TRANSITIONS: VIBRATIONS, KUNDALINI AND SOUND

Although transitionless OBEs are common, many OBEs *are* accompanied by transitions, or pre-onset, features such as energy sensations, which are sometimes likened to tingles, voltage, energy, wind, waves, currents, buzzing and vibrations. Although the experience can be intense, as if the bed is shaking (on one occasion I was convinced it was an earthquake), anyone looking from the outside will report that your body has been still. I have found in my research that the vibrational state generally manifests in the following ways:

1. In motion, repeating either (a) back and forth, or (b) in one direction, typically from the toes to the head, before starting at the toes again. Its course generally repeats back and forth or goes in one direction all the way through the body or in only a section of the body, such as feet to waist.
2. A stationary buzzing, either confined to one part of the body (e.g. the left pinkie toe for me) or in the entire body at once.

Other pre-onset features can include sounds, such as whooshing or mechanical noises, and the feeling of touch or pressure. Transition phenomena usually cease once the exit from the body is complete. Similar phenomena are also reported in meditation or spiritual contexts, which may or may not be accompanied by out-of-body experiences, but are known by different names depending on the culture or discipline.

Mystical beliefs in bodily energy flows are found in many cultures, known, for example, as *chi* in China, *ki* in Korea, and *Kundalini*, or *prana*, in the vedantic and tantric traditions of India. In the tantric tradition, the inner Kundalini is visualized as a serpent in the root chakra, and can be awakened through spiritual practices such as meditation, allowing the individual to also be awakened to their true nature.[1] This energy force is thought to be an 'all-encompassing consciousness' with an outer form – the physical universe, physiological processes – and an inner form – spiritual awareness.

In scientific and religious disciplines, these transition sensations are known as Spiritually Transformative Energetic Experiences (STEs) or Energy-Like Somatic Experiences (ELSEs), which are triggered by concentration on spiritual matters, the presence of a spiritually developed person, and intense meditation or prayer.[2] In psychiatry, these symptoms are referred to as 'cenesthesias', which can include 'vibrating,' 'migrating sensations' through the body, and 'sensations of movement, pulling and pressure' which start at the feet and move towards the head. In the psychiatric literature, cenesthesias are often associated with schizophrenia spectrum disorders.[3] This does not necessarily mean that these symptoms are signifiers of mental illness, but that the symptoms were unmanageable enough to seek medical attention.

A team of psychiatrists and religious scholars at Brown University published a 2021 study on the ELSEs – mainly reported as vibration sensations – as experienced by Western Buddhist meditators. The authors found that the frequency of these experiences was nearly identical across the three Buddhist traditions they looked at (Zen, Tibetan and Theravāda), with around 62 per cent of practitioners spontaneously reporting them. The term most commonly used to describe these sensations was 'Kundalini', and they were often accompanied by inner sounds, light or a feeling of joy or interconnectedness. One practitioner of Tibetan Buddhism described Kundalini as like 'standing next to a 747 as it is firing up its engines on the end of the runway' due to the intensity of vibrations, while another practitioner said it's like 'if you put your hand in front of the exhaust when the car engine is running'. Other explanations include 'like being a rocket ship', and 'like a machine with gears – it felt like, all of a sudden, all the gears started to grind'. These sensations can be described as smooth, neutral and pleasant, or as grinding and painful ('just this horrific, grinding discomfort').[4]

Now compare this with the following account from astral projector Sylvan Muldoon:

I could feel a tremendous pressure being exerted in the back of my head, in the medulla oblongata region. This pressure was very impressive, and came in regular spurts, the force of which seemed to pulsate my whole body. … I began to hear somewhat familiar and seemingly far-distant sounds. … No sooner had the sense of hearing come into being than that of sight followed. When able to see, I was more than astonished! No words could possibly explain my wonderment. I was floating![5]

My OBEs have usually started as soon as my head hit the pillow, without a break in consciousness. The transition would usually involve one or more features, like full-body, partial or undulating vibrations, the feeling of someone touching or pulling my hand, or strange noises. One night, it started with mechanical whirring sounds that reminded me of an aeroplane, as one limb floated up of its own volition. This was followed by a period of silence as it floated as if on water, before the process started again. The vibrations and sounds would end either gradually or abruptly after the bodily exit. I would often shake off my pre-onset experiences by forcing myself to physically move around, either because I was tired and wanted to sleep, or because the transition was so intense that it startled me. I've never been good with roller coasters, and the anticipation I felt reminded me of being at the front of the queue at the wildest ride in the theme park. But interrupting the process would often only serve to delay it to later in the night. So, sometimes, I would wake up with the same sensations again and, this time, more rested and less anxious, I would allow the experience to unfold. Otherwise, I would 'wake up' to find myself already standing or floating 'out there' somewhere, with no transition and no recollection of how I got there. Curiously, if I induced an OBE from a lucid dream or sleep paralysis, these transitions would often still lead to vibrations *within* the dream state, until I floated out of my dream body. I've heard people suggest that this might be explained by what is known as the continuity hypothesis, which is where you dream about what you experience in 'real life', so if you've experienced vibrations from the waking or pre-OBE state, for example, this might make it into your dream content. It's also possible that these sensations result specifically from the transfer between body schemas in different states of consciousness, rather than another feature specific to the transition between the waking and OBE state.

THE LOCATION OF TRANSITION SENSATIONS

Curiously, the vibration sensations can be concentrated in just one area of the body. For me, it tends to be limited to my left pinkie toe, if it's limited at all. The first time this happened, it was followed by a blackout period and then five consecutive OBEs.

In *The Out-of-Body Experience* (2011), Anthony Peake describes an experience with the Lucia Light device, which caused him to feel vibrations in his eyes. This device works by flashing stroboscopic white light at different brightness levels, which has been found to lead to brain wave patterns similar to those in advanced meditators; it can even induce visions. Supervised by its inventors, Austrian psychologist Dr Engelbert Winkler and neurologist Dr Dirk Proeckl, Anthony sat in a reclining chair about three feet away from the Lucia device, facing it with his eyes closed. He then watched as blue, then yellow lights exploded onto his visual field, and opened his eyes slightly to see whether the inventors had switched the colour of the lights, but it was still only flashing white light. It was now obvious to him that his mind was generating these colours. He continues:

[W]hat happened next began to disturb me. My eyes started to vibrate in my head. It was a very unpleasant sensation. I told Dr Winkler about this. I then heard the voice of Dr Proeckl, the neurologist, who had clearly just entered the room. He told me not to worry and that what I was experiencing was a physiological, not neurological, reaction to the stroboscopic effects. After a few seconds, and much to my relief, the vibrating stopped ...

Now, he saw movement in his right peripheral visual field, which continued when he moved his head toward it, as instructed.

I was looking down on a vast plain made up of a chessboard-like series of black and white squares. I could see the squares running off to a distant horizon that seemed to glow with a faint bluish light. I then realized that I was suspended many thousands of feet above the surface of the plain. My mind simply couldn't comprehend the sensation of dual location. However, my hands decided that this was a dangerous place to be and they grabbed the sides of the chair in a vice-like grip. The sensation of vertigo was palpable. Just as I was trying to come to terms with this, the vibrations started again, but this time it was not only my eyes but my whole body.

The vibration increased, and Anthony felt an intense rush of blood to his head. He felt as though part of himself was vibrating in and out of his body, and was concerned that the inventors could observe him twitching. He explains, 'I felt like an astronaut sitting at the top of an Apollo launch rocket as it accelerated into space. It was extremely scary but also stupendously amazing.' Although the experience was impressive, it also disturbed him, and he asked for the device to be switched off.[6]

Ukrainian astral projector Pasha has also felt vibrations in his eyes as a result of his 'ten-second tunnel' technique which he outlines here: 'In the morning, after awakening, you have just a few seconds to realize that you have woken up. With your eyes closed, consciously gaze into the darkness behind your closed eyelids, shifting your focus from the tip of your nose to the horizon. And you will see this tunnel! Calm your mind and consciousness, and allow yourself to enter inside.'

Pasha was inspired by a 17th-century Tibetan Lukhang Temple mural, which features various vision scenes that were induced by the Tibetan Buddhist prayer practice of Tögal (from the Dzogchen tradition). This practice was traditionally done in the seated *nirmanakaya* pose and employed both breathing and gaze direction, although Pasha adapted it to a supine position post-sleep. The images in the mural show faces and coloured lights, which are common images seen during hypnagogia (the transition between wakefulness and sleep). But although others have suggested to Pasha that he is seeing hypnagogic images, he thinks that it is more than that, because the tunnel was always the same each time. Pasha would also see light particles rotate counterclockwise in the tunnel, which would bring on the vibrations in his eyes, followed by OBEs which seemed to feature past or alternate lives, including those in bird and fish form.

Recently, Pasha experienced coloured grid-like images like the ones depicted in the Tibetan illustration. Because of this, it seems like there are discrete stages of consciousness that may be triggered by certain techniques. 'It seems the stages are step by step,' he says, 'and each stage needs multiple steps. And then a new stage appears. I see no more tunnel; it seems it's been replaced with another step. It's very interesting how it works. Our growth is staged.'

In addition to his eyes, Pasha has also experienced the vibrations in the area *between* his eyes. 'I felt [the vibrations] like some force drawing vibrational vertical lines from the left to the right part of my forehead in the 3rd eye area only,' he explains. 'This force is conscious, just like whatever made my eyes vibrate. I moved my head a bit aside as the vibrations in my eyes were painful enough and not comfortable, but it moved back and continued to make my eyes vibrate. Moreover, each eye vibrated separately; first the left, then the right. Only later, in subsequent experiences, did they vibrate together.'

The third eye is an important point of focus in several religions such as Hinduism, Buddhism, Taoism and Theosophy, and is associated with attuning one's vibrations to a higher state. Tibetans and Theosophists further place importance on the pineal gland that sits behind the third eye as the engine of this process, and it is thought to be the producer of endogenous (internally generated) DMT (Dimethyltryptamine).[7] Much more research needs to be done before we fully understand the 'geography' of these vibrations, but we do have a few hints of what could be behind them.

In 1983, US Army Lieutenant Colonel Wayne M. McDonnell submitted a report to the CIA detailing his research on the Monroe Institute's Gateway process, a program that uses binaural beats to induce astral projection (see page 84). Although many refer to this CIA report as the official government stance on astral projection, it's worth noting that it only reflects the conclusions of one individual, and much of it has been criticized as pseudoscience. However, it refers to an interesting theory developed by biomedical engineer Itzhak Bentov, which is also explored in his book *Stalking the Wild Pendulum* (1977). The report concluded that techniques such as hypnosis, transcendental meditation and the aforementioned Gateway process developed by the Monroe Institute allow us to bypass the cultural and psychological baggage of the left brain (a bypassing which Muldoon and others argue is necessary to have an OBE). According to Bentov, once the left brain is bypassed in this way, there are two processes which can be triggered.

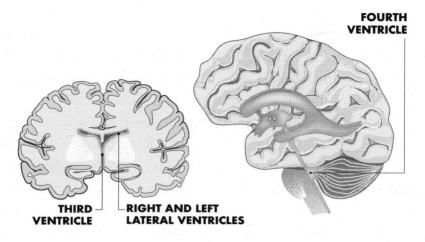

The four cerebral ventricles of the human brain.

To understand this theory, it helps to know a bit about brain anatomy. The brain contains four cavities called cerebral ventricles (see diagram above), which circulate cerebrospinal fluid, helping to cushion the brain, remove waste and maintain its chemical balance. The two largest ventricles, known as the lateral ventricles, sit near the parietal lobe, which are responsible for processing touch and bodily awareness, and the corpus callosum, which bridges the brain's two hemispheres. The third ventricle, which is smaller in size, lies beneath these structures, and is surrounded by the corpus callosum, the hypothalamus (which regulates vital functions) and the pineal gland, which, as mentioned, has been linked to mystical experiences. Finally, the fourth ventricle is located lower down, near the brainstem, specifically the pons and upper medulla oblongata, which in yogic traditions is associated with the 'Spiritual Eye'.

Bentov theorized that acoustical standing waves – created when two sound waves of the same frequency travel in opposite directions

– could create the cerebrospinal fluid to vibrate, particularly in the first three ventricles. This would occur in much the same way that a tuning fork creates vibrations in the air around it. He proposed that these vibrations might also generate currents along the sensory and motor cortices (areas that control sensation and movement), especially in the right hemisphere of the brain, stimulating the brain's pleasure centres. This could explain the blissful sensations often reported during Kundalini experiences, particularly in individuals with sensitive nervous systems. In essence, Bentov suggested that the brain's natural resonance might play a central role in mystical experiences. He referred to this phenomenon as 'physio-kundalini syndrome'.

Amazingly, Bentov suggested that these responses could cause a signal to move from the toes upward, similar to some OBE pre-onset experiences and cenesthesia reports. Bentov suggested that these sensations often begin on the left side of the body, which the CIA report puts forward as evidence that this phenomenon originates in the right hemisphere of the brain (as the left side of the body correlates to the right hemisphere of the brain, and vice versa).[8] This made me think of my 'left pinkie toe' vibrations, my childhood 'out-of-arm' experience (which occurred in my left arm only), and Pasha's vibrations, which swept from the left to the right side of his forehead.*

Continuing this enquiry, medical doctor and member of IANDS (International Association for Near-death Studies), France, Jean

---

* Not everyone, however, will necessarily experience vibrations starting on the same side. After a lab-based OBE induction, one subject of Charles McCreery's study noted, 'my right leg below knee and hip felt "crawly" as if something was about to happen'.[9]

Pierre Jourdan, writes:

> The first stages of transcendental experiences might be induced by blocking or saturating sensory input to the brain at the level of the hippocampus. This could be accomplished during near-death experiences by blockade of hippocampal NMDA receptors by endopsychosins and during meditation by alteration of the hippocampal theta rhythm. Mystical practices described in ancient Yogic or Taoist texts may also alter hippocampal theta by breath exercises or labyrinthine stimulation. Many accounts of kundalini awakenings are consistent with this theory, as is an extended version of Itzhak Bentov's physio-kundalini model.[10]

In his book *Near-Death Experiences* (2024), Anthony Peake explores the link between the Kundalini experience and descriptions in Vedanta (a Hindu philosophy) of the bodily channels in which *prana* flows and the primo vascular system (PVS) in modern science[11]. According to Gene Kieffer, then President of the Kundalini Research Foundation, near-death conditions could trigger Kundalini as a final attempt to direct *prana*, or life-giving currents of energy, towards the dying brain, which can also bring on visions.[12] Indeed, a study by Bruce Greyson showed that Kundalini was more common in near-death experiencers than in a control group. Greyson mentions that Eastern traditions have long claimed that when the brain is oxygen-deprived, Kundalini can move towards it to keep the person alive.[13] Similarly, parapsychologists Caroline Watt and Harvey Irwin suggest that OBE onset sensations may be 'innate biological warning signals'.[14] In 2013, a team from Bulgaria and South Korea published a paper entitled 'The primo vascular system as a new anatomical system', which suggests that it is the anatomical basis for vital energy or *qi* in

Eastern medicine, and is in accordance with traditional acupuncture points and meridian lines. The threadlike primo vascular structures are especially found in the ventricles,[15] tying in with Bentov's theory. As we will see in Chapter 8, Eastern medicine may also shed light on movement and the 'cord' reported in some OBEs.

BELIEFS RELATED TO VIBRATIONS AND SOUND

Understandably, a diverse body of spiritual lore has emerged from these sensations, which are often seen as a natural part of one's spiritual evolution or 'awakening'.[16] According to the Sant Mat tradition originating in India, the Absolute Supreme Being is made up of sound vibrations, which their *Surat Shabd* ('sound current') Yoga practice aims to unite with by focusing on the Third Eye and listening out for inner sound and light. A prominent initiate of this tradition, Kirpal Singh (1894–1974), went on to found his own movement called Ruhani Satsang, which recommended a minimum of two hours meditation per day and taught students how to have out-of-body experiences. According to Singh, while *prana* practices limited students to mental and astral worlds, Shabd Yoga allowed one to reach more open and free realms, because, as he put it, 'Shabd pervades everywhere without ever any limitations'.[17]

Although many of those who experience Kundalini vibrations as an effect of meditation adopt a Western psychiatric or psychological framework alongside spiritual frameworks, many astral projectors refuse to liken pre-onset vibrations to biological processes or medical diagnoses, instead seeing them as properties of spiritual bodies and worlds. There is a widespread belief among experiencers that the nature of one's personal 'frequency' determines the nature of one's experience. For example, YouTuber Natam found that sometimes she could go through the walls of her house, while other times this ability seemed to be blocked, and she concluded that there were different levels of materiality or density that she needed the right frequency or vibration to pass through.[18] This alludes to a different kind of transportation involving fine matter and multiple dimensions rather than the linear mechanics of the day-to-day three-dimensional world. (Chapter 8 discusses mental, physical and emotional methods of navigating these spaces.)

During one of my astral projection phases when I was 13, a friend told me that unusual physical sensations signalled the presence of a nearby spirit, and that the nature of the sensation could reveal its intentions. One afternoon, while we were listening to music in her room (specifically Onyx), I decided to attempt an OBE induction. Although many traditions recommend a quiet environment for such practices, I found the music oddly helpful for focusing my mind. As I concentrated, a tingling sensation gradually washed over me, intensifying until it became full-body vibrations. *It was finally happening!* Just as the vibrations reached their peak, however, her mum called us to the dinner table, cutting the experience short. Assuming that a spirit must have been involved in my experience, my friend explained that it was important to discern the type of vibrations I felt: dull sensations were associated with malevolent spirits, she said, while tingling vibrations were a sign of benevolent spirits.

Transition phenomena can also change over time, which might be related to the kindling process described on page 61. Sohee, a voice actress based in the United States, had not yet achieved an OBE but was actively practising meditation-based induction techniques with this aim. At first, she experienced vibrations when she meditated right after waking, which she described as tingles that flowed through her entire body and face. This was occasionally accompanied by a cold nose or teeth chattering, despite it not being cold. Around this time, she began to also hear a low-frequency chord or ping coming from her right ear, which she likened to an angelic symphony. Over time, this sound changed in two ways. At first, she would only hear it during meditation, but, as time went on, the sound occurred at random times. Secondly, while it started in her right ear cavern, she would later hear it as though it surrounded her, and found herself looking for the source of the noise before recognizing it as a spiritual perception. Sohee noticed that this noise seemed connected with her mental clarity, because although it usually took about 20 minutes of meditating to overcome her 'ADHD thoughts' and get into the vibrational state, whenever the sound was present, she noticed that this would take only five minutes or less. She concluded that the sound meant that there was 'less muck' in her mind, effectively paving a clearer path to another mode of consciousness.

While Sohee's experiences highlight how personal practice and mental states can shape these phenomena, my experiences in scientific settings – ranging from targeted brain stimulation to psychedelic-induced states – offered unique perspectives on the shift into alternate modes of consciousness. In a 2019 study on OBEs in France, I had my right TPJ stimulated to see if it would trigger an OBE as suggested in the neuroscience literature.[19] But instead of an experience similar to my OBEs 'in the wild' (as described in chapter 1), it made me feel as though my body disappeared and 'I' was floating peacefully in nothingness. I suppose this could be seen as a type of 'out-of-body' – or 'no-body' – experience, but there was no crossing the threshold into a new 'Story of Experience' like in most reports from the field. Later, in another study in Belgium, I was given a small dose of the psychedelic drug DMT (Dimethyltryptamine) to see if it could help induce an OBE. I noticed that my body felt as though it were 'pixelating', which reminded me of full-body vibrations before OBE onset. It felt like the DMT had thrown my body into a state of flux, somewhere in the static between radio stations. Once my body knew where it was again, it would settle into a coherent body model. However, sustained by the drug, this 'pixelation' went on for too long, and no amount of concentration could override it. This made me think that the vibrations that occur during pre-onset are a sign of the body schema being in flux. It could explain why the sensations cease after exit, as we have already switched into an alternate or 'astral' body, like the quieting of radio static once we snap into a new channel.

7.

'STEALTH MODE'

Let's return to our protagonist from *The Twilight Zone* pilot episode at the start of Chapter 3, and imagine that he is wandering the same small town, but now there are people present, but nobody can see or hear him. He goes from street to street and room to room, trying to speak to one woman here, shaking a man there, but nobody pays him any attention. This is yet another eerie and commonly reported feature of OBEs (but curiously, not often found in other states of consciousness such as lucid dreams or sleep paralysis). On the astral projection subreddit, I've seen this referred to by the gaming term 'stealth mode', which usually makes the character crouch around quietly without being seen. Another apt term is 'ghost mode', in which the player is a point of awareness that can move freely in all directions without being seen. In Chapter 2, we saw an example of this with Dr Wiltse, who was surprised that his friends couldn't see him as he moved around, and that he even seemed to go *through* other people. Writing in 1939, Oliver Fox also described a 'ghost mode' experience:

> As a rule I am quite invisible to the people I meet and therefore cannot talk to them. In a restaurant I cannot order a meal, because the waiter is unaware of my presence. If I spoke to him, he would not hear; but if I touched him, he would feel me and give such a start that the trance would be broken. However, if I do not

concentrate my attention upon people, I can pass through their bodies without their becoming aware of my presence. Only very rarely have I been visible to another person and able to enter into conversation. And in these exceptional cases our talk has been of very brief duration; for the act of speaking divided my attention and upset my mental control, and the trance was broken.[1]

In their analysis of hundreds of OBE reports, Celia Green and Charles McCreery found that the experiencer is typically invisible to people who are present in the actual physical environment, while the people or beings who *are* responsive are usually *not* physically present.[2] In 2018, I decided to explore this feature further in a preliminary multiple-choice questionnaire on my blog, which had 35 responses:

Have you ever seen people, animals or other beings whilst out of body who COULDN'T see or hear you? Please select all that apply.

Yes, humans: 56 per cent

Yes, animals: 15 per cent

Yes, other beings: 12 per cent

No: 18 per cent

Unsure: 12 per cent

Respondents elaborated further on these events:

> *The most remembered is going to a mall and no one could see me.*

> *They look right through me, walk through me and generally ignore me.*

> *I was flying in a street and I started to spot a guy walking. He did not know I was there. I tried to 'manipulate' him energetically before realizing it was not okay and stopping. The guy kept walking as if nothing had happened.*

> *I was a sphere of energy and guiding a man on a horse. He couldn't see me but I don't know about the horse.*

> *I've been out of body and my animals cannot see me.*

> *I was at a friend's house. I am a Reiki healer and saw my friend in his kitchen, with his back towards me. When I saw his whole aura, I instantly started doing a healing session on him – what I would call astral healing.*

> *They spoke to me as if I was at the end of their bed in physical form, they acted as though all was normal and communicated by asking what I was doing, for example. One witness spoke to me and when they realized it was not really me they became temporarily paralyzed in their bed, unable to move or utter another word until they saw me slowly fade away.*[3]

My stepmother, Trish, shared a personal testimony of her three OBEs, all of which featured this ghost-like quality. It started when she was a teenager in 1980, while standing in the queue at McDonald's. She was famished, not having eaten all day. As she waited to place her order, she turned to her friend. 'Everything sounds weird,' she said.

'What do you mean?' her friend asked.

'Like there's a ghostly echo,' she replied. 'I don't feel good.'

The moment she uttered these words, Trish felt herself zip above her body, and watched as it collapsed on the floor below. The surrounding customers panicked and somebody screamed.

Call an ambulance!

Is she on any drugs?

Trish wondered if this was what it felt like to die. She watched as the paramedics arrived, and one of them pushed his knuckles into her chest, hard enough to leave a bruise later. They placed an oxygen mask on her face and someone pressed two fingers on her wrist. *Weak pulse!* The second time the knuckles went into her chest, she felt herself sweep back into her body.

Trish's second experience occurred in the summer of 1987 while on a date. As soon as she entered the restaurant, she was hit with a wave of heat, despite the air-conditioning. The voices around her changed in quality like the first time, before *poof!*, she saw her body on the floor and heard someone shout, *Call an ambulance!* According to her date, she was unconscious for five to seven minutes, but to her it felt like much longer. Once the ambulance arrived, the paramedics slapped her awake, and her mind and body were reunited once again. In both of these cases, Trish was able to confirm what had happened and what people had said while she was unconscious. She was unsure of what had caused these fainting spells, but suspects that it was a lack of nutrition or low blood pressure.

Trish's last OBE occurred in 2004 while sleeping at home. Although she had not been under any stress at the time, she was plagued one night by a series of 'freaky, unsettling' dreams about mutated animals and being chased. Then the dreams stopped, and she found herself in her bedroom, looking down at herself sleeping in bed. Terrified, she left the room and began walking around the house, when the front door opened and my sister Sarah* arrived home from work. As Sarah took off her jacket and shoes, Trish greeted her, but received no response in return, as if she were invisible. She followed my sister for a while, taking note of what she was doing, before wandering into the powder room alone.

Trish had always felt safe and comfortable at that house, with no 'ghostly' feelings to speak of, until now. Glancing in the mirror, she was shocked to see a strange figure. 'It wasn't me. I'm not sure what I saw, but it was scary,' she said.

Once she had glimpsed it, she immediately felt herself thrown into the air and slammed between the ceiling and the floor repeatedly, which she assumed was caused by the entity in the mirror. Trish screamed, at which point she woke up in bed. Later, when her therapist asked whether she had experienced any unexplained phenomena or dreams, she told him about this experience, and he suggested that these violent movements had been caused by her desire to return to her body. Still, she was not sure what had caused this experience in the first place.

The next morning, she relayed her experience to Sarah, who confirmed the list of things she had done after coming home. If not for this confirmation, Trish said, she wouldn't have known whether this was a true out-of-body experience.

In my bachelor's dissertation on encounters with OBE figures, I found that experiencers tended to interpret unresponsive figures as people who were currently busy in their physical bodies, sleepwalkers (similar to Muldoon's astral somnambulist described in the next chapter), zombies or 'dudes stuck in purgatory'. Astral projector and High Priestess Witch Tree Carr described an OBE in which she visited a warehouse party where nobody seemed to notice her presence, including the friend she had arrived there with. She shook him to get his attention, but he was non-responsive and seemed 'stoned'. 'Maybe he was sleeping, maybe I was in his dream,' she suggested. Before nearly being pulled into the bathroom, Samuel* also tried to get the attention of his flatmate, who was in his room studying at the time. When he nipped his arm, he seemed to respond by glancing towards it before returning back to his book. Samuel wasn't sure if this was just a coincidence or if he had actually felt him pinching his arm, and felt awkward about asking him.[4]

VISIBILITY

Not everyone will experience invisibility in their OBEs; there can also be a combination of humans or other-than-humans that can and cannot perceive you within the same experience. This is an example from a 2016 entry in the OBE journal that I had decided to keep since 2009 to record my experiences.

I'm in a type of massive utilities place, gas or something, in a smaller room with big pipes and high ceilings. I have the sense that I'm in Europe somewhere, and it seems to be night (or underground and dimly lit). There is a group of people meeting there and I listen in for a moment, out of curiosity – they can't see me. But I can't quite make out what they are saying. There are also about seven people nearby who can see me and who, like me, seem confused about why they are here. I tell them that they are out of body, and tell one girl my name and to look me up when she wakes up.

It's not unusual for me to feel confident in assessing whether someone is 'in' or 'out' of body while the OBE is taking place – there is a sense of 'knowing' which I am normally more critical of once awake. But it is also natural for experiencers to speculate on who they are encountering, and what the differences are between the ones who can see and the ones who can't.

Nearly a century ago, Theosophist Charles Webster Leadbeater (1854–1934) listed the various beings one could interact with during astral projection in his book *The Astral Plane* (1933). This included both the living and the dead, which he insisted were equally alive on the astral plane. Among the living, there were ordinary people in astral form who float about semi-consciously, and the psychically developed ones who have no spiritual master and might be limited to, and tricked by, certain experiences. Then there were black magicians and their pupils, from traditions like Obeah, Voodoo and Tibetan black magic, themselves mainly earnest seekers of truth, he adds. Finally, you could meet adept students in their *Mayavirupa*, similar to the concept of the double. This was a temporary body which was 'usually formed for the pupil by his Master on the first occasion' after which he could learn to create it himself.

Besides humans, the experiencer could also meet nature-spirits or fairies, as well as 'artificial' inhabitants, including 'elementals formed unconsciously', 'Guardian Angels' and 'Human Artificials'. Leadbeater claimed that one could project an elemental or thoughtform to oneself or someone else by thinking good or ill of them. This could include projecting an angelic being to someone through prayer, who could be visible on the astral plane.[5]

In the questionnaire I posted on my blog, I also asked participants if they had been seemingly seen by anyone while out of body, and I received 25 responses:

Yes, human: 28 per cent

Yes, animal: 20 per cent

Yes, other beings: 36 per cent

No: 40 per cent

Unsure: 8 per cent

I next asked, *If you answered yes to the above, what was their reaction to you?* and I received the following responses:

They were not surprised to see me. Took it in stride.

In-the-body people either completely ignore me [or] avoid eye contact, 'talk' to me telepathically, and seem very distracted, as if I was talking to their subconscious mind only.

Afterward, they never have recollection of the conversation.

Animals often see my astral form and react to it.

*A memorable one appeared to be terrified. I gave her
a small pinch, and the reaction was one of horror.*

It's interesting that, from my first question (on page 100), 56 per
cent of respondents had experienced being 'invisible' to humans,
and 12 per cent to other beings, while, here, 28 per cent were seen
by humans and 36 per cent were seen by other beings.[6] Respondents
didn't elaborate on what they meant by 'other beings', but the
entities in this category in my dissertation findings included shadow
figures, nature spirits, insects, a floating tadpole with the face of the
interviewee's father and, in one case, a fictional character (Mickey
Mouse). These 'other beings' tended to be more interactive than the
humans, or they at least acknowledged the experiencer's presence,
which may have contributed to a belief in the OB environment as
a supernatural space.

On the other hand, the humans who *did* react in some way
were seen either as deceased spirits, the subconscious part of a
waking person's mind, other astral projectors (including those
from other dimensions or times) and, interestingly, regular waking
people. This last interpretation was especially common when the
OB figure seemed shocked or scared of them.[7] Similarly, occultist
Oliver Fox wrote that, although he was rarely seen or heard during
his experiences, he seemed able to get a reaction from OB figures by
touching them. However, this seemed to frighten the person, which
would then shock him back to his body.[8]

Some people *only* experience visibility in their OBEs. As of 2024, modern 'hedge witch' Jane is one of them, although hearing her next experience, maybe this *isn't* for the best. Jane told me that after only having OBEs that were absent of any people or beings (besides a felt presence) until the age of 21, she then saw a mother and daughter who seemed normal and lucid. She was excited to finally encounter someone else in an OBE and approached them. 'I thought they were looking behind me, and they got really scared and started running, the woman was pulling the child – they weren't flying, they were walking, and I was flying after them – and I kept looking back, thinking "there must be something scary there", but the closer I got, the more they were running away, and then I realized that they were running from me. And then I stopped. I wanted to tell them, "You don't have to be afraid", but they were so terrified.' In another experience, Jane had looked in the mirror while out of body, and saw a headless, winged, three-breasted woman in her reflection, and we wondered if perhaps the mother and daughter had seen the same![9] Examples like these point to burgeoning beliefs among experiencers that, whether OB figures are responsive or not, or present in the location or not, they are real external agents.

I had a similar experience of someone looking at me with fear, as if I were a ghost, during an OBE. I had woken up at 4:30 a.m. and went back to sleep at 6 a.m. Just before this experience, I briefly woke up feeling vibrations.

I suddenly find myself in the TV room of an apartment with no recall of how I got there. I'm watching a film on the sofa, not quite lucid, just on autopilot. At first, I assume that I'm in my flat (although the layout is different) and worry that the noise from the TV will disturb my flatmate. I notice a little girl in the room who keeps looking at me – she seems so real, and I am sure I'm seeing a ghost, although she looks solid and doesn't disappear. I can't believe my eyes that I'm seeing this little ghost girl in 'my flat'. I watch her pace against the wall, looking at me like she doesn't know what to make of me. She answers my simple questions shyly but when I reach out to comfort her, she recoils in absolute horror and is frozen in fear. Then she gathers her courage, and says, 'You're in somebody's lounge, you know,' as if I'm not supposed to be there.

In a split second, I realize that I must be dreaming and try to wake myself up. This seems to do something, but I'm still in the same room, although the little girl is now gone. I try to open the door and escape, super freaked out like I'm in a haunted home (but maybe I'm the one doing the haunting – and also, maybe I'm not the only one). I can barely move and get the door open, as if I'm moving through treacle. I recognize this from previous OBEs and realize that I'm out of body. Still in panic mode, I try to scream out for help, but nothing comes out. Strangely, I even feel my heart beat harder as if I'm in my physical body, which makes me uncomfortable. I calm myself down by telling myself to focus on positive feelings, which makes it easier to move, or at least float, and I'm able to grab the door handle and pull it open. On the other side of the door is a big living room, but just as I considered going in, each light inside turns off rhythmically one by one, getting darker, darker, DARKER. NOT GOING IN THERE, I think to myself. Try the window.

I float up higher, towards the ceiling, which feels much nicer, and I wonder if I'll get pulled somewhere else. I go out the window and start to float somewhere, slowly, without directing my own movements. It's lighter out, and I see maybe about ten people here and there floating in different directions, and wonder if they're dreaming. I get close to a lady in a white hijab and get the impression that she wants to go somewhere in particular – Indonesia, I think. It seems like she is willing herself there, but her eyes are closed as if she's sleeping.

THEN, I hear the voice, the same little girl from before, LOUD, as if she's at my physical ear. I don't know what she said, but she shouted something and I woke up in my body with my heart pounding.

NAVIGATION

In the movies, out-of-body experiences are often depicted as being easily controllable or navigable. However, many experiencers have told me that, like in my experience above, they can rarely direct their own movements. Upon exit, they might float or sink, in a straight line, side to side, or up and down, as if caught in a current. In the beginning of the experience, they might find it hard to move their second body, other than, perhaps, their head and eyes. In this way, an OBE is similar to sleep paralysis as, although the body is moving through the environment, they are unable to steer it (a feature sometimes found in alien abduction reports). This is an entry from my OBE journal which describes what navigating an OBE can be like:

I float out of my body and swivel near the door so that I'm standing upright, though still not quite touching the ground. I want to go upstairs to the ground floor, and out the front door to explore the streets of London. On the corner across the street is an old diner, the Astral Café, and it strikes me as a fun goal to visit it 'in the astral'. However, efforts to will myself upstairs are futile – I am going too slow. Frustrated, I think to myself, 'This is boring!' Instantly, I feel a hand squeeze the back of my waist, as if telling me to smarten up. Now I'm curious about who touched me, and start to rotate at a snail's pace to check. But it then occurs to me that I might see something scary, and I return to face the direction of the front door. It feels almost like turning in water with only the force of my torso. When I get to the top of the stairs, I turn to the right against my will, as if someone else has turned me, and everything goes black. In the distance, I can see a rectangular area that is lit up, which slowly gets bigger, although I cannot tell if I'm moving towards it, or if it's moving towards me. Finally, I see that it's the scene of a traditional Japanese living room. Two men are sitting on the floor as a woman serves them tea. It is as if I'm watching a stage from a pitch-black theatre.

It was esoterist Sylvan Muldoon who called the inability to move in this state 'astral catalepsy' (as also mentioned on page 76). He proposed this was due to 'direct subconscious control'.

Astral catalepsy reigns from the beginning of exteriorization until it progresses to that point where the phantom is in the vertical or standing position.[1]

It can sometimes seem as though you are being led or tugged by a hand, a draft or another force, which can give the impression that the journey is being facilitated by a spirit guide, helper or other sentient being.

I explored this sense of being pulled in OBEs within my online questionnaire:

Have you ever felt as though you were being pulled out of your body by someone or something else?

Yes, often: 6 per cent

Yes, sometimes: 44 per cent

No: 48 per cent

Have you ever felt as though someone or something else was directing your OBEs (e.g. from location to location, etc.)?

Yes, often: 10 per cent

Yes, sometimes: 35 per cent

No: 55 per cent

In summary, half of the respondents felt that their OBE exit had been facilitated by someone or something else at least once, while 45 per cent felt directed *within* the OBE itself.[2] Some people reported catching a glimpse of this force or agent, which can contribute to beliefs about who is doing the 'directing'. In 1953, a sculptor known as 'Mrs Robertson' was interviewed by the Society for Psychical Research about the OBEs that accompanied her narcolepsy-induced blackouts. She reported feeling that she was 'drawn out of her body' by what she described as 'little folk', which she occasionally saw, while at other times she only felt their tiny hands. The little folk would take her to a place she called 'the island', where she could conjure up anything that she wished. Mrs Robertson used these occasions to see her deceased husband, but felt that this was nothing more than 'an empty phantom', a 'joke' of the little people on the island, and not her husband's spirit.'[3]

Spirit agents can also be seemingly involved in the return to the body. As entrepreneur Ji Yeon describes, 'You know after riding one of those free-drop [things] at a theme park? It feels like that at the end. … it was, like, *thwoop*! I came in, but the last three seconds or whatever, they were gently putting my soul back to my body.'

THE 'CORD'

The astral 'cord' is a well-known feature in New Age OBE lore, popularized by writers like Sylvan Muldoon. In his first experience in childhood, he reported seeing his body lying below him, with his 'two identical bodies … joined by means of an elastic-like cable'. Muldoon wandered around for about 15 minutes, unsuccessfully trying to wake the others in the house, until he felt the cord increase in resistance, and was again unable to move as it pulled him backwards to his body.[4] He calls this the 'Silver Cord', after the Biblical reference in Ecclesiastes, although there is debate about what this originally referred to. Author and OBE instructor Graham Nicholls tells me that in his decades of experience, he has only met a few people who have mentioned this feature to him. Although geologist and experiencer Robert Crookall claimed that a cord was seen in 20 per cent of 242 cases,[5] as Charles McCreery observed, most of Crookall's correspondents came from spiritualist publications, which may have influenced their experiences.[6] Parapsychologist Carlos Alvarado further found that many of Crookall's cases mentioned feeling pulled, but not seeing a cord, and came to a more conservative figure of 11 per cent. His own studies showed that a cord was seen in between 0 and 2 per cent of cases,[7] and Celia Green found a prevalence of 3.5 per cent when recruiting from mainstream news sources.[8] I also asked about this feature in my questionnaire, which recruited participants from social media.

Do you recall seeing or sensing any attachment between your physical and 'second' bodies?

Yes, seen: 23 per cent

Yes, felt: 9 per cent

No: 59 per cent

I asked those who answered 'yes' what purpose they thought this cord or attachment served. This is a selection of their answers:

To keep you in your body.

Potentially so that you can return to your body if you stray too far?

Thought form created by projector to ease fear of losing body.

I think there is some sort of energy attachment that 'feeds' our physical body with the necessary energy we need to be 'alive' in the physical body on Earth. Once we die, cord severed. Logically, there has to be some sort of connection from the beyond to the physical.

Curiously, some people experience this 'cord' attachment, while others do not, perhaps due to a psychological need, as suggested above. The main ideas that emerged were of the cord as either a safety tether keeping the physical and spiritual bodies together, or as an energy conduit. Two respondents also suggested that the limit of the cord was based on what you were ready for.[9] The Rigo and Samarai sorceresses in Papua New Guinea hold similar beliefs, as researcher Alaistair McIntosh reports:

> During separation the physical body and the spirit remain attached by a 'magic cotton'. It acts 'like a fishing line', in that it is usually taut but will extend indefinitely to allow the spirit to travel freely.

McIntosh suggested that the cord might be 'inspired by the idea of a foetus being attached to its mother by the umbilical cord'.[10] There is a widespread belief that if this line is broken while the spirit is far away, the physical body will die, and that it is dangerous to wake someone while they are travelling. However, there are reports of people who have seen this 'cord' cut during their experiences and did not seem to suffer any negative consequences.

Like the location of the pre-onset vibration sensations and sounds (as described in Chapter 6), what intrigues me most of all about the potential cord feature of an OBE is that some see or feel it in one particular part of their body, or get pulled in certain directions. My friend Tree gets pulled out by her feet if she gets pulled out at all, while some move forwards or backwards, float upwards or sink down. Sylvan Muldoon 'saw a cord stretch between his physical eyes and the medulla oblongata (the base of the skull) area of his double, which got thinner the further away he was from his body. Dr Wiltse and Robert Monroe perceived the cord nearby, behind their shoulders. In my interviews, I have heard of an attachment felt or seen between the shoulders, on the forehead or at the crown. I have never seen a cord between bodies personally, but whenever

I feel 'pulled', it is almost always from my lower back – perhaps a cord or attachment of some sort *is* there, but out of my field of view, and I am going too fast to even think to look back. One respondent to my questionnaire likened the attachment to Wi-Fi, invisible but ever-present. I would describe this pulling similarly, more like a focused magnetic force than something material, but again, this seems to depend on the person, although nobody seems sure why that is.

Muldoon had also felt pulled backwards during his experiences, as did Robert Monroe, who was curious whether this was caused by the 'cord' he had heard of from other astral projectors. The next time Monroe had an experience, he decided to check:

I turned to look for the 'cord' but it was not visible to me; either it was too dark or not there. Then I reached around my head to see if I could feel it coming out the front, top or back of my head. I reached the back of my head, my hand brushed against something and I felt behind me with both hands. Whatever it was extended out from a spot in my back directly between my shoulder blades, as nearly as I can determine, not from the head, as expected. I felt the base, and it felt exactly like the spread-out roots of a tree radiating out from the basic trunk. The roots slanted outward and into my back down as far as the middle of my torso, up to my neck, and into the shoulders on each side. I reached outward, and it formed into a 'cord', if you can call a two-inch-thick cable a 'cord'. It was hanging loosely, and I could feel its texture very definitely. It was body-warm to the touch and seemed to be composed of hundreds (thousands?) of tendon-like strands packed neatly together, but not twisted or spiralled. It was flexible and seemed to have no skin covering.[11]

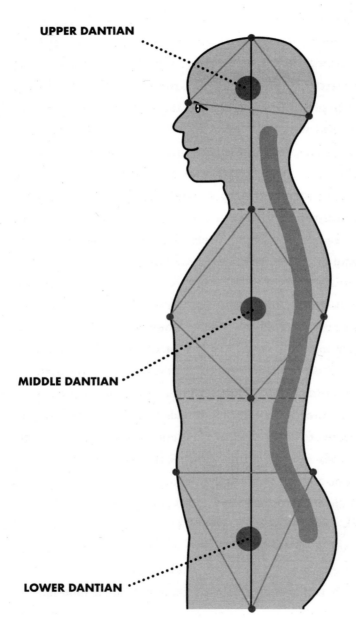

UPPER DANTIAN

MIDDLE DANTIAN

LOWER DANTIAN

The location of the dantian *and their front and back gates.*

When telling a friend about my experiences, he suggested that these points might coincide with the gates, or energy centres in the body, as described in traditional Chinese medicine (TCM) and Qi Gong practice, which are called *dantian* and are important in breathing and meditation practices. As you can see in the illustration opposite, there are three *dantian* ('elixir of life field') or centres of *qi*, each with a front and back gate. It is believed that the thoughtform, or *qi*, connected to the subconscious, can project out of the front gate of a *dantian*, and return through the back gate. The upper *dantian* gates are located between the eyes (*yingtang* or 'hall of inspiration') and the back of the head (*fengfu* or 'wind palace'), the middle *dantian* gates are at the chest (*shanzhong* or 'centre alter') and between the shoulders (*shendao* or 'spirit path'), and the lower *dantian* gates are located below the navel (*qihai* or 'sea of energy') and on the middle of the lower back (*mingmen* or 'gate of destiny').[12] The *mingmen* ('gate of destiny') on the middle of the lower back, just opposite the navel, is where I normally feel pulled from. This lower *dantian* is considered to contain the whole cosmos and is the seat of *qi* or *prana*, the origin point of one's life force, whereas the middle *dantian* is said to be where *qi* is refined into spirit and is related to emotions and thoughts, and the upper *dantian* is where spirit is refined into emptiness or consciousness.[13]

THE 'SUBCONSCIOUS WILL'

In general, the attachment or cord is seen as *part* of oneself, although the directing force does not often seem explicitly attached to the self. While Muldoon acknowledged that the force behind the cord felt like a sentient external agent, he suggested that it was instead directed by one's 'subconscious will',[14] comparing the relationship between the subconscious and astral body to that of a mother and a child:

> It has always impressed me as being very like a mother allowing her child to go to some distant place. The mother (subconscious) allows the child (astral body) to go a short distance away from her, then brings him back; the child is allowed to go farther and farther, coming back each time. Eventually the child is allowed to go to such a distance that his mother can no longer call him back (outside cord-activity range) and the child can do as he pleases. However, after a while, his mother will come after him and bring him home again. But the subconscious (like most mothers) sometimes permits the child to go away from home without repeatedly calling him back.[15]

Sylvan Muldoon described the astral cord as 'the very foundation of the phenomenon', noting that it could either stabilize or disrupt an experiencer's movement within the astral environment.[16] He identified a critical feature he called the 'cord-activity range', where navigation was most difficult because the cord – or the subconscious will – was in charge of movement. Beyond this range, he found it easier to move freely. After a year of experimentation, Muldoon observed that the cord-activity range was longer when his body was in good health, as more energy seemed stored in his astral body and cord, making it stronger. In other words, he only had full freedom of movement when he was farther from his physical body. Conversely, when his physical health was weaker, the cord offered less resistance, making it easier for him to navigate the astral realm even at close distances.[17] According to Muldoon, one could 'skip' this step by projecting from a dream, as presumably one was already beyond cord-activity range.[18]

Muldoon also found other ways to make it easier to induce an out-of-body experience. The experiencer could prompt the subconscious will to move out of the body by 'tensing' it through suppressed thoughts, emotions and certain desires. Once the conscious mind was asleep, Muldoon explained, it no longer stood between the subconscious will and its desires, leaving it free to project to where it wanted to go. This is why practices like fasting were so effective in achieving astral projection, he added, because hunger or thirst could rouse the subconscious will into action. He did not recommend the use of sexual desire, however, as this could stimulate blood flow, which would keep the person in the body.[19]

Muldoon stated that it was also possible – and common – for the subconscious will to wander outside of the physical body without conscious awareness, which he called 'astral somnambulism'. He credits these experiences with giving us a sense of déjà vu when visiting a place we've never been before, suggesting that 'the future, contemplating, subconscious mind sometimes projects the astral body to places that the subject, later, visits in the physical' – either that or clairvoyance, he added. The conscious mind can sometimes become active for short or long periods during this time,[20] but if this leads to excitement, shock or fear, it may signal to the subconscious to end the experience. This could be overcome through learning to control the emotions.[21] More recently, David Wilde, a lecturer at Nottingham Trent University, concluded in his doctorate on OBEs that cognitive skills such as emotional regulation could lead to better control of their onset and navigation.[22]

Sometimes, there seems to be a kind of 'dialogue' between the conscious and subconscious mind while directing the OBE, with interesting results. On a recent visit to Canada, I was staying in my dad's guestroom when I had an OBE and floated out the window. For a moment, I was confused about where I was, and seemingly in response, the force turned my body so that I could have a glimpse of the room. I was baffled to see that there were two rooms: the one on the left was the proper view of the guestroom from my perspective, but right next to it was a mirror image of the room, with no delineation in between. Other times, one might feel a strong resistance to the direction of movement, which can redirect the experiencer. For example, philosophy graduate Samuel describes feeling himself being pulled towards the bathroom during one of his OBEs, but as his female flatmate had just walked in, for the sake of her privacy he tried to stop himself. 'There was a time when I was a bit deluded in the mind when I did want to go and spy on people,' he said. 'I never actually did.' He felt that this was a test of his morality, as if to see how he would react emotionally to the direction he was being pulled in.

These accounts highlight how the experiencer can gain a degree of control over navigating their OBE, whether by overcoming the cord-activity range or confronting moral challenges. Yet, even with mastery in these aspects, the experiencer may still find themselves transported to unpredictable and seemingly random locations, hinting at the presence of deeper motivations guiding the experience.

THE MOTIVES OF THE SUBCONSCIOUS WILL

Author and OBE instructor Graham Nicholls tells me that, although it is rare for experiencers to successfully go where they consciously choose to, their odds improve when they are emotionally invested in the location. However, he finds that the more experienced one becomes, the more likely the person is to allow the OBE to unfold naturally, without trying to influence its direction, and that these are often the most fulfilling journeys. Although the belief in astral guides is popular, and there might be a reason for an external agent to show an experiencer something, it is also worth considering that the subconscious will might have priorities beyond the reach of the conscious mind that is leading to these so-called 'random' locations.

One of the most heart-warming examples of this comes from the incredible Saroo Brierley whose story was depicted in the film *Lion* (2016). At the age of five, Saroo was lost at the train station, when he embarked on the wrong train and fell asleep. When he woke up, he was on the other side of the country in Calcutta, unable to understand the language. After a difficult life on the streets, he was taken to an orphanage and adopted by a couple in Australia, where he spent the next 25 years. In the film and book, Saroo recounts how he spent years searching for his home using Google Earth and his childhood memories. However, during an interview with Talks at Google, he revealed another intriguing detail that helped him crack the case.

'I don't tell a lot of people about it,' he says. 'I had astral projections when I came to Australia, always had that sort of, the out-of-body experience upon going to sleep, hence why I woke up in the morning with a sore head, because I never really slept.' He described his experiences as 'going out of body into space, and then materializing at the door of my house where I was born, and going in and hovering over my family to tell them that I'm okay'. These experiences ceased when he was finally reunited with his birth family at the age of 30.[23] Although he could no longer consciously recall his original home, perhaps it was coded in his spatial memory as suggested by my biologist and OBE specialist friend Cecilia earlier (on page 48) – or the collective unconscious, as many experiencers believe.

MY 'FUTURE TOKYO' EXPERIENCES

I was sometimes wary of continuing with astral travel after my rather alarming Three Intruders experience, as outlined on pages 25–8, but my 'kindled' OBEs continued to happen anyway. Two main things helped me overcome my fear and allowed me to continue to embrace and explore them. Firstly, I learned how to induce OBEs from lucid dreams, which was less nerve-wracking, and helped me get used to the OBEs that occurred from the waking state. Secondly, a helpful thought popped into my mind during an exit one night. I had heard people say that our souls existed before birth and will continue to exist after death. If this was the case, then technically I will have spent more time *out* of this body than inside of it – *right?* If so, then it was perfectly natural to have out-of-body experiences – *a birthright* some might say. I'm not sure if I still believe this, or whether to be comforted or disturbed by the thought of everlasting eternity, but it helped me to overcome the fear of OBEs that had developed for me at that time.

Once I started to embrace the OBEs that happened both as soon as I lay down to sleep and in the middle of the night, I noticed that more often than not, I would feel pulled from my lower back quickly until I ended up in what I came to call 'Future Tokyo', for reasons that will soon become clear. I have had dozens of these experiences, to the point where I was worried at times that I was going to lose my mind if they continued, as they seemed so real. I felt hesitant to include this part of my journey in this book, but it's an honest, albeit slightly off-the-wall illustration of what can happen when you practise astral projection. I imagine that some readers will think that it's a great adventure, while others will be horrified; basically, I came to the realization that I may have been seeing the same world that featured in my recurring childhood dreams (which started when I was a toddler).

In these dreams, I am in a shopping mall – a common dream template in our consumerist world, according to anthropologist Robin Sheriff.[1] However, they were different from most dreams in that they were stable and had no symbolic or bizarre content. The mall is always the same. It is open in the centre, with a long escalator to the food court on the 2nd floor. Above the shopping mall is a hotel, and below, in the half-lit basement, there's a multi-storey cinema with a garish entrance. If you continue down a low-ceilinged hall and make a left, there is a video arcade with faux rock walls, and an ice cream parlour across from it, where everything is painted in primary colours. There are winding stairs that go up to a small shop. And this has an entrance to a grassy area with low pools of water, where the glass walls of the main building loom overhead. Over the years, this dream mall fleshed out to include an airport annex, a square wood and glass building of four storeys or so, with a conference centre at the top. (I once read a sign there that said 'Nebulus Place'.) Two types of planes fly from this airport: one seats around six passengers, while the other seats around 20. They are taken as casually as buses, and there are no customs or security areas to clear.

Most of my dreams set here were pretty uneventful: I would simply walk around trying to recall what was around the next corner, and seeing if I could hear what language people were speaking – usually Japanese or Korean, but I also heard French twice. For some reason, though, I felt like I was in Japan, but I wasn't sure why at the time. Over the years, the shopping mall dreams expanded, and it was either in my late teens or early twenties when I first explored the city outside, which confirmed that I was indeed in Tokyo. The sky was grey, and the canal and buildings were drab, but I felt like I was home and it was exhilarating. A few years later, while living in Vancouver, my mum advised me to move to China or Japan to look for work. Although I initially wanted to move to South Korea, I decided on Tokyo because I'd studied programming and there was a good job market there. However, while living in Tokyo, I did not get déjà vu or feel any particular affinity with the place like I did in my dreams, which occasionally still happened.

These dreams were both a comfort and a source of entertainment throughout my life, but I never thought of them as anything more than a psychological creation of my brain. I reasoned that the mall evolved from my favourite show as a kid, *Today's Special*, which was set in a department store, and that it was located in Tokyo because I was obsessed with the anime *Sailor Moon* as a pre-teen, which revolves around a group of superhero schoolgirls living in Tokyo. I usually saw everything from the first-person perspective, but other times I would see myself from outside, usually from right above and behind, like in a video game. I was most often in my late teens or twenties, with long blonde hair. Even though my hair went from light blonde to a darker colour in my teens, I figured that this was always 'me' that I was seeing. Why would I think otherwise? Why would I keep dreaming that I was another person?

To my surprise, when I started to have regular OBEs from my mid-twenties onwards, two significant things happened. Firstly, the dreams continued but the world expanded even more to include other countries like England, the United States, India, South Africa, Tanzania and even a human colony on a pink, dusty planet. But it always *felt* like I was in the same world, and the same time, in the future. Secondly, my OBEs were often located in these same locations. It is difficult to put into words, but both the dreams and OBEs had the same quality of realness that 'felt' different from any other experience. The OBEs were different from the dreams in the way that they started, and they had a different level of immersion or embodiment in the environment, which made it feel more like being awake than anything else. Like my other OBEs, these ones would normally start with vibrations and mechanical or whirring noises until I floated out of my body in the immediate environment. But then, I would feel a sudden tug from my lower back, accelerating until I landed in one of the locations from the 'Future Tokyo' series. In transitionless OBEs, I would simply find myself already there.

In my 'normal' OBEs, my second body was either exactly like my own (or a close approximation), or almost invisible. When floating, I would have varying degrees of control over my movements; walking was easier, except for rare occasions when it felt like I could only walk slowly, as if through treacle. As discussed in Chapter 7, there were also the 'stealth mode' experiences, in which others couldn't see or hear me, as well as experiences in which I could interact with others.However, in these 'Future Tokyo' experiences, it was like wandering around the physical world, usually seen and heard by others. Although it took me a while to realize it, I seemed to have varying levels of agency about where I went or what I said. It was like

I was a silent passenger in another person's body, and I wondered if this was what it was like to be the semi-dormant subconscious during wakefulness, taking a back seat to my left-brain dominant waking mind. My assumption that I was always 'me' changed after an experience that took place in a small hair salon, which made me pay more attention to how much agency I had during these experiences. I seemed to be dropping something off at this salon, and caught my reflection in the mirror, which surprised me. My face looked completely different. What had felt like 'me' wasn't 'me'!

I became more curious about these 'Future Tokyo' experiences and tried to piece each of them together to see just how consistent they were. I still saw the mall occasionally, but less and less frequently. The locations and technology, such as the thin, scroll-like phones, were consistent, and so was this woman with the light blonde hair. Her activities, however, seemed inconsistent at first: her jobs included working in a hospital spa, fixing the water utilities of the city and off-shore, questioning an old lady who ran an insectarium in a city swamp while people in hazmat suits waded in the water, and I sometimes saw her swimming, or running track in a military facility. At first, these locations were all completely different in my mind, but when I wrote this list, one theme jumped out at me: *water*. There seemed to be minor flooding here and there, swamps located inside and outside the city, and worries about water-borne illness.

I've also seen other recurring figures during these experiences, but not nearly as often: a pilot, for example; an athlete who looks genetically modified; and my favourite, an android. In my 'Future Tokyo', corporations seem to govern different parts of the city, and some of them have their own militaries; there is definitely a problematic, dystopian undercurrent to this world, with squats, refugees, and even a cult. But there are also funny things, like people who pray to Santa Claus; and strangely cheerful androids, who seem to be popular with teenagers but make the adults cringe. At this point, I thought about writing a sci-fi novel based on these experiences, for my eyes only.

But then I started to wonder whether there was something more to these experiences after meeting Lana*, a woman from Romania who, in what was probably the most extreme synchronicity in my life, worked at the same bar as me in both Tokyo and London, three years apart (the businesses are unrelated). We became friends after working together in London, and over lunch one day, she mentioned recurring dreams of a hotel with a shopping mall underneath, which she had been seeing since childhood. In some of these dreams, the lower level had flooded and a group of people were climbing the staircase to get to the next floor of the mall. The man in front of her told her his name, and when she looked it up later, she learned that it was the name of a Korean water god. Lana had also heard Korean in these dreams, but like me, somehow knew that it was Tokyo. The more she spoke about her dreams, the more I realized that they matched with mine. We finished each other's sentences and napkin sketches over the next hour, during which I started to wonder whether this world had really been created by my mind, or whether we were tapping into – or remembering – something more.

In *Journeys Out of the Body* (1971), American radio executive Robert Monroe discussed what he called his '"I" There', whose body he seemed to take over each time he went to 'Locale III', a term he used for Earth or Earth-like places which do not seem to be in our past but are not necessarily more advanced than us. During these experiences, Monroe had no access to the memories of this 'I' but was aware of 'the emotional patterns of his past' and observed his world at several points in his life, which sounded similar to my 'Future Tokyo' experiences. Monroe dismissed the idea of this being a vicarious escape from reality, as the circumstances there were 'less than idyllic' (again, similar to my experiences). Instead, he wrote:

> It might be a memory, racial or otherwise, of a physical earth civilization that predates known history. It might be another earth-type world located in another part of the universe which is somehow accessible through mental manipulation. It might be an antimatter duplicate of this physical earth-world where we are the same but different, bonded together unit for unit by a force beyond our present comprehension.[2]

In *The Out-of-Body Experience* (2011), Anthony Peake refers to Hugh Everett III's many-worlds interpretation to solve this. Everett thought that it was absurd to believe that Schrödinger's cat is both dead and alive until you observe it. Instead, Everett proposed that at the point of observation, the observer and his world split in two, one observing a dead cat while the other observes it living. This suggests that all possible choices are playing out somewhere in the expanding multiverse. Peake proposes that we can apply the many-worlds interpretation to OBEs, which could explain the inconsistent details they sometimes feature (like the writing on the window mentioned earlier, or a misplaced door). Peake suggests that Monroe had somehow 'meld[ed] his mind into that of his "I" There associate' in one of these other worlds.[3] In terms of why he merged with this person in particular, it might have been because they were similar in some way, as Monroe suggested. Later, as his experiences and beliefs developed over time, he described an '"I" There cluster' that might be made of thousands (or hundreds of thousands) of personalities, which seemed to have a purpose or action that remained beyond their comprehension as long as they remained human. Monroe believed that these personalities, who were bonded together in this cluster, had to be united somehow, which these experiences could achieve.[4]

As I continued to have my recurring experiences, I could feel myself, like Monroe, shifting from a 'monophasic' cosmology (i.e. one that only considers experiences in one state of consciousness, usually waking) to a 'polyphasic' cosmology (i.e. one that also recognizes the ontological reality of other states of consciousness).[5] Personally, the idea that I was tapping into a parallel world existing alongside this one didn't resonate for some reason. All signs pointed to this being set in the future. I also didn't resonate with the idea that this was an 'astral city', which OBE author Jurgen Ziewe later suggested to me. I have heard of astral cities or worlds from many experiencers; they are believed to be thought-produced and accessible via astral projection. But I cannot change anything with my mind or emotions in my experiences. Still, I tried to cling to the idea that this was nothing more than a creation of my mind – after all, there is still a lot we don't know about the brain. I was also aware that I clung to this belief for the sake of my sanity. What would it mean if I allowed myself to fully believe that this was real? But sometimes, I entertained the idea that I was peering into a future life, or connecting with a future descendant of mine who had settled in Japan.

After meeting Lana, my suspicion that I was experiencing an objectively real place increased ten-fold. In some of these experiences, I felt like I was completely in control of both mind and body, and now I used these opportunities to try to gather clues about where – or *when* – I was. At the beginning of one OBE (which was about an hour long), I walked into a dingy hospital room near a busy overpass and saw an android inside the entrance. I didn't want to waste any time, and immediately asked her, 'What year is it?'

'Well, we're not entirely sure,' she replied, 'but our best estimate is the year 2545.'

'What do you mean you don't know what year it is? Did something happen? What happened?'

'Well, they aren't sure, but they *do* know that in 1993 a statue in Washington fell.'

'That isn't true,' I said, 'I was alive then.' She didn't seem to be of much help, so I continued on my way.

In 2016, I was off work for two weeks with bronchitis, and during this time I had lucid dreams and OBEs about once every other day. This included three experiences in which I met the blonde woman face to face, which had never happened before, and, as of 2024, has never happened since.

The first of these experiences started with vibrations and floating out of my body into my bedroom. I had taken a 'Dream Leaf' capsule, which included valerian root, mugwort and other oneirogens (dream enhancers). After floating out of my bedroom, I found myself going through a tunnel and meeting with the woman face to face on the other side, on a pink, dusty planet. This was the first time that I could see her from the outside, and she could also see *me*. She approached me and I was able to ask her some questions before the experience ended. She looked so *real*, and I was amazed as I looked at her in detail, noticing the cracks in her skin from the dry climate, and the green glimmer in her hair, which I thought must have come from the minerals in the surrounding rocks.

I was finally able to ask a question that had been on my mind for a long time. 'So, are you my descendant?' I asked. 'Because I see you a lot.'

'No, I'm you,' she said matter-of-factly, as if it was a question that she had already worked out the answer to. 'But my [...] is the descendant of your [...]. I'm the only one who doesn't see you. Well, I've only seen you two or three times. She feels you around her a lot.' I got the impression that our minds were automatically translating for us, but that there was no English equivalent for the people or roles she was wanting to refer to. I am still not entirely sure what she meant by all of this.

'Is she on Earth?' I asked, still not knowing who *she* was.

'Oh, no,' she said, as if this should have been obvious. We spoke some more. She was interested in talking about the engine of a space vessel, and she was just starting to explain how it's possible for us to be the same person when two young women walked in and handed her something in the shape of a credit card. They didn't seem to see me. I remember feeling weird and emotional, and wanted to connect with the blonde woman on a deeper level. I stared at her as she spoke with the two women, thinking of how business-like and unemotional she seemed with me. For me, this was a huge deal. She noticed me watching her and gave me a warm smile, which comforted me a little. Then, everything faded.

During the next two experiences, I suddenly found myself 'awake' and wasn't sure if I was in a lucid dream or an OBE. In the second direct encounter with this woman, I suddenly 'woke up' sitting next to her on black rocks facing a bleak landscape. I knew that I probably didn't have much time, and asked her, 'What is it like being you?'

'Well, there's two things,' she replied. 'One, we're so mechanized, how do we know we're not machines? And two, how did we get like this?' She indicated the environment around her. I asked what she meant, and she clarified that they didn't have any history of how humanity got to where it was. In an exhausted tone of voice, she also told me that she had been in the military for nine years.

A week later, I had my final face-to-face encounter with her in a computer room. It seemed as though this was an archive of the 'old' (non-virtual) Internet with large flat monitors, and she was answering my questions about the people I had seen in my previous experiences. I can't recall much of this conversation, to be honest. It was as if my conscious mind had briefly peered into the world that another part of me inhabited. All I remember was that she answered my questions about the 'genetically modified' athlete and an underwater tunnel I had seen.

The experience of being pulled from my back is definitely one of the main features of these 'Future Tokyo' experiences, and might have something to do with the *dantian* (Chinese energy centres), as discussed in Chapter 8. In one of these experiences, I began in my bedroom and flew out the window with some difficulty, before floating above the garden outside. Again, I was pulled from my lower back rapidly until I slowed, and saw blue skies and pristine buildings. I saw what I can only describe as tall (30 storeys or so) sticks of coloured blocks stacked on top of each other in front of a large (40-storey +) building, swaying back and forth, like stiff leaves in the wind. As I floated high in the air, I noticed an old man hovering in front of me with a black box on his lower back. I also felt like something was on my back, not strapped on but like a small square board stuck on by a weak force, and I felt like I might fall if I slowed too much. I am still baffled as to what exactly it could mean.

Soon after recovering from bronchitis, I visited Jane (I interview her in Chapter 12) for a long chat to try to make sense of my experiences. If not related to reincarnation or descendants, what could it mean? After several crumpled Post-it notes and mugs of tea, I concluded that, if I was to take these experiences as more than my imagination, it *could* indicate that *future* Tokyo was actually the present day, and that we were in some sort of simulation. In terms of the function of this simulation, I liked the idea that it could be an immigration test (to enter a country or planet, perhaps) or a witness protection programme (one that blocks telepathic signals). As Robert Monroe and Anthony Peake suggest, it might even be a quest to retrieve other parts of my '"I" There cluster' from multiple worlds. My favourite idea of all was that there were countless 'ancestor' simulations running in parallel – which would create 'parallel worlds' – and that if the events in one of these leads to the situation outside of the simulation, this is the one that goes in the history books. After all, my '"I" There' had said that they were missing history.

But there was another, more down-to-earth explanation. As I tried to wrestle some logic out of all of this, I thought about how OBEs often seem to be reconstructed from spatial memory. They often begin in the most recent (immediate) environment, but some sleep-induced OBEs can also begin from one's childhood bedroom or another area, as if they had somehow teleported during the night. It occurred to me that since I moved around so much, both in childhood and adulthood, my recurring dream world may have been the most stable (or consistent) spatial model to choose from. There are other possibilities, too. In Chapter 3, Argentina-based biologist Cecilia suggested that maybe we jump from the eerie immediate environment to remote places that are less frightening, in order to protect our emotions. Despite the potholes, flooding and slightly dystopian vibe of my recurring OBE world, these experiences were fun and comforting, and it might have satisfied some psychological need, functioning as a hero's journey of sorts. In these scenarios, perhaps the overlap with Lana and I was a mere coincidence?

Although I loved these experiences and always felt like I was coming home, as I mentioned earlier, I started to worry at one point that I would lose the plot if they continued. The world I experienced there was so realistic that I found it hard not to integrate it into my wider views on reality, but I couldn't do that without seeing *this* daily world in a different light. The explanation that seemed to fit the most was that *this* world that I am currently writing from was a simulation, and that the place I was returning to in my OBEs was the *real* world. So, what if I embraced these beliefs? Would I even have the self-awareness to notice how this huge shift in perspective would shape my decisions, relationships and general daily life?

Before I delved deeper into my own OBE practice to get answers about my personal experiences, I decided to explore the journeys that other people were having with OBEs, and how they interpreted them, which revealed just how diverse and fascinating this phenomenon can be.

10.

ALIEN CONTACTEES

In 2013, I was majoring in geology and was holding a chunk of granite in my hand when it suddenly occurred to me: here I was, having had over a hundred out-of-body experiences already, and I was studying rocks. I felt like I was studying the pixels of a video game instead of learning the programming, which I was now much more interested in. I quit university and took some time out to think about what to do. During this time, I consulted with retired psychology professors and scientists at the Society for Psychical Research to choose another discipline to study in order to better understand OBEs. I was surprised when, more often than not, they recommended anthropology: the study of the origin and development of human societies and cultures. So, I took the decision to start from scratch in 2015, attending night classes while working full-time at the university next door.

Before classes started, I wanted to hone my listening skills, particularly with people who had different views from mine. I had always considered myself open-minded, but I was aware of one bias in particular: *aliens*. While I believed that they must exist out there *somewhere*, I found it hard to believe that they were interacting with us, or that, if they were, people would admit it publicly – unless they wanted the attention. At the same time, I'd had alienesque dreams and synchronicities myself – and weirdly, so had Lana, who had shared the same 'Future Tokyo' type of experiences. However, I had not given aliens much thought, and wondered what had led some people to develop such strong beliefs in these beings.

First, I found some alien-related events to attend in London, and met people who identified as 'Starseeds', or aliens reincarnated as humans, to meditate with and chat to in the park. I attended an intergalactic séance in a sparsely furnished flat in South Kensington where, through incense smoke and New Age beats, we sat holding hands and asked the extraterrestrials known as Pleiadeans to come down and help our species. I decided to create a discussion group for alien 'contactees' (i.e. those who believe they have made contact with extraterrestrials or interdimensional beings), in order to discuss their views on these experiences. These semi-regular meetings in the art deco café of a quiet hotel failed spectacularly. Although I had clearly stated that the gatherings were meant to be for contactees, it was ultimately an open group and was flooded by alien enthusiasts from the beginning, who dominated the conversation. They enthusiastically listed dates and locations of second-hand UFO reports, while the quiet ones wrung their hands, obviously uncomfortable sharing their private experiences.

This caught the attention of Isobela*, an Italian computer scientist and contactee, who suggested that we open a new, closed group together and meet members one-on-one. I met Isobela for lunch and immediately took to her intelligent and down-to-earth nature. We opened a new group, as she had suggested, and were soon meeting one to two people a week, often for several hours at a time. The meetings usually occurred in the nook of a cosy Moroccan restaurant over fresh mint tea and hummus, with only the odd wandering belly dancer to interrupt the flow of conversation. In addition to our in-person meetings, we corresponded via email with one local man, and via Skype with a woman in Saudi Arabia.

Each week, I was astonished at how wrong my stereotype of alien contactees had been. They didn't strike me as attention-seekers as I had mistakenly thought they might be. In fact, far from it, we were often the only ones that they had disclosed their experiences to. In my opinion, the only thing that stood out about them was that they seemed more sensitive or gentle than the average person. Although Isobela and I oscillated between being sceptics and believers ourselves – often at opposite times – regardless of personal opinion, we let them know that we were there for them at any time and could connect them with professional assistance or other experiencers if they wished. (They did not, preferring instead to share their stories once, ask a few questions about the others, and then go back 'into hiding' so to speak.) The month-long project I had initially planned stretched to a year, and to my surprise led me right back to OBEs.

BETWEEN THE EXTRAPHYSICAL AND THE PHYSICAL

In starting the group, I had expected to hear tales of physical abductions and spaceship voyages, but instead, most of the contactees we spoke with believed that they were not being taken *physically*, but that contact was happening on another level of reality that was hard to articulate. Similarly, John E. Mack (1929–2004), a psychiatrist at Harvard University who focused on alien abduction phenomena, noted:

> Quite a few abductees have spoken to me of their sense that at least some of their experiences are not occurring within the physical space/time dimensions of the universe as we comprehend it. They speak of aliens breaking through from another dimension, through

a 'slit' or 'crack' in some sort of barrier, entering our world from 'beyond the veil' . . . They experience the aliens, indeed their abductions themselves, as happening in another reality, although one that is as powerfully actual to them as – or more so than – the familiar physical world.[1]

Isobela and I hopped on a train to Farnborough to meet Hilary Porter and Kenneth Parsons of the British Earth and Aerial Mysteries Society (BEAMS), or 'the British Mulder and Scully', as the tabloids called them. We sat in their front room as Kenneth served tea and showed us a presentation of their research, and Hilary described her personal abduction experiences. While we were chatting, Hilary abruptly fell asleep, and Kenneth explained that this was part of her abduction phenomenon. This reminded me of narcolepsy sleep attacks, which can happen during monotonous tasks such as watching television, eating, walking or listening to a lecture. It can feel as if you are being rapidly drained of energy, which can sometimes seem as though another intelligence is behind it. As narcolepsy disrupts the sleep cycle, sufferers are also more likely to experience sleep paralysis and out-of-body experiences than the general population.[2] We saw one example of this in Chapter 8 with Mrs Robertson, who felt little people take her soul to another land during her narcolepsy episodes.

Like the overlap between OBEs and apparitions, OBEs also share features with alien contactee reports, such as seeing a blue light, encounters with 'doubles' and deceased loved ones, and the OBE itself. In terms of the double, three contactees told me that others had reported seeing or hearing them when they weren't there, although they hadn't been personally aware of any unusual experiences at the time. Ryan Sprague, author of *Somewhere in the Skies* (2016), joins researchers Joshua Cutchin, John Keel and Preston Dennett in noticing a cross-over between UFO and spirit phenomena, 'to the point where now, I'm having individuals come to me and say that they have seen [deceased] loved ones aboard the craft when they're abducted,' he says.

Sprague continues, 'The out-of-body thing is very prevalent in our field. I mean one guy said that he was in his bed and this blue light showed up. He put the covers over his head because he was scared, and then he started to hear wind in the room, and smell the trees from outside, and literally felt like he was somehow transported outside of his bedroom. I was like, "What are you saying, you and your bed were sucked out of your room?" and he said, "I don't know how to explain it." I've had so many people say, "I felt like I was looking at myself having the experience," literally separated from their body.'

When speaking with social worker Beatrix* for my dissertation later, she kept saying, 'Stop me if this isn't related,' as some of her experiences skirted on the boundaries between states. Trying to take a similar approach to parapsychologist Celia Green (see Chapter 2), I remembered that our categories don't always 'fit' the phenomena, and tried to listen to these experiences without judgement. As a child, Beatrix would sometimes wake up to see beings in her room between 2 and 6 a.m., when coming out of a vivid dream or sleep paralysis. These included seeing her deceased grandfather one night, and 'alien greys' on multiple occasions. 'When I was 19, I woke up from a vivid dream, in sleep paralysis, I looked over into the corner of my room, and there was a hooded figure, four-foot, and I don't know if it was an alien, a being, I don't know. He was looking at me and communicating telepathically and he was amused that I could see him. His face started to transform and then he just dissolved. When I learned about OBEs, I thought I must have been peering into that space.'

In her private life, Beatrix felt a strong emotional connection with the 'greys', and once even cried to her dad that she didn't want to be human. It's easier to keep these experiences to herself, she says. She described her friend group as 'Barbies' who live for cocktails, manicures and hen-dos, who think that she is completely 'normal' and have no idea about the alien side of her life. Beatrix thinks that they wouldn't understand.

THE ALIENS

I later visited author David McCready at his office in the heart of London, where he teaches and consults on OBEs. He's a tall, pleasant gentleman with a background in engineering, whose first words to me were: 'You have a nice pink and red aura.' As mentioned earlier, members of the Golden Dawn had used astral projection to connect with beings from other planets. McCready has written an entire encyclopaedia on such encounters, entitled *Real Alien Worlds* (2016). Among the beings that travellers might encounter, he says, are alien grasshoppers, goblins, greys, lizards, Nordics, ants, jellies, star children, mechanoids, and my personal favourites, lobsters and dinosaurs. According to McCready, ant beings are human-sized alien neighbours who are 'trying to help humans evolve', while Big Jelly 1, an organism which has stretched over the universe, is interested in accessing human experiences while we're in deep sleep. Meanwhile, lobsters are a highly telepathic species on an ocean planet who 'have access to some of the best space-time craft technology available', but unfortunately are not well adapted to visit the Earth plane. Finally, he suggests that the dinosaurs may have been recreated through a 'genetic code library for extinct species' and allowed to evolve to a sophisticated level on another planet. In a most delightful sentence, McCready states, 'Technologically, the urban Dinosaurs 1 are similar to human beings of the mid-1800s or Victorians, whilst the forest dwellers remain in the Stone Age, but nevertheless make basic tools and typically cook using fire.'[3]

Isobela and I did not come across any reports of beings like this in our interviews with contactees; the entities described looked human or humanoid, like the popular 'alien greys', but beliefs that they could potentially shapeshift were also common. Most of the contactees that we met with didn't know what to make of their encounters, while others believed that they were part of a breeding programme, particularly one that involved human–alien hybrids. In terms of their goals, some suggested that they were here to monitor, experiment or interact with our species in order to mimic us (to influence our actions or harvest our energy), or to extract Earth's resources. One woman we spoke to, Chun*, said that her most frequent experience was the sense that aliens were using her eyes to watch her as she worked. She was employed by a foreign government, and believed that they were keeping an eye on her country through her. Chun had also seen what she thought might have been an alien hybrid at a church in Leicester. The boy was about six years old, she said, with big eyes and sharp ears that were smooth inside like a bat. His mother looked normal.

Some criticize such reports, and suggest that they are misinterpreting people who merely have physical or behavioural differences. Over that year, two people even said that *I* looked like a hybrid. I think my favourite comment was that this was probably why I was drawn to anthropology – what better way to study humans?

THE PHYSICAL EFFECTS OF THESE PHENOMENA

In his book *Alien Chic* (2004), English literature professor Neil Badmington suggests that the alien contact phenomenon is a modern defence mechanism: we are living at a time of great uncertainty, and contact with something alien serves as a contrast that emphasizes our humanity. 'When "our" difference from machines and animals is no longer obvious,' he writes, 'we turn to the alien for its instant difference ("I may be a cyborg, but at least I'm not one of those.")'[4] In contrast, according to UFO researcher Paul Devereux, any hostile experiences reflect the fact that we live in a materialistic and machine-oriented society that's essentially hostile to such experiences.[5] If the alien contact phenomenon is purely psychological, it makes sense that it could be a manifestation of our fears: we had just come out of two world wars and were in the midst of a cold war and space race when reports of alien encounters became popular, and we are now dealing with mechanization, scientism and AI.

However, the physical phenomena in some contactee reports make it harder for them to be brushed off as purely psychological in nature. These can include waking up with unexplained pain that lasts for days, unexplained growths or marks on the body, or encountering UFOs, sometimes along with other witnesses. 'Almost every person I've spoken to says it felt like a dream,' Sprague says. 'So, I automatically want to say, well then it probably was a dream. However, when someone wakes up and has physical markings – I mean the mind is a powerful thing, you can think yourself to be healthy and it can happen – but I don't know.'

He tells me of a case he's currently investigating of a man who saw a massive UFO over a nuclear missile silo that he was working on. As he was looking up at it, he looked to his right and saw shadowy figures approaching him before he blacked out. He woke up in the security vehicle with his partner five hours later, and eight miles away, with neither of them able to recall having moved the vehicle. We find an instance of an OBE in this case, too, which happened *after* the main event. The man was brought back to the base and interrogated. He was so overwhelmed that he went to the bathroom for a break. And as he sat in the stall, he felt himself rising from his body until someone came into the bathroom to check on him.

The 'alien' group that Isobela and I had created ended strangely. Week by week, one by one, each person cancelled their meetings with us due to migraines or other reasons. After a couple of weeks of this, it was Isobela's turn to cancel, when she suddenly needed to lie down just before heading out. 'I suddenly felt like I had been drained of all energy,' she said. I went alone to meet with Chun again at a quiet pub. She was noticeably flustered as she walked in from the cold and sat down. After a minute or two of catching up, her eyes started to water. 'I'm sorry,' she said, collecting her scarf, 'I feel like they know that I'm talking to you about this, and they don't want me talking about it.' She excused herself and rushed outside. We never heard from her again.

The week after, I planned to meet Isobela alone one afternoon when I suddenly felt drained of all energy a few minutes before heading out. I texted Isobela to let her know, struggling to even press 'send' before being overcome with sleep. Was this just a coincidence? Was it the power of suggestion, like a kind of contagious narcolepsy?

Or was there another species out there that could induce sleep and other states of consciousness?

CONTACTEES AND SHAMANISM

Devereux suggests that abductions are a type of 'spontaneous shamanism occurring in an unprepared person',[6] and he is far from the only one to come to this conclusion. In the year 2000, the late social scientist Simon Brian Harvey-Wilson presented his master's dissertation comparing shamanism and alien abductions, using an Australian abduction support group as his fieldwork site. He found that many of his interlocutors' encounters took place in altered states, such as lucid, realistic or 'weird' dreams, visions and OBEs. Harvey-Wilson noted that although this doesn't fit the mainstream idea of consciousness in the West, it does align with shamanic worldviews. Both can be said to be polyphasic, in that experiences in multiple states of consciousness are seen as real and meaningful. There are other similarities, too, like spiritual relationships with birds or animals, and an emphasis on using altered states for healing. One of Harvey-Wilson's interlocutors, Ruth, describes the following experience. (Note that it begins with shaking, which might allude to the vibrational state.)

> I woke up one day and I just felt like everything was shaking .... As I looked up I saw this being and it was all dressed in [a] gold cape, and it told me to go and sit in the chair in the lounge. So I sat in the chair in the lounge ... and I started flying, and I flew to South Australia, where I used to live, from Queensland, and I ended up at the hospital there.

There, Ruth described being taught how to heal a patient who had suffered a bad accident, using only her hands.[7] Author and contactee Mike Clelland, who has been interviewing alien experiencers for over 16 years, tells me that one of the main effects of alien encounters is often feeling a calling to become a healer, either full-time or on the side. Besides the ability to heal others, another similarity that abduction experiences share with shamanism is the period of illness and denial of spiritual experiences that often afflicts experiencers. Acceptance through shamanic initiation or by joining an alien abduction support group tended to usher in a turning point, after which these experiences became less traumatic.[8] Importantly, Clelland emphasizes that despite pop culture depictions, aliens are *alien* more in the sense of being 'alien to *us*', rather than physically originating from a place beyond Earth. Thus, rather than merely keeping an eye on the sky, we might look closer to home for signs of their existence – including in our dreams and OBEs.

At a Society for Psychical Research banquet nearly a year after my alien work with Isobela, I was sitting next to an astrophysics professor who asked how my research on OBEs was going. When I mentioned the interviews with contactees, he said, 'I've always thought that if aliens were going to communicate with us, they would do so via dreams and out-of-body experiences. That would be the most economical way.' If such a thing is possible, it would indeed be faster and safer than using a spaceship. Perhaps it is preferable because, as David Bowie sings, the Starman waiting in the sky would 'like to come and meet us, but he thinks he'd blow our minds'. Perhaps humans are easier contactees in these altered states. But, of course, the question would still remain of who is getting in contact, and why?

I had started this project with the question as to why alien contactees had developed their beliefs. Now I knew that the real question wasn't why *they* believed what they did, it was why *I* didn't believe. I also knew the answer to that question now: I was afraid of the implications. I didn't want to feel like an ant in some suburban kid's plastic ant colony. It was bad enough that my 'Future Tokyo' experiences had led me to think that we exist within a human-made simulation. I knew why the people Isobela and I spoke to believed so strongly – because they were having OBEs or OBE-like experiences, and I personally knew how realistic that could be.

11.

ECKANKAR AND SOUL TRAVEL™

'As you put your body to rest, you (Soul) awaken in the
Atma Sarup, the Soul body. You are now free to roam in
the fields of eternity, beyond the shadow of death. This is
part of the spiritual freedom spoken of in Eckankar.'
– Sri Harold Klemp, *Past Lives, Dreams, and Soul Travel* (2003)

It's October 2018 – the final year of my bachelor's degree. In the
lecture hall of my New Religious Movements class, the lecturer
presses her clicker, revealing a building captioned with the words
'Temple of Eck'. The religious movement practises 'Soul Travel', she
explains, in which members – 'Eckists' or *chelas* (students) – leave
their bodies as part of their spiritual path. Needless to say, I now
know my subject for this term's fieldwork project, and spend the next
two months (and a few years intermittently) attending Eckankar's
events in London and Milton Keynes. This is my first encounter with
out-of-body experiences as a *religious* practice, and I wonder how
being part of this community might affect the interpretation and
nature of this experience.

At an event entitled 'An Afternoon of ECK Soul Travel to
Experience God's Love', I take a seat among 40 other adults with
ages ranging from their early twenties to late sixties. The chairs are

arranged in circles of five, and one corner of the room is made into a tea station while another is set up to sell books. In my circle, there is a man in his thirties from Nigeria, a British woman in her forties, and two women in their sixties from Poland and Ghana. After brief introductions, we are asked to take turns sharing the first moment we knew that we were 'Soul'. The others seem reluctant to speak first, so I share one of my most vanilla out-of-body experiences. Next, the Polish and British women recount stories involving synchronicities and a sudden feeling of oneness, followed by the two Eckists from West Africa who describe their first out-of-body experience. This is actually what led to their conversion to Eckankar, they both say.

One of them, Barbara*, shares an incredible story. She had woken up in the middle of the night to see a door appear in the middle of her bedroom wall. A man emerged from it and invited her to go with him. She accepted his invitation, and he showed her various locations over what seemed like several hours, before returning her to bed in the morning. The next day, Barbara told her family about this experience and they tried to find answers within her religion, but nobody seemed able to explain what had happened. Within a day or two, her world changed when she saw a TV advert for the local Temple of Eck, and recognized the man from her experience – the leader of the local Eckankar branch. This was proof enough that there was something special about this religion, Barbara says, and she joined shortly after.

Eckankar was founded in San Diego in 1965 by Paul Twitchell, whose spiritual journey included years as a Scientology staff member, during which he claimed to have helped followers achieve OBEs.[1] He also spent years of instruction with the Ruhani Satsang movement mentioned earlier, meeting and corresponding with its leader Kirpal Singh and honing his astral projection practice. Besides his involvement in Scientology and Ruhani Satsang, Twitchell also held OBE courses for the general public, building his student base before declaring his new religion. He claimed to have encounters with spiritual teachers in the out-of-body state, the most important of whom was Rebazar Tarzs, a Tibetan monk who left his body from a hut in the Himalayas in a quest to aid others.[2] An older version of Eckankar's history states that the teachings were originally brought from a city on Venus millions of years ago by a spiritual force called Gakko.[3]

Twitchell claimed that Rebazar Tarzs had handed him 'the Rod of Power', which officially made him the 971st 'Living ECK Master',[4] a title that made him the emissary for these ancient teachings. This also imbued him with the same God- or 'Mahanta-'* consciousness as his predecessors. In his first article on his newly established (or old and Venusian) religion, Twitchell wrote:

Eckankar, the philosophy of out of body experience, is the understanding which I have gained from bi-location excursions similar to those in the lives of saints of all faiths.[5]

Eckankar has gone through several name changes since its inception: Eckankar Corporation, The Religion of the Light and Sound of God, the Secret Science of Soul Travel, and finally its current name, which officially means 'Coworker with God'. (The name was likely inspired by *Ik Onkar* or *Ek Oankar*, Punjabi for 'One God'.) The leader of their UK branch tells me that Eckankar has

---

* The Mahanta is the inner form of the Living ECK Master, and the 'highest state of God Consciousness known to man'.[6]

an organizational structure with the Living Eck Master at the top, supported by the Eck Spiritual Centre, and various centres dotted across the globe which organize events for members and the public. Their annual conference is held at their headquarters, the Golden Wisdom Temple in Chanhassen, Minnesota, which features a golden step-pyramid on its roof. Annual membership, which includes access to discourses, requires a donation of US$60, or US$50 in developing countries. Initiations are free but by invitation only.

Today, Eckankar boasts over 50,000 members globally, with a large fellowship in the United States and Nigeria. The members don't wear distinctive clothing, but sometimes wear jewellery with the words ECK, or HU, 'the most ancient, secret name for God',[7] which many Eckists chant in daily meditations. San Francisco-based novelist and ex-Eckist Dodie Bellamy explains what drew her to Eckankar:

> Besides my straight As, I had nothing to give me a sense of self-worth. In Eckankar, since everyone is Soul, everyone is worthy. As Eckankar filled my life, I felt like I was entering Shangri-La: a new glistening world of love, of possibility opened before me.

Dodie noted that although her perfect grades suffered as a result of her focus on Eckankar, it also helped her to give up drugs.[8]

The cornerstone of Eckankar is the belief and practice of 'Soul Travel' (a term they've trademarked), illustrated in Eckist materials with pictures of souls flying out of their bodies, and personal accounts of meeting the ECK Masters in other realms. Soul Travel is said to help the *chela* (student) to expand their consciousness, remember who they are and who they were in past lives, learn about the future, and most importantly, connect with God. Spiritual exercises to this end are practised at home, with the HU app, and at community events. An exercise on Eckankar's website instructs the *chela* to close their eyes and focus on the 'Spiritual Eye' between their eyebrows, and sing HU while calling forth a feeling of deep love. Next, they should look into their Spiritual Eye for the holy person of their choice, either an ECK Master or a non-Eckist figure such as Christ, and give them permission to guide them to the location best suited for their spiritual growth. Finally, they chant HU a second time while imagining themselves in a familiar place with the guide.[9]

Eckankar acknowledges both male and female ECK Masters, stating:

> Any woman or man can attain God-Realization and become an ECK Master in this lifetime. The ECK teachings recognize that the true identity of each individual is Soul, which, like God Itself, has no gender.

These ECK Masters presumably inhabit spiritual realms – unfortunately, it doesn't look like we will see a female *Living* ECK Master anytime soon, as the website states:

> Every Soul who is in training for the role of the MAHANTA, the Living ECK Master in that lifetime chooses a male body. Soul needs the atom structure of a male body in the physical world to become the spiritual leader.[10]

At the Soul Travel-related event I attend, the crackle of a microphone draws our attention to the stage, where a married couple introduce themselves and recount moments when they had felt blessed by the Holy Spirit. This includes being upgraded to first class and synchronicities involving people with the same name. The musical performance that follows includes a song entitled 'In Soul I'm Free', sung by a keyboardist, a casually dressed man in his fifties, and a woman in her twenties with fur draped elegantly around her shoulders. Some attendees sing along quietly or sway to the music. After a tea break, we are asked to switch off our phones and take our seats, now arranged into neat rows. The projector whirs into action for an hour-long talk by the current Living ECK Master, Harold Klemp, pre-recorded at their Chanhassen headquarters. Each ECK Master has a spiritual name that makes them sound like mythical hip-hop artists: Paul Twitchell was Peddar Zaskq, Klemp's predecessor Darwin Gross was Dap Ren, and Klemp himself is also known as Wah Z.

Sri Harold shares the stage with a couple of large houseplants and a silver backdrop that wouldn't look out of place in a disco. Decked in a suit and tie, he sits comfortably in an office chair and cups the microphone with his slender fingers, addressing the audience with a smile. The way he speaks – his accent, his relaxed and gentle demeanour – reminds me of the American children's TV presenter Mr Rogers (who incidentally was ordained as a Presbyterian minister). Klemp often pauses to sip from a straw, to admire the flowers displayed beside him or to indulge in self-deprecating humour. In my interactions with members, they seemed to have internalized his rhetoric, sharing a similar way of telling stories in a calm and unrushed manner.

The audiences in both London and Chanhassen listen with rapt attention; at one point he stops to ask if the 'youth' are present, and receives whoops and applause in response. The video ends with a recommendation for a supplement called 'Turmeric Forte' for various health benefits.

Given the title of the event and the pictures in their literature, I had been expecting more tales of out-of-body travel. I soon learned that the concept of Soul Travel was much broader and seems to have transformed over time.

THE EVOLUTION OF SOUL TRAVEL

In a snug café tucked within the glass office block where he works, I meet with an Eckankar member in his forties called Daniel*, to learn about what drew him to this religion. Over a mug of hot apple cider, he shares the story of how he converted to Eckankar when he was 13, while still living in Nigeria. His father had just passed away, and with ten children to raise and a series of life-shattering incidences that followed, his religious mother began searching for spiritual answers in other faiths. Eckankar resonated with her as she felt its teachings went into more depth than her former religion, helping her to better understand her purpose in life. She introduced Eckankar to her children, and they soon began attending events together. As a teenager, Daniel appreciated Eckankar's lack of 'you musts' and the emphasis on the Holy Spirit, which made him feel spiritually free while still being held morally accountable. He also became fascinated by Twitchell's writings on telepathy, and practised cultivating this ability with his friends. However, as he got older, this interest waned as he became interested in communicating telepathically only with the Mahanta, because as he explains, 'the objective [of Eckankar] is to have the most direct relationship with the Holy Spirit'.

Daniel felt the same about Soul Travel, which, for him, was 'a higher and more direct communication method with the Holy Spirit'. He tells me that his first experience with Soul Travel occurred when he was a teenager at an event with around 200 people singing the HU song. Daniel thought that he could hear an orchestra playing alongside them, but he couldn't find the source of the noise, either in the room or behind the curtains. He later came to realize that this was an *aspect* of Soul Travel: *a shift in consciousness*. Daniel has never felt that he was actually *leaving* the physical body, but has instead experienced a *muting* of the body when shutting his eyes and focusing on his 'inner screen' in which the sense of other realms can leak into the foreground. It was as though, rather than an on–off switch, this phenomenon existed on a spectrum.

According to Daniel, Eckankar allows scope for change with each Master, and this includes the concept of Soul Travel. Daniel explains that psychic phenomena were more prominent in the teachings of Eckankar when Paul Twitchell was the Living ECK Master. Since Klemp's time, there has been a shift away from esoteric practices like out-of-body experiences and telepathy, and a focus on more subtle or common experiences as *aspects* of Soul Travel, like Daniel's experience of an unexplained sound, which he interpreted as a 'shift in consciousness' or 'muting of the body'.

Religious scholar and Eckankar critic David Christopher Lane suggests that this change may have been a rebranding strategy to appeal to a wider membership. I wonder the same: this shift acknowledges the importance of more subtle experiences, which can be spiritually meaningful to many people. As Lane notes, the *chela* now has a higher success rate in achieving spiritual states, as it's easier to recall dreams than to induce an OBE. This change in direction might also reflect how the Living ECK Masters Twitchell and Klemp personally experienced Soul Travel, as even when practising the same spiritual exercise, results can differ depending on individual biologies and personal histories, and this, in turn, can affect what one thinks is meaningful or possible.

The clash in teachings might also be a reflection of what Lane calls Twitchell's 'spiritual shoplifting' in his book *The Making of a Spiritual Movement* (2017).[11] In his later book entitled *Gakko Came From Venus* (2020), he lists examples of original passages from other writers side by side with Twitchell's writings, which sometimes even include the grammatical mistakes of the original. Lane traces Twitchell's main sources to Theosophy, the self-realization fellowship of Swami Premananda, the work of author Julian Johnson, Scientology and, in particular, the Ruhani Satsang movement. From what I can tell, however, these examples are limited to general spiritual concepts, and not his spiritual experiences themselves, although Lane suggests that Rebazar Tarzs was a composite character based on his astral meetings with Kirpal Singh and others.[12] The impression I get from Lane is that Twitchell, an avid spiritual seeker, was more of a rascal than the villain he is sometimes portrayed as being. Although thousands left the religion as a result of Lane's first book on Eckankar in the 1970s, many chose to stay on, and Eckankar continues to attract new members to this day.

Some maintain that Eckankar's teachings were revealed to Paul Twitchell by Rebazar Tarzs, and that is the end of it. Eckankar's official website calls Twitchell a master compiler, skilled at recycling lost material to meet the needs of a new audience. Many Eckists are of the opinion that their religion's past is unimportant because, in effect, they are simply taking teachings that 'work' and making them more accessible. But there are also concerns of cultural appropriation, as Eckankar is said to have profited from Indian spiritual teachings (which were originally free of charge), putting its own spin on these traditions. The sense of meaning that accompanies the resulting experience is also redirected towards a Living Master.

I wondered what other Eckists thought of this shift towards a more subtle concept of Soul Travel, particularly those who had joined because of their out-of-body experiences. Jeff* and his friend had also converted to Eckankar in this way. As a teenager, his friend had told him about his out-of-body experiences, which Jeff didn't take seriously at the time. Shortly thereafter, his friend joined Eckankar, impressed by the group's knowledge of the phenomenon. Several years later, Jeff fell ill while camping, which triggered his own OBE. This changed everything, he says, as he immediately stopped identifying with his body once he'd floated away from it. Jeff got in touch with his old friend and soon after followed him to Eckankar. He still continues to enjoy out-of-body experiences both from the waking state and through dreams.

Jeff and the other Eckists I spoke to seemed to accept Klemp's more nuanced and broader approach to Soul Travel. It was also clear that, while some converts initially focused on repeating their OBEs for various purposes, Eckankar gradually redirected their focus towards a broader range of experiences, all centred on a single goal: connecting with the Mahanta (the inner form of the Living ECK Master, and the 'highest state of God Consciousness known to man'). Views on dreams could also change after conversion, with some converts reframing prior dreams as Soul Travel within an Eckist model. According to Eckankar's website, dreams are a 'daily report card', a real and meaningful way to achieve a higher perspective on what matters to the dreamer, as well as to connect to the Mahanta and to bring about actual changes such as healing.[13] As Emma*, a young German Eckist tells me, the dreams that seem 'real' are the ones they deem Soul Travel, while others can be 'message dreams'.

'A BOAT WITHOUT SAILS'

Although my interviewees do not seem conflicted about the ways in which Eckankar frames dreams or Soul Travel, I find that some Eckists at the public events react negatively when I mention out-of-body experiences. When I introduce myself to the facilitator of one event, he replies in a jaded and somewhat disapproving tone, 'Oh yes, we sometimes get PhD students who want to know about astral travel.' Later, I join an event to sing the HU and get chatting to the cheerful woman beside me, Gabriella*, who enthusiastically lists all the things that she loves about Eckankar. At the top of this list is Soul Travel. When I tell her that I have had out-of-body experiences, Gabriella immediately looks uncomfortable and tells me to be careful, explaining that 'it can sometimes be dangerous'. She gives me an example of doing things the safe way: after attending the HU meditations before she converted, she began to see the Mahanta in her dreams, and allowed him to guide her through these realms.

'Otherwise,' she explains, 'out-of-body experiences are like being on a boat without sails – drifting.'

Twitchell's approach to OBE guidance differed from those of Scientology and Ruhani Satsang. Scientology encouraged independence from spiritual gurus, while advising members of what to do before and after exteriorization (for a fee),[14] while Ruhani Satsang founder Kirpal Singh highlighted the importance of the guru's role in safely guiding the student with their journeys (without charge). In contrast, the Eckist is guided by the Mahanta he encounters *within* the Soul Travel experience, reflecting Twitchell's personal encounters with out-of-body figures, such as Rebazar Tarzs and others.

However, not everyone is convinced that what one sees during these experiences is real. Shortly after founding Eckankar, Twitchell wrote to Kirpal Singh to let him know that he had been receiving visits from Singh's 'light body', during which he was dictating extra teachings to him. While Singh was polite about it, he seems to have distanced himself from his student thereafter.[15] In her work *The Guru in America* (2015), religious scholar Andrea Diem-Lane suggests that the differences between Twitchell and his guru lay in their conflicting views about dreams versus authentic out-of-body experiences. Diem-Lane notes that, while Twitchell encouraged 20 minutes of daily meditation and Soul Travel from both sleep and dreams, Radhasoami, which Ruhani Satsang is rooted within, advised at least two and a half hours of daily meditation and emphasized OBEs from conscious wakefulness.[16] This is perhaps due to the association between the waking state and verifiable information, whereas sleep and dreams, largely dominated by an untethered imagination, are a less reliable gauge of reality. In other words, Singh may not have been convinced that Twitchell's experiences had any grounding in reality, spiritual or otherwise.

When I ask Gabriella what the dangers of OBEs might be, in relation to her 'boat without a sail' comment, she wrings her hands and catches the eye of Amber*, the organizer of the event. I redirect my question to Amber, and although I have not mentioned any details of my experiences yet, she tells me that I probably experienced *astral* travel, not Soul Travel, which is what Eckists aim for. So I tell her about an unmistakably positive experience during which I encountered another person, hoping to hear a more detailed interpretation of my experience. Now she tells me that this person could have been the Mahanta in disguise. When I ask about the difference between astral travel and Soul Travel, she directs me to their FAQ page, although this is likely due to the meditation starting rather than her avoiding my question.

As we get comfortable in our seats, we're instructed to close our eyes and focus on the light of our Third Eye as we chant *HU*. The velvety hum of our voices reverberates in the small community hall, with some varying the pitch while others hold a constant note. After a few minutes, I notice a slight buzzing course through me, and my body feels so relaxed that I barely register its presence. The organizer's voice eventually drops from the chorus, and one by one we follow her into a moment of silence. I look up at the clock and can't believe my eyes. Twenty minutes has passed – it had felt like less than ten.

I am told that Light and Sound are the main components used in the creation of both physical and non-physical planes. The closing of the eyes, the buzzing of the repeated sound and the visualization of light between my eyes do seem to reconstruct my world, transporting me away from the meditation circle, the body I inhabit, and even the song itself. I can see how this practice could result in a sense of connection with something otherworldly, and even trigger a full-blown OBE.

A few years later, I attend an Eckankar meeting in Milton Keynes which involves a HU song followed by tea and discussion time. The COVID-19 lockdown has eased, but attendee numbers are much lower than before the pandemic, when events were held more frequently in London. The group takes turns sharing our meditation experiences, paying particular attention to any sensory aspects such as lights, sounds or bodily sensations, as well as any impressions that come to mind. This time, the sensations are not as strong as the first time, and I wonder if this is due to the smaller number of attendees, leading to a less acoustic 'buzz' in the room.

As the event draws to a close, the organizer hands me a free copy of the *Spiritual Experiences Guidebook* (2012). I flip through it while finishing my tea, and stumble upon a table of 'soul travel planes', mapping them into two categories: the Higher worlds, which are predominantly positive and associated with God-realization, and the Lower worlds, which are predominantly negative and linked to self-realization. The booklet describes the sounds one might hear during an experience, helping Eckists identify which plane they are on. It also assigns chants to facilitate intentional journeys to each location; for example, the sound of humming denotes that the Eckist is in the 'Alaya Lok' Higher world, which can be entered by chanting *Hum*.[17] The Theosophists had also created similar categories influenced by the Kabbalistic sephiroth (or spheres, levels).[18]

The booklet goes on to describe the astral plane as the 'source of all psychic phenomena – ghosts, flying saucers, spirits, [and] ESP', which can be reached 'by astral projection and most occult sciences'. In contrast, the physical plane is the realm of 'time, space, and matter … where the Soul is trapped by the five passions: lust, anger, greed, vanity, and attachment'. Unsurprisingly, each of these planes is relegated to the 'Lower world'.[19] In contrast, in the glossary of the guidebook, Soul Travel is defined as:

The expansion of consciousness. The ability of SOUL to transcend the physical body and travel into the spiritual worlds of God. *Soul travel is taught only by the Living ECK Master.* It helps people unfold spiritually and can provide proof of the existence of God and life after death.[20] (The emphasis here is my own.)

Its website further states that 'Soul Travel transcends astral or mind travel, and rote prayer, elevating one into profound spiritual areas.'[21] For me, the downgrading of astral projection in preference of Mahanta-guided Soul Travel echoes the elevated status of Hubbard's exteriorization. Curiously, although some members have told me that Soul Travel is the highest form of communication with the Holy Spirit, in his book *Past Lives, Dreams, and Soul Travel*, Klemp states that Soul Travel may become no longer possible after an initiation, or when the ECK *chela* becomes advanced enough.[22] When I ask Jeff about this passage, he tells me that he could not say what the initiations do, but that simply put, they allow more Light and Sound into one's life.

For me, I find that trying to make sense of what Soul Travel means in Eckankar can be confusing. At the very least, Eckankar serves a population looking for answers after they have had a spontaneous out-of-body experience. As one Eckist tells writer and ex-Eckist Dodie Bellamy:

We don't rely on the written word. I had out-of-the-body experiences, I had contact with spirit, I saw the blue light, saw all the things they talk about in the books – prior to coming to Eckankar. A lot of people have.[23]

Encounters with ECK Masters in dreams and Soul Travel are also cited as evidence of their religion's authenticity. Eckankar critic Lane has also dreamt of the ECK Masters, but attributes this to nothing more than his imagination after spending a long time studying them. However, some Eckists swear that they have encountered these figures *before* they knew about Eckankar,[24] like in Barbara's case, earlier on page 156, with the leader of the local temple of ECK. It's hard to argue against the power of such experiences.

Although I have not had any Eckankar-themed dreams or OBEs (unless Amber was right and I was visited by the Mahanta in disguise, which I mention on page 167), I have been affected in other ways by my short time with Eckankar. Mostly, I remember the warmth and humanity that I encountered in their community, and the relief I felt in being able to talk about my experiences more openly than usual (with a couple of exceptions). I came to appreciate Soul Travel as a broad umbrella term for both full-blown OBEs and subtle experiences alike, both of which can contribute to spiritual meaning. I do think that trying to box highly personal and complex experiences into neat categories with associated sounds might be too limiting for some people, and it sometimes felt that this impactful experience was being used to funnel loyalty into their specific spiritual mould. However, in my conversations with Eckists, it seemed that there was scope to focus only on what was useful at the time, enabling them to be part of a largely supportive community in which to make sense of their spiritual experiences, which is especially important with stigmatized subjects like OBEs.

12.

ASTRAL PROJECTION AND WITCHCRAFT

Witches flying on broomsticks. The benandanti *in out-of-body battle with rival witches. Satan-worshipping television witches who astral project to chat with friends and interrogate enemies.* There is no shortage of lore, both on-screen and in history books, of stories connecting witchcraft to astral travel. In Papua New Guinea, anthropologists write about flying sorceresses and chiefs that travel at will with the aid of magic and medicine, for both benevolent and malevolent purposes. In Europe, there is a long history of spirit journeys undertaken by witches, a tradition that still continues to this day. Meanwhile, today, pastors from the United States to South Africa are warning their followers about astral projectors infiltrating their churches to break up families and assault congregants.

I dug into these resources to find out more about the enduring link between witchcraft and astral travel, exploring how these narratives have evolved over time and why they continue to captivate the public imagination. This revealed a fascinating interplay between folklore, cultural fears and personal transformation, where astral projection is often seen as both a mystical gift and a potential threat. This duality – of power and peril – reveals much about society's shifting views in the unseen realms and the people who claim to traverse them.

CLAIMS OF ASTRAL ATTACKS

I recently read *Wake Up, Church! The Enemy Is Within Your Gates* (2009) by Marilyn Schrock, a Kansas-based pastor and member of the End-Time Handmaidens – a controversial Christian ministry which some call a cult. Schrock was hosting a pastor from Jamaica in her home when he revealed that Christians were under attack from astral projectors, some of whom were pretending to be believers. He claimed that in order to acquire and keep their astral abilities, witches would give money to demons and sacrifice family members while out of body.[1] Schrock wrote the book at the behest of Gwen Shaw, the founder of the End-Time Handmaidens, who told her that the Lord wanted her to write a book on astral projection.[2]

Although the book acknowledges that astral projection can happen spontaneously as a defence mechanism, especially in children suffering from physical or sexual abuse, she conflates astral projection with witchcraft and argues that both are the work of the devil. She argues that this is even the case when one's intentions are good, as while the experiencer might believe that they are doing it of their own will, the journeys are actually facilitated by demons who can kidnap one's soul.[3] Referencing Rebecca Brown, an author and former medical doctor (she had her license revoked), Schrock argues that demons have forged a link between our soul and spirit, whereas the Lord wants our spirit 'linked with His Holy Spirit'.[4]

The book is full of claims about the threats that astral projectors pose against Christians, including secret meetings held in New York City to 'pre-determine spousal changes' in order to break up Christian families.[5] Schrock also describes a man she met at a sales leadership conference who admitted to using astral projection to become a successful salesman. There are also two accounts of mysterious illnesses and hallucinations that began after marrying Christian men. Although there is mention of carbon monoxide and black mould in these homes (both of which can cause hallucinations), the husbands' astral projection experiences are deemed to be the problem.[6]

According to Schrock, some church members believed that astral projectors had infiltrated the church after reports of physical and sexual attacks both during church services and while sleeping. In 2019, Reverend Gopal Koopan focused on this phenomenon for his doctoral thesis at the University of Pretoria, interviewing victims, spiritual counsellors and former practitioners. It was his hope that his research could bring awareness of these experiences to the Church and better prepare religious leaders to counsel traumatized victims. In his interviews, he heard that astral projection was used by witches and Satanists for molesting women, committing murder and espionage. Koopan's case studies include women who reported being assaulted by an unseen force during sleep, sometimes with alleged physical evidence like bruising or blood. One woman even reported to her Pastor that after a night attack, a man in a suit came to her house in broad daylight, turned into an animal and attempted to assault her again. When she screamed, the man disappeared.[7] In households that believe in astral intrusions such as these, measures are taken to identify the activities or objects that have left them vulnerable, which can range from abuse, martial arts and pornography,[8] to a strand of hair placed in the home by the attacker.[9]

Although astral projection was normally associated with people from occult backgrounds, Koopan interviewed a Christian man named Medic who practises 'spirit travel', which he defined as 'travel during dreams, translation by faith, when in a trance and the physical body is moved by God to another location'. According to Medic, spirit travel comes from God, unlike astral projection, and Christians who don't practise it are 'suffering from spiritual amnesia'. The experience can also happen to Christians spontaneously, like when praying or meditating. Koopan interviewed a Pastor who was meditating when he suddenly found himself in the spirit version of his room, with different sensory perceptions that overwhelmed and frightened him. When he later met someone who experienced astral projection, he realized that this was what he had experienced. Koopan suggested that 'meditating the "Eastern Way"' may have caused demons to enter his life, triggering the experience.[10]

It seems that this negative view of astral projection largely stems from reports of nocturnal sexual attacks by invisible or supernatural assailants, which are reported around the world. In psychiatry, this is classed as a sleep-related disorder called the 'incubus phenomenon', which is linked to REM intrusions during apparent wakefulness, OBEs and especially sleep paralysis.[11] Every night when we sleep, the movement of our skeletal muscles is inhibited, including our ability to speak, which stops us from acting out our dreams. Usually, we are blissfully unaware of this mechanism, but for a number of reasons related to sleep disruption, we can sometimes 'wake up' before we are released from this sleep paralysis. In between this dreaming and waking state, it is common to hallucinate visions, sounds, smells and tactile sensations in the room with us, usually relating to an Intruder.

Neuroscientists Jalal Baland and V.S. Ramachandran argue that this 'bedroom intruder' comes about due to an interruption in the brain's temporoparietal junction (TPJ). As discussed in Chapter 3, the TPJ, which processes information of the self and the body, is also thought to be interrupted during an OBE, but in the case of the bedroom intruder, this interruption occurs in a different part of this brain region, and the body image is projected *outwards* from the self, usually as an undeveloped, shadowy form.[12] Studies have found that the incubus phenomenon is more common in students and people diagnosed with schizophrenia, narcolepsy, sleep apnea and PTSD, as well as people with a history of sexual abuse, people who consume alcohol or amphetamines, and people from non-Western European backgrounds. In students, risk factors include anxiety, sleeping disorders, eating disorders and psychotropic medication.[13]

Despite scientific attention, the traumatic and realistic nature of this experience can greatly influence core beliefs, and strangely, just hearing about them can trigger similar experiences in others. For example, in the early 1980s, Eckankar's Harold Klemp wrote an article about black magic practitioners who can invade dreams and attack a person's astral body, which the Eckist could prevent by singing HU and ensuring that they get enough sleep. David Lane interviewed several Eckists who claimed that they had never had such an experience until they heard Klemp's warning. Ten Eckists told him that they felt they had become mentally unbalanced since, and that they felt they had been 'haunted by internal beings and powers taking away the inner recesses of their personality'.[14] This could well be the 'nocebo effect' in action; i.e. when the belief that you are going to have a bad experience triggers a bad experience.

In extreme cases, this phenomenon can cause collective hysteria, and even lead to violence. One of the most popular cases of the nocebo effect relevant to this topic is the *Popobawa* ('bat wings') crisis in Zanzibar, in which witnesses reported seeing bats turn into men, or vice versa, during sleep. Like a haunting or contagion, the

Popobawa swept through communities, sexually assaulting both men and women. This period started during a local revolution in the 1960s and 70s, with other outbreaks occurring in 1995 and 2007. Several innocent people were beaten or killed after locals suspected them of being sorcerers responsible for the attacks, as they stood out from the crowd due to their odd behaviour. Tragically, it turned out that these were psychiatric patients visiting the island hospital from the mainland.

This illustrates that, although they are claimed by some to be evil and used to spy on or harm others, many of the negative views of astral projection and witches come from certain interpretations of sleep-related phenomena. These views can lead to the chaos and negativity they are claiming to avoid, contributing towards discrimination and persecution against innocent people, some of whom are practising indigenous traditions, as well as those who have spontaneous experiences. This is not to say, however, that there are not people who attempt to learn astral projection for nefarious purposes. But in reality, the experiences can also be used for healing, protecting and recharging, and connecting with both supernatural beings and loved ones. For this reason, it is important to remember that, just like waking and dreaming consciousness, astral travel is a human capacity which can be used for either benevolent *or* harmful purposes, depending on how we view it and what we choose to do with it.

THE FLYING WITCHES OF PAPUA NEW GUINEA

Although I don't advertise myself as an astral projection instructor, people sometimes reach out to me to ask if I can teach them this skill. I generally enjoy a friendly conversation with them and ask what their motivation is, out of personal interest in what draws others to this topic. The reasons given range from keeping their spontaneous experiences under control to simple curiosity, but a significant number are also hoping to use astral projection to visit 'physical' people and places, like a kind of astral stalker. I've been told by instructors that they don't really come across this. Maybe it's a kind of karma that these people find me; after all, my childhood fascination with astral projection began with my brother spying our neighbour approaching our house with a cherry cheesecake!

I received such a message one day from a man in Papua New Guinea who I ended up video-chatting with. He gave me a vague answer about coming across the subject online, and after stumbling upon a comment I left on an astral projection group on Facebook, he decided to reach out to me. As he walked on the edges of his small town, dodging the dense flora and parked cars on the side of the road, he came to what seemed to be his main question: 'So, if I go out of my body, I can go and visit someone, right?'

'Visit?' I asked.

'I mean, if I was to visit someone, alive like you, in any country in the world, I would be able to if I astral travel, right?'

I told him that while I had heard of people successfully visiting people and places out of body, I had personally never had much luck directing where I ended up outside of whatever building I was in. I was also curious about why he didn't look for a teacher in his country; weren't there a lot of people there with knowledge on this topic? He looked at me like I was crazy. 'The people who do that here – they're scary. They're witches,' he replied. As I would come to find out, there have been several papers written about soul-travelling witches in Papua New Guinea.

From 1978 to 1980, Alastair McIntosh was working as a volunteer teacher at a secondary school in the Gulf Province of Papua New Guinea, and with an interest in astral projection, he used this time to interview students from the Elema, Rigo and Gulf Kamea cultures about local beliefs on this subject. He found that this varied between individuals: sometimes beliefs were unanimous, sometimes contested, and sometimes completely unique to one person. The Elema students, who lived by the coast, believed that sorcerers could leave their body at will, but when McIntosh spoke to one of their grandfathers who was a sorcerer, he was told that, regardless if one was a sorcerer or not, the spirit leaves the body during sleep but is never conscious of it. These nocturnal soul journeys were different from dreams, which were received by their ancestors, he said. Some of the boys McIntosh spoke to said that OBEs can only happen to regular people during deep sleep, while others believed that they could happen in recallable dreams as well.

In contrast, the Gulf Kamea students lived a traditional mountain life, with hunting and subsistence agriculture, and were very secretive about their beliefs. After some coaxing, the students revealed that when a person dies, the spirit dies too. They considered spirits to belong to living humans or non-humans of mysterious origin, rather than the dead. Some sorcerers, not ordinary people, could use magic to leave their bodies, often taking on an animal form to 'travel to any place in the world, use their invisibility to steal things, and communicate with spirits'.

McIntosh also interviewed five Rigo workers who told them of two different types of OBEs: the 'dreaming and sleeping type', and the 'magic type'. They said that everyone leaves their body at night, and that dreams reflect the soul's wanderings while the body rests. However, dreaming OBEs were thought to be less 'real' than magic-induced OBEs. The latter were induced mainly by young female sorceresses who were often chosen as a baby, after which magical spells were recited by the sorceress mother. Later, the young sorceress would retreat to the bush with her elders to learn the induction techniques, which include 'magic incantations and either swallowing or having under one's pillow a charm made from the roots and leaves of magic plants'.[15] Another technique, written about in 1920, was to warm the body by rubbing it with heated *tutumuna* leaves before lying down in a place where she would not be disturbed.[16] The OBE would occur while the body slept, during which the sorceress would appear either identical to the physical body, as a bird or fruit bat (which is strangely reminiscent of the *Popobawa*), or if extra magic is applied, as light.

In all three cultures, there was a majority belief that sorcerers can travel to other places on Earth and communicate with spirits during astral travel, with some believing that the transportation of goods (including theft) was possible. In terms of the form that the 'astral body' takes, the most prevalent belief was that it was invisible, followed by animal form, a facsimile of the physical body, and a ball of light. Several people affirmed that this tradition comes from the Samarai people who live in the south-eastern tip of New Guinea and surrounding islands, prompting McIntosh to later travel to Milne Bay to interview Samarai people about their OBE beliefs. This is where he learned of the 'flying witches' of Milne Bay, which he notes anthropologist Bronisław Malinowski and others had written about decades earlier.[17] Malinowski had heard that the flying witches were believed to harass men at sea while out of body, eating them before returning home, but could be fought with a spell using ginger root and magical incantations.[18] McIntosh suggested this was nothing more than a fun story, like the ghost stories he heard back home.

In talks with locals, he also heard that there were serious practitioners who aimed to retrieve information or food during their travels. In one case, a trade union official told him a story about a run-in with one as a child, who used her powers to threaten him. He had beaten up a friend one day after fighting over a cricket bat, and that night was visited in his dreams by the friend's grandmother, who he described as 'a champion flying witch'. As she lived half a day's journey away, she couldn't have known about the fight through normal means, and yet there she was in his dreams. Two days later, the woman arrived by boat and warned him in person, and even mentioned the dream warning. She made sure that the two boys reconciled as friends over a picnic before she left.[19]

A man named Rex Yapi Epei told me a story about his grandfather, the chief of the Mele clan in the Southern Highlands of Papua New Guinea, which had become somewhat of a legend in their family. 'My paternal grandfather Epei lived a life where a lot of mysteries surrounded him,' he said. 'He lived a secluded life up in the jungles and high places in the mountains [and] married many wives, domesticated lots of pigs and amassed high valuable kina shells [traditional Wiru currency].' In 2020, Rex lugged a video camera into Kumiane village to interview his father and some of his uncles about the rumours that his grandfather had flown in the air above Mount Ialibu. He had heard of cryptids in the area – 'large monster birds' called *Iaineya* (similar to a flying pterosaur). It was also said that villagers saw a bioluminescent light shoot across the sky, and that they figured this was Grandpa Epei, a 'flying fire' and 'his Iaineya flying'. Rex wondered if his grandfather had been airlifted by such a creature. How else could he have defied gravity in such a way?

His grandfather did not disclose his experience to either his first- or last-born son, and only his middle son Nareh had heard it first-hand. Nareh said that his father claimed that, after climbing a wild pandanus nut tree at the top of Mount Ialibu, he had been airlifted across the mountain tops by rushing, thick mountain clouds. A cloud approached him in the form of a man and grabbed him, pulling him away from the pandanus tree branches. At the time, Rex explained, 'Grandpa Epei's brothers thought that he had gone for a hunting trip and gotten lost, so they searched for him until darkness, until returning back to their mountain hut without him. In the early morning the next day, Grandpa Epei arrived to the hut with his eyes hot and red like a glowing fire, which frightened his brothers.' It turned out that he had ingested wild taro, which made his eyes glow like fire and allowed him to 'read people, knowing what evil deeds they had committed'.

'So, in conclusion,' Rex said, 'I would say that my own grandfather was into hardcore paranormal activities during those early days.' He suggested that it was his loyalty to this spiritual force that blessed him with such material wealth.

HEDGE WITCHCRAFT AND 'FAIRY FLIGHT'

London-based receptionist Jane has had over 200 OBEs since childhood and is a practising hedge witch, a term that refers to travels 'over the hedge' into other realms, such as the astral planes. The ability to leave one's body has a long history in European witchcraft. In north-eastern Italy, the *benandanti* or 'good walkers' were farmers and healers who claimed to go out of body to serve their community. Sometimes in animal form, male *benandanti* would battle 'bad' witches in the sky to protect crops and fertility, while female *benandanti* would attend feasts in which they learned about the future from supernatural beings. *Benandanti* were often identified from birth, from the presence of a caul (membrane) over their face, or some other sign, and taught the practice by their mothers. During the 16th- and 17th-century Inquisitions, many of them accused others of witchcraft and were also themselves accused.[20]

As anthropologist Charles Stewart said, 'the Inquisition was the final solution to European shamanism'.[21] According to historian and author Emma Wilby's 2005 book *Cunning Folk and Familiar Spirits*, descriptions of witchcraft cosmologies and spirit journeys share more similarities with shamanism than with Christianity,[22] making them a target for persecution when the Church had a hold on the State. Besides the Earth plane, these witches believed that there were also upper and lower worlds that could be entered through a natural feature such as a hole in the ground, where they could then converse with both deceased humans and other-than-humans.[23] In Scotland, witches described visiting a fairyland and being 'transported in "fairy whirlwinds"'. Fairies were (and still are) believed to travel in the air, and even carry humans with them.[24]

Jane's experiences started when she was a child, before she knew about astral projection. These would normally start with her suddenly becoming aware that she was flying, as opposed to either having a non-lucid dream and becoming lucid, or an OBE with a conscious transition stage. She called these experiences 'fairy flight' because she had read about elementals and nature spirits in books about witchcraft. 'I remember doing little rituals in the woods, similar to guided meditation,' she says. When she seemed to have more flying experiences, this confirmed to her that the rituals must have worked.

'I don't remember seeing anyone,' Jane says, 'but I could sense presences around me, helping me fly or doing things with energy. I used to be taken to a cottage type of place sometimes, and there were definitely these beings around me, but I could never see them. It was very much teacher–student, but in a detached way.'

As an adult, Jane can direct her own movements in around half of her OBEs, while others seem to be facilitated by other beings. In the ones that she can control, her favourite thing to do is to fly around outside, which makes her feel recharged. Although many of Jane's earlier experiences were spontaneous, she has since learned to induce them, which will often begin with vibrations. Around 90 per cent of her experiences start with these vibrations and climbing out of her body in her bedroom, but as soon as she steps through a door or a window, she will find herself somewhere else. She has had months and years when she has multiple OBEs per week, but can also go months without having any. What seems to bring the most results is a combination of 16:8 intermittent fasting, intention and Robert Bruce's 'tactile imagining' technique from his book *Astral Dynamics* (2009). This starts by focusing on building and sensing energy at your feet, and over the next few weeks, focusing on bringing this sensation up higher, before finally circulating the energy throughout the body from the feet to the crown and finally to the solar plexus. She also has good results from imagining that she is breathing from her throat or solar plexus chakras.

Jane's mother has also had OBEs since childhood, but these stopped after suffering from recurrent episodes of vertigo. Now, she says, she will still get the pre-onset vibrations, but this is accompanied by nausea that stops her from exiting her body. Like Jane, her mother would use her OBEs to fly around outside, particularly in the nearby forest. During her last experience, the trees in the forest seemed dead in some way, and she wonders what this could mean.

Jane shares some of her encounters after the one described earlier, in which the mother and daughter seemed to be running away from her. 'In one experience, I climbed out of my body and went into the hallway, and there were two women there. They were discussing, "Oh look at her, but she's asleep, she's useless like this." I wanted to tell them, "*Hello*, I'm not asleep, I've just climbed out of my body, and you're in *my* house, so if you want to talk, let's talk. Because this is kind of a big deal now." And that's it, they kind of dismissed me and I couldn't communicate normally.' Jane felt that these women weren't human because, as she explains, their image intermittently 'fell apart, as if a signal was interrupted – not blurry, just, I can't remember why, but I came to the conclusion that it was because that wasn't their real form.' She wasn't sure if they intended to change their form so as not to frighten her, or if her mind interpreted their appearance that way.

'Did you ever end up seeing a fairy in an OBE?' I ask.

'Not a typical Victorian-era fairy,' she replies, 'but I've met some kind of earth elemental, which looked like a small troll or gnome. He lived underground in a cave, but somehow the cave still had light and lush greenery. Another time I met what I think were water elementals, two or three women with really dark skin. When I flew to their lake and wanted to take a dip, they warned me not to, but I really fancied a swim so went in and got stuck. They helped me get out, giggling, and told me that my "skin" was not the right type to swim there. They made me look at myself and I think I had pearly, rainbowy skin – I've had that at other times, so that didn't surprise me. They were super nice about it though.'

Jane would later use her OBE ability for more solemn purposes, which would have a big impact on her and her family's life. After a tragic accident, Jane's younger sister went into a coma before sadly passing away a couple of weeks later. When Jane heard the news that she was in a coma, she was in another country but was desperate to connect with her as quickly as she could – quicker than she could board a plane. Jane began her technique to have an OBE, but fell asleep before she was able to induce it. However, she instead had a touching dream in which her sister suddenly appeared, 'not like the other dream persons, who walked in through the door'. Jane realized that she was dreaming as soon as she saw her, and tried to persuade her to return to her body, as the healing might not have the full effect if she was out of body. Her sister answered that this was not how it worked, and that she just wanted to meet before going on a long 'vacation'. Overcome with emotion, Jane woke up.

Within a week of her sister passing on, Jane had an OBE that started with the usual vibrating sensations. As soon as she could, she called out her sister's name, and a few seconds later she saw her enter the room. 'She looked very different, as in her features were the same, but it looked like she was somehow made of a rainbow,' Jane said. 'To date, that is the only time I saw anybody appear like that.' They had a short conversation, and her sister indicated outside of the window, where a ship was being prepared for a journey (which did not align with what was physically outside the window). The next morning, her mother told her that she dreamt of walking with Jane's sister in the woods that night, when suddenly she had stopped and said, 'Do you hear that?' She didn't hear anything. She continued. 'Jane's calling me,' she said, before leaving the dream. This proved to Jane and her mum that they had both been visited by her sister's spirit that night.

THE ASTRAL MARKETPLACE IN THE 21ST CENTURY

You are more than your physical body! screams an ad from an Instagram carousel. *DM me with the code word ASTRAL and get 20 per cent off my course!*

My team and I are on a mission to reach as many people as possible, reads a newsletter, with promises of reuniting with deceased loved ones 'in the astral'.

Enter the astral supermarket, where online courses and discounted e-books sell alongside conference hall pep talks and expensive retreats in tropical locations. Yet beneath the glossy marketing and dazzling promises lies a deeper question: what is lost when the sacred becomes a commodity? As enticing as the idea of astral projection may be, as we have seen in the previous chapters, it can also have some unexpected effects. This chapter will illustrate some of the real-world risks of selling New Age promises, from the leveraging of authority and the creation of out-groups, to the handling of this phenomenon's more frightening aspects.

THE ASTRAL AISLE

Over the years, astral projection has been dusted off and displayed in the spiritual marketplace in different formats. Once confined to mystical orders, which have thankfully shed much of their colonialist baggage, and exclusive groups like Scientology – where 'exteriorization' is now reserved for advanced (and highly paying) members,[1] it is now accessible to anyone with an Internet connection. Thanks to this technology, astral projection can now be broadcast across platforms like YouTube, TikTok, Instagram, Zoom and Discord, and social media algorithms ensure that curious users are funnelled into an endless stream of content with a simple swipe or click.

Unlike many occult groups and traditional cultures, today's spiritual marketplace aims to democratize astral projection. Some resources are free, but many come with a price tag ranging from £20 to over £2,000 per course. One of the most well-known institutions in this field is the Monroe Institute, founded by Robert Monroe in Virginia, which has also held events in the UK, Europe, Brazil and Japan. As of 2024, the institute charges between US\$1,065 for a virtual retreat and US\$2,495 for the five-day, six-night residential programme, which includes semi-private rooms, meals and shuttle transportation. For the same fee, they offer several other programmes, such as an advanced course called 'Starlines', which promises to help you 'discover your relationship with other life forms' and 'begin your new role as a "galactic ambassador"'.

The International Academy of Consciousness (IAC), with origins in Brazil and classes worldwide, runs courses on what they call 'conscientiology', or the science of consciousness, with out-of-body experiences at its core.[2] When I first encountered the IAC's London branch, its proximity to the Church of Scientology Centre and professional, business-like attire of its staff (as well as the fact that the staff are volunteers) made me wonder whether the IAC is a secret branch of Scientology created to recruit the best and brightest voyagers. In reality, they are likely just making the most of the proximity to multiple universities and their wide-eyed students. Curious about what they teach, I signed up for their Consciousness Development Program (CDP) which ran over four weekends, Saturday and Sunday, morning to night. In addition to OBE techniques, the course covers topics such as the history of OBEs, bioenergy, chakras and auras, paranormal phenomena and findings from their OBE questionnaire, which had thousands of participants. The other students from my cohort talked about their motivations for taking the course, which ranged from supplementing an already established personal practice, to wanting to learn more about life after death, which this experience can presumably give a sneak peak to.

It's inspiring that people can make a living exploring astral projection full-time, allowing them to become adept in this area while providing a service to those who don't have the time to curate the practices or information they seek. However, it's often difficult to know which courses are the result of genuine altruism and which are born from opportunism in a growing money-making niche. While some instructors clearly have integrity and years of experience behind them, some enthusiastically begin teaching after only a handful of personal experiences. In an open online astral projection group on the South Korean platform KakaoChat, experiencers express concern about the rise of these 'astral influencers'. Given South Korea's recent history with cults, many are understandably cautious about anything that feels cult-adjacent or spiritually hierarchical. Yet some express hope that these influencers could help normalize the experience of astral travel, making it easier to discuss openly. One member writes: 'Imagine if I can walk out the house one day and tell my neighbour about my experience the night before?'

Both online platforms and in-person communities like those fostered by the Monroe Institute, the IAC and independent instructors offer experiencers a vital sense of connection. They create sanctuaries where people can share their journeys without fear of stigma, an essential component of mental well-being. However, the wider world may still view these experiences with scepticism, especially when they are marketed in flashy or gimmicky ways. In the days of TV domination, bikinis, buzzwords and icons of prosperity were used to stop viewers from changing the channel; the same things are now used to stop people from scrolling to the next thing on their phone, and to encourage them to stare at their digital ads instead. In this quest for visibility, an experience which is spiritual and priceless to many can easily start to feel cheesy or hokey, which can reflect back on experiencers in general, and potentially even worsen the stigma of altered states.

But beyond the packaging, what exactly are these marketeers advertising, and what promises do they claim to deliver?

THE CURE FOR PERSONAL AND SOCIETAL ILLS

After immersing myself in the study of OBEs through parapsychology, I was keen to explore New Age approaches to astral projection. New Age spirituality is often defined by its focus on personal and cosmic 'transformation',[3] which often incorporates psychic powers while seeking legitimacy through modern scientific language.[4] It tends to be optimistic and focus on Western values like individual freedom, equality, self-reliance and material prosperity. As anthropologist Paul

Heelas argues, in this climate, the New Age itself has become a product, sold in the aisles of the 'spiritual marketplace'.[5]

After purchasing one of these 'products' in the form of a lecture, I descend the stairs of an occult bookstore to a cramped room that smells of old carpet and sweat, where I hear how astral projection is the key to understanding our true selves. I have to admit that I tend to feel a little suspicious of self-styled astral projection instructors, who can sometimes have a combination of game show host enthusiasm and televangelist authority, with the evasion skills of a well-trained politician. The speaker's charismatic delivery paints astral projection in an attractive light, but he deftly avoids addressing many of the concerns that attendees express (like the fear of not returning to the body[*]). He then announces an upcoming week-long retreat, and my ears perk up; this could be a wonderful way to explore my experiences with others like me.

At the retreat, I join an eclectic group of attendees in front of the fireplace. There are two software engineers, two flight attendants, a cabaret singer, an osteopath, a tax attorney, a film effects technician, a social worker, a sound healer and a mysterious fruitarian from Sweden. Some are here because they've had a spontaneous OBE and want to have more, while for others, this is just one stop on their personal spiritual journey which might also include yoga, tarot or psychedelics. During dinner, eaten at long wooden tables at the back of the house, people drop into a conversation while someone's telling a story, and unironically ask, 'Did this happen in the body or out of body?' This makes me

---

[*] When I asked OBEr and author Jurgen Ziewe about this, he said that this fear is unfounded, as 'you'll need to go to the loo eventually', which will bring the person back to their body.

smile – I feel like I've just entered a secret world operating just under the surface of normal reality.

I first met Florentin Ionita when we attended this same retreat; he has since switched careers from visual effects and cinematography to teaching OBEs. On anthropologist Kim McCaul's astral projection podcast, Florentin says that OBEs can help us find out why we're here, what our mission is in life and what happens after death – they're a way to see the nature of reality for yourself, rather than taking somebody else's word for it. OBEs can also lead to the belief that loved ones don't disappear after death, which is more of a transition than an end. This sounds like a therapeutic outcome to me, especially for people who are grieving.

One of the most common claims made about the benefits of OBEs is that they can help us get over the fear of death, because they suggest that we are 'more than our physical body'. Some claim this can even lead to insights brilliant enough to cure racism and sexism. The reasoning behind this is, since many of our interpersonal conflicts stem from identification with the human body – its gender, sexuality, colour and birthplace, among other features – it makes sense that perceiving the world from the outside will lead to wider perspectives. For Sohee, a voice actress who felt pressured to conform to the beauty standards in South Korea, her astral projection practice had led to freedom in knowing that she is more than her looks specifically. And this was just from OBE transition sensations; she hadn't yet had a full OBE. Similarly, many of the people I've spoken to over the years have said that they feel more like their 'original' self after their OBEs, without all of the cultural and psychological baggage they've accumulated over their lives. Another interviewee, a South Korean artist, even credited her OBE with saving her life. After contemplating suicide due to financial struggles, she had an OBE in which a 'soul guide' conveyed a message about internal power, which gave her the strength to continue living.

If these are the outcomes of an OBE, then it sounds like a pretty good 'product' to me! A sense of community, a deeper connection to oneself and others (even, potentially, deceased loved ones), a decreased fear of death, increased purpose in life and courage to keep living make this all sound worth any price tag. But like with any medicine comes the fine print – and there was suspiciously little coming from astral projection instructors. I found this curious due to the frightening experiences I'd heard about from others (and experienced for myself). It was all good vibes and discount codes, and, as it would turn out, quite a lot of ego.

THE CREATION OF ASTRAL GURUS

At the retreat I mentioned earlier, not everything felt harmonious. At one point, the retreat facilitators sat in fold-out chairs in the living room while attendees sat at their feet, despite having plenty of sofas available. One of the attendees had taken this position in a half-joking show of deference, and the others followed. The pair regaled us with stories of their astral adventures, including one that revealed that they'd shared a past life as king and queen. In general, there was a feeling of oneness and camaraderie between the facilitators and attendees, but for me, there was also a sense of pervasive hierarchy.

This dynamic isn't always intentional – people sometimes project authority onto instructors, seeking a guru to guide them. I experienced this firsthand in 2013 when I started an astral projection discussion group in Tokyo. Although I made an effort to foster an open dialogue, attendees plied me with questions and seemed willing to accept whatever

I would say to them, without necessarily having a critical ear. While such dynamics can create a sense of belonging and safety, there is always the chance that somebody will take advantage and abuse their power.

On several occasions, I witnessed how vulnerable these settings can be, with the danger coming from other attendees, instructors, certain features of the event, or the outcome of the experiences themselves. For example, at one event, another attendee offered me a free Reiki session, only to pressure me into allowing an invasive procedure with a crystal wand as soon as he was done. I declined and got out of there fast, but when I reported the incident to the event organizers, they merely charged the man for a private counselling course instead of banning him to protect other students. Not only did this make me lose my trust in them, but it disturbed me to think that other students would continue to be exposed to these environments. Other stories I've heard are even more troubling. A woman at an astral projection workshop later confided to the instructor that another attendee had sexually assaulted her afterwards. The student, viewing the instructor as a wise spiritual teacher, was hoping that he could offer advice or intervene in some way, but the instructor admitted to me that he was in over his head and felt powerless to act.

This is another thing to keep in mind – even if the facilitator or instructor has good intentions, it may be difficult to ensure a safe space to explore such personal experiences. Unfortunately, the instructors themselves don't always have the best of intentions. Someone at another event had warned me that a certain instructor had a reputation for telling his female followers that he could 'transfer spiritual energy' to them during sex. Disturbingly, years later I was told by three women on separate occasions that they had been approached by this same instructor who had asked them to sleep with him during an event – after curating a relaxed setting that had attendees let their guard down.

This brings us to our next factor to consider: how the environment or the states of consciousness fostered can play a role in shaping the group dynamic. For example, group activities like heart-chakra meditation (to open your heart), music and dancing can make you feel good – and also help with embodiment, which can strengthen your OBE ability (see Chapter 4) – but it can also make you associate these feelings with the instructor, group or practice, and this can sometimes discourage critical thinking.[6] There are also concerns about what can happen as a result of the technique taught to students, which can include meditations and the use of substances that require care and expertise. For example, meditation sickness (discussed more on page 235) and negative psychological effects of the phenomenon itself can be avoided through spiritual training under an experienced and well-informed teacher,[7] and some of the substances taken at workshops – like mugwort – should not be taken when pregnant or breastfeeding, yet attendees are rarely warned about things like this.

Then there is the question of what can happen when people start having the experiences they train for. Neuroscientific research suggests that exceptional human experiences like OBEs might trigger the release of hormones such as oxytocin, the 'love hormone', enhancing feelings of connection and trust, while decreasing the sense of an individual self.[8] While this can sometimes be beneficial, it can also be exploited. Cults will sometimes promote altered states to manipulate followers, then encourage their own interpretations of these experiences, as I learned from researchers at the International Cultic Studies Association (ICSA) conference in Manchester in 2018. At this conference, I spoke with a professor of sociology, Eileen Barker, who lived with the leader of the Unification Church, colloquially called the 'Moonies' cult, along with some of his followers. We spoke about the hierarchical nature of this group, and she told me that the interpretation of dreams was sometimes used to manipulate its members. For example, the first thing the leader would do when he came to the kitchen in the morning was to ask his followers about their dreams. He was especially interested in any sexual dreams of his female followers that involved him.

Barker encouraged me to investigate this utilization of altered states to leverage authority more, as it is an overlooked part of cult-like dynamics. As we saw in previous chapters, out-of-body experiences are often perceived by experiencers as glimpses of deeper truths, which makes them even more potent than dreams as the basis for beliefs. And, just as the Mahanta can appear to Eckists in their Soul Travel experiences, astral projection instructors sometimes feature in their students' OBEs, enhancing their perceived status and abilities. I came across one such case during my bachelor's dissertation, when Beatrix shared that she saw her astral projection instructor – the same one who the women warned me about earlier – in two of her OBEs. Wondering if these had been objectively real, shared experiences, she shared these with him, and he replied that he didn't have any recollection of the first, but did recall teaching in the astral that night when she asked the second time. For Beatrix, this confirmed his authority as a spiritual teacher. As we will see, this aspect of the OBE – as a source of truth – is an important factor that can amplify the guru-like power of instructors.

OBEs AS A SOURCE OF TRUTH

In the modern astral marketplace, instructors sometimes make claims based on their personal OBEs, such as assertions of being royalty in their past lives, with the same effect. Because the content of these experiences is unprovable, people are free to make any claim they want, and even use it in their advertising. A decade after this retreat, a different instructor shared an Instagram post claiming that a mysterious being had appeared to her in an OBE, declaring that she had been chosen to teach astral projection to the masses.

Incredibly, OBEs have even been leveraged to support politicians. An anthropologist sent me a link to a Facebook page where an OBE instructor described seeing Donald Trump during an OBE. Trump appeared to be asleep, guarded by what the instructor described as an astral guard who permitted his presence. For at least one follower, this confirmed Trump's spiritual importance, leading her to comment, 'Trump is a powerful lightworker.' The idea of Donald Trump as a lightworker was popularized by Lorie Ladd, a popular 'ascension teacher' on YouTube, who claims to have received a divine message that Trump is here to help humanity spiritually awaken. This is part of a wider trend combining mysticism with the far right, which worries some political commentators as there was a similar trend with the Nazis.

In some instances, OBEs can also be used to create divisions or out-groups, such as between experiencers and non-experiencers, or between loved ones. In one extreme example, a netizen argued on a Facebook forum that people who are unable to have OBEs probably have no soul. His reasoning was that if their soul cannot leave the body, perhaps there was no soul to begin with. Luckily, this is the only time that I've come across such a belief, but it's worrying that OBEs can affect beliefs in such problematic ways.

In another case, a popular astral projection instructor posted that he had seen someone he knows in waking life 'in the astral', and observed negative energy or thoughtforms around them. He announced to his followers that, having already had his suspicions about this person in real life, this astral sighting proved to him that he was up to no good. Out-of-body observations can also affect romantic relationships: on Reddit, a woman shared that her boyfriend broke up with her after claiming to observe her cheat on him from the astral plane – and she is adamant that she had been perfectly faithful!

In an era dominated by fake news, clickbait and deep fakes, it is perhaps unsurprising that more people are turning within – or out of body – for answers that they feel they can rely on. This is especially the case when it is impossible to go somewhere in the body – and of course this makes these claims almost impossible to prove. Content creator Imkingcash, for example, recounts an astral journey to a place called Maldek, or Phaeton, which he claims is a planet between Mars and Jupiter that was destroyed long ago. He also claims to have visited a city on ancient Mars, reporting details of its technology and society to his followers with the authority of a news anchor. Even in the more cautious South Korean KakaoChat group that I mentioned earlier, participants often respond to questions about the nature of reality with the advice: 'Have an OBE and find out!' It's not just that people are selling OBEs – the OBEs are selling something in return: ideas and information that we can't always prove, but which have the power to affect who we date and, potentially, even who we vote for.

THE FINE PRINT

The potential therapeutic role of altered states has been noted by anthropologists like Erika Bourguignon to the point that some psychiatrists have proposed it for clinical use.[9] And parapsychologist Rhea White, who coined the term 'exceptional human experience'

(EHE) argued that these experiences – including OBEs – 'extend the limits of who we are and what we perceive reality to be (i.e. what is). They extend our human being in ways that enable us to know more and do more.'[10] However, although the risks may be uncommon and there are likely a lot more benefits of astral projection than risks, these kinds of experiences can affect us on so many different levels, including in unpredictable ways – so they can have a big impact on a person's life. For the record, this is why I never became an astral evangelist. I want to emphasize that I think that astral projection is worth it – at least for some people, if not all – but we need to be aware of what claims we make, and keep in mind how this experience might alter our beliefs and behaviours. Author Erik Davis made a great point about psychedelics in the wellness sphere, which I think also applies to OBEs: he talked about how we are in the midst of a mental health crisis, and that people are therefore grappling for solutions anywhere they can find them. But some of these cures end up being weird – an aspect that nobody wants to talk about. Exceptions include psychedelic researchers like Jules Evans, David Luke, David Jay Brown, Pascal Michael and a few others who have explored entities in depth in these states.[11]

So, despite my life-long obsession with OBEs and enriching personal experiences that I wouldn't trade for the world, I found myself feeling uncomfortable promoting this practice to people who hadn't already experienced it. Hedge witch Jane has also had offers to teach courses, but has declined. 'It's like teaching someone to swim online,' she says, 'you can't be in the water with them at the time and stop them from drowning.' In other words, you can't accompany them into the actual OBE. The instructor may have 'swam' hundreds or thousands of times but only in calm, pleasant waters, and not know how to help their student navigate the 'astral wildlife' or other challenging features. And although courses are sometimes labelled as being for 'beginners', this doesn't stop a student from having an experience which could be thought of as 'advanced'.

It's difficult to know the prevalence of negative OBEs. In one study in this subject, psychologist Susan Blackmore found that only around 5 per cent of experiencers describe negative OBEs,[12] and the reigning narrative in Western astral projection communities is that they are overwhelmingly positive. However, seeking the true prevalence of negative experiences in these sources may be like looking for the prevalence of caffeine consumption by only surveying café customers, which can inevitably lead to skewed results. In paranormal and UFO circles, in groups like Eckankar and the IAC (International Academy of Consciousness), and when speaking to the general population in the UK or South Korea, my impression is that the number of negative OBE experiences is much higher. These views can be missed by researchers who only look to astral projection workshops for interviewees, which people often attend because they want to have more experiences. While some might attend to learn to control their experiences or deal with fear of the experience, many who have negative experiences will want nothing more to do with astral projection.

However, as there were plenty of people who had confidently taught hundreds of others how to astral project, I was sure that they must know something I don't. So, I met up with astral projection instructor Hannah*, who has made it her mission to teach this skill after having a life-changing experience of her own. I gave her a few examples of the negative experiences I had heard of, including one from a friend who saw a shadow person before feeling himself pushed out of his body, only to then see his body yelling at his friends to leave.

'Aren't you worried that some of the people you teach might have a bad experience?' I asked, hoping to hear some tips from her about how to prevent or escape from them.

Hannah shrugged. 'I just get them to sign a waiver so that if anyone does have a psychotic break, they can't sue me.' I had asked how she protects her students from the potential risks of astral projection, and she replied with how she protects *herself* from her students.

I had seen social media posts that advertise astral projection courses as if they were revealing ancient techniques that have been hitherto hidden from the masses. One website I had noticed read: 'FOR CENTURIES, ASTRAL PROJECTION WAS TAUGHT TO MONKS, ROYALTY AND SHAMANS IN SECRET – UNTIL NOW…' These pioneering souls, on a mission to spread the word, assert that the out-of-body experience is a natural state to be in – a birthright. And to be fair, this line of thinking was actually what helped me get over my early fear of OBEs, and, as such, has led to some incredibly meaningful and satisfying experiences in my life.

However, I've noticed that some social media influencers misrepresent out-of-body experiences as practised in other cultures, by misquoting anthropological and shamanic sources, saying things like: 'It's normal, every culture does it,' while skipping over the cultural context. I thought back to Shiels' study, which showed that voluntary OBEs were restricted to a certain type of person, like a shaman or witch (see Chapter 4). Might there be some wisdom that these cultures had that we were missing in the modern world that can explain why some are better prepared for OBEs? It turns out that cultural context can give us some clues as to why only some people are encouraged to take up this practice.

In 2018, I gave a presentation on lucid dreams and OBEs at SOAS University of London, and an academic approached me afterwards with a disapproving look on her face. 'You can't just teach these things that are so sacred in so many cultures,' she said. I told her that I wasn't actually teaching how to achieve these states; I was simply comparing the differences between them. She grumbled about the commodification of spirituality, and I agreed with her. She said that she had conducted fieldwork in Western Australia with indigenous people who limited the knowledge of out-of-body experiences to a select few who were first tested through an initiation process. The first initiation involved physical pain, and the second initiation was unknown to outsiders. Her point was that it is not our place to go around sharing this kind of sacred knowledge to everyone.

I also understood her worry about the commodification of spirituality – potentially stripping it of its rich cultural context and nuance, like the point I just mentioned. She proceeded to share some of this cultural context with me. During her fieldwork, she was told that the reason for these initiations and cautiousness about who has OBEs was that during this experience, it is sometimes difficult to distinguish what is ontologically real and what is part of your subconscious. This can have a big effect and even be potentially dangerous, she added – and I think that this chapter has illustrated some of the reasons why. How do we know if we are truly encountering the instructor, politician or lover, rather than an imaginary projection of them?

As we saw in the previous chapter, there is certainly no shortage of fear-mongering about astral experiences, often laden with religious beliefs, false assumptions and biases, without a critical eye. But there is clearly also evidence that we are missing some fine print on this type of 'medicine'. There are organizations that deal with spiritual emergencies, which can occur with sudden or drastic changes to one's worldview. I now volunteer for the Spiritual Crisis Network and was pleasantly surprised by how well informed, unbiased and helpful they are for people in this position. However, I have found that some organizations promote the same instructors that I have concerns about, and there is still much we don't know about the effects of OBEs. For example, earlier I gave examples of how OBEs can lead to a reduced fear of death. But this really depends on *why* the person is afraid of death in the first place. If they fear that death is the end, then the experience of subjectively existing apart from their physical body might cure their fear. But for someone who believes in a straightforward afterlife, and believes that the out-of-body environment is a preview to this, such an experience can have the opposite effect if they encounter something frightening or hostile. At least, this was the case with me: my Three Intruders experience made me afraid of death, when I wasn't before.

This leads us to the main concern of many experiencers: the entities. The term 'entity' here is used to refer to any seemingly sentient or animate being, whether human or other-than-human, including animals, robots and any people or supernatural beings encountered. And in the astral marketplace, advice on dealing with these beings is scarce and fraught with disagreement.

ADVICE ON ENCOUNTERING ASTRAL ENTITIES

Like in my Three Intruders experience discussed in the first chapter, I have been told by several people that they've been grappled by shadow figures and other beings during their OBE. Some in the astral marketplace and astral projection communities insist that these seemingly negative encounters are not with independent astral agents, but with parts of the 'shadow self' which should be integrated to self-heal. As New Age spirituality has been heavily influenced by Tibetan Buddhism and Carl Jung, which focus on inner content and illusion, it's not surprising that many Western astral projectors believe that the entities we encounter in OBEs are aspects of ourselves. For renowned occultist Aleister Crowley, it didn't matter whether these environments were real or not; what mattered to him was that 'by doing certain things, certain results will follow'.[13] Crowley likened frightening astral realms to the dangerous city slums: intimidating yet thrilling. Although there was a risk of carelessness (one might walk 'into the traffic' or contract dysentery, for example), he advised students to 'take the bull by the horns' and use the experience to challenge their fears. This, he concluded, was 'the essence of the practice' of astral travel.[14] He encouraged his students to avoid attributing objective reality to them, and to challenge the reality of the beings they met; for example, the use of an appropriate pentagram could reveal a hostile entity who would then 'shrivel or decay'.[15]

I can see the positive side to this. Often, especially in the case of nightmares and sleep paralysis, fear can make the experience even more frightening than it already is, and the practice of embracing frightening dream content in lucid dreams often turns it into a positive experience. However, although there is a large body of research on dream characters, I couldn't find anything on OBE entities, despite the impact that OBEs can have on beliefs. Instead, OBE-related research has largely been confined to the experience of the self and the body.[16] I decided to make this the focus of my 2019 bachelor's thesis, and found that while lucid dream figures often feel like projections of the self, OBE entities feel ontologically real. My interlocutors described a visceral 'knowing' about whether an entity was internal or external – a deeply social sense, akin to recognizing another person's presence. This can make embracing seemingly hostile beings feel especially uncomfortable in an OBE.[17] In contrast, the realness of the OBE can make some encounters incredibly meaningful and therapeutic, like in Jane's case in the previous chapter, who believed she and her mother encountered her late sister during an OBE. But not all such experiences have this comforting effect. Some report feeling that the entities they meet, even deceased loved ones, seem hollow or different in an unsettling way, as though it is only the likeness of the person, with no real association to the person's spirit or soul. This might go against their expectations if they've been told that they can meet deceased loved ones in this state.

As mentioned earlier, in biologist Dr Cecilia Forcato's research, she had found that although her participants found it easy to alter the content of their lucid dreams, this did not seem to be the case with OBEs, and participants instead escaped into another scene. As there are too many 'weird things' that one can encounter in this state which might trouble the experiencer, in particular entities, Cecilia has come to believe that OBEs should only be taught in a controlled medical environment, and only for pain management or escaping sleep paralysis. This suggestion is not meant to gatekeep, but to safeguard experiencers.

However, of course this will not stop many people from trying, and it's important to thoroughly explore the various approaches to such challenging OBEs, keeping in mind the impact that this realness factor can have on experiencers.

Besides either being fearful or openly embracing out-of-body entities, a calm and curious approach might lead to a more positive outcome. Graham Nicholls, an experienced OBE instructor and author who I interview in Chapter 16, said that although he is open to the possibility of negative entities in the OBE environment, he has not yet come across anything that can actually harm you. He suggested that this might be because he seems to attract students with a more scientific outlook, who tend not to believe in negative entities. If his students do see something like a shadow figure, they keep an open mind instead of assuming that it's something negative – and in some cases, the shadow figure has turned out to be someone they know who is also having an OBE. Hence, the experience turns out to be positive. Nicholls also noted that he doesn't teach sleep paralysis-based techniques, which might lead to what might be called 'waking nightmares' – this could also be the reason for students' overwhelmingly positive experiences.

However, there is one more thing to consider: how these approaches might transfer into our daily lives. It is possible that for most people, approaches of embracing or reframing entities also influences them to be more open in their day-to-day interactions. But this might not always be desirable. In 2019, High Priestess Witch Tree Carr told me that boundary-setting with astral entities may be especially important for women who are largely socialized to not have strong boundaries in waking life.

Unfortunately, astral instructors and community leaders often dismiss concerns about such challenges, and sometimes accuse people of 'fear-mongering' for bringing it up. In these spaces, fear, not entities, is viewed as the primary obstacle. According to the Theosophists, we can be affected by the astral world – said to be made of vibrations, along with the physical world – and affect the astral world and astral bodies by altering these vibrations with our emotions; it is said that we attract astral beings that vibrate similarly to us, or that are 'in tune' with us.[18] According to this logic, being afraid during the experience can attract more fearful situations, while embracing something with love will see this reflected back to us. This is a common answer given by astral instructors and others in astral projection communities when someone has a bad experience: their 'vibration' must not be high enough, they say, placing the blame on the experiencer for attracting the negativity to them. This smacks of victim-blaming to me, and I also don't think it applies to most OBEs. Based on my personal experiences and interviews with experiencers, OBEs often do not seem to coincide with what's happening in the person's life at the time. The narratives of astral teachers instructing their followers to embrace such astral figures, as mentioned in the beginning of this section, reminded me of what followers of the infamous cult NXIVM were taught: that by ignoring the instinct to escape, they were reaching their full potential. In the quest for self-development, is it possible that attempting to 'integrate' scary entities could also be conditioning us to ignore our fight or flight response?

Even if the entity is a part of oneself, is it a good idea to fully embrace it? In the next chapter, we meet Aisa, a Tuvan shaman, who mentioned having her *ereng* (staff) with her in some of her dreams, which she used to protect herself against snakes and other creatures. Interestingly, she saw the snakes and other creatures as negative aspects of herself (she could feel that they were a part of her rather than external spirits), and, as such, the rejection of these elements was important in solidifying her path as a white shaman.

In the next chapter, we will dig deeper into this subject from the perspective of Tuvan shamans, where the out-of-body environment and beings are seen as both existing independently from the experiencer.

14.

SUNEZIN TRAVEL IN THE REPUBLIC OF TUVA

Many people thought that I was crazy for visiting Russia in 2024, when political relations between the UK and Russia were so dire – and to the republic of Tuva no less, as there is no shortage of sensationalist videos calling it 'the most dangerous place in Russia'. But as the last republic to join the Soviet Union, Tuva has kept its language, culture and shamanic traditions more intact than other parts of Siberia. In anthropology, shamanic flight has been associated with this region of the world more than others, but I was never able to find details describing how they experienced it. Were the features similar to Western astral projection reports? My friend Sayana, the daughter of a Tuvan shaman, had kindly invited me to her hometown and offered to help me interview shamans both in Tuvan and in Russian to learn more – I could hardly pass the opportunity up. Besides hearing about their experiences, I was also keen to know what they thought about regular people like me having out-of-body experiences, and further investigate some of the questions I raised in the previous chapter.

So, there I was – in a small office cabin in Kyzyl, the geographical centre of Asia and the largest city in the republic of Tuva, with a shaman named Ainara, who was firing off a few quick text messages from her swivel chair. On the wall behind her, between the drum, animal furs and wolf pictures, was a shelf with small plush toys, a skull and a photo of a soldier. In her Looney Tune's t-shirt, Ainara looked unassuming and ordinary, but her eyes revealed an intense depth and knowledge. She asked if I would like her to wear her shaman dress for the photos. It was over 30° C, so I replied okay, but just for a couple of minutes. She picked up the heavy animal skin coat and first put it on like a cape, covering her head while shaking it and saying a few words in Tuvan. Although today was her day off, a few desperate clients tried to enter without knocking, and a barrel-chested man admitted one woman to perform a ritual in the next room. *Probably a family emergency*, Sayana whispered. When the ritual was over, we explained to Ainara that we were here to ask her questions about out-of-body experiences, and she nodded in understanding. 'I do that all the time for work,' she said.

The term 'shaman' is derived from *šaman* in the Evenki language (an endangered language spoken in central Asia), but some scholars prefer to use local terms to refer to specialists who can go into 'trance' or altered states at will. Here in Tuva, in south-western Siberia, the word *kham* is used when speaking Tuvan, while *shaman* is used when speaking Russian. Among shamans, or *kham*, altered states of consciousness are generally for community use, such as for healing or bringing back useful information, rather than for personal development or self-exploration, like the examples in the previous chapter.[1] In 1968, anthropologist Erika Bourguignon published a report for the National Institute of Mental Health that reviewed the incidence of trance in a sample of 488 societies, using Murdock's 1967 Ethnographic Atlas and other sources.[2] This atlas is an anthropological database of over 1,200 pre-industrial societies, and is one of the sources of the Human Relations Area Files (HRAF), which has been used in economics and anthropology publications for decades. Although it has been criticized by anthropologists due to having been recorded from a mostly European male point of view (as briefly mentioned earlier), a recent review has argued that the data are nevertheless informative about the diversity of human societies.[3]

In Bourguignon's report, she found that at least one type of trance was established as a part of sacred rituals or practices in 90 per cent* of these cultures, a finding that helped to shift the opinion of trance in the West from being a symptom of mental illness to being a natural human ability.[4] In the anthropological literature on shamanic communities, two trance modalities are utilized in particular: possession trance, in which another spirit or soul is said to enter the shaman's body, or shamanic flight (also called ecstatic or magical flight), which involves the soul leaving the body; some use both, sometimes simultaneously.[5] Bourguignon also found that the type of trance that shamans enter seems to depend on the societal structure: possession trance, for example, which 'involves the enactment of multiple roles', is more common in permanent (i.e. non-nomadic) communities, which have more varied and rigid social roles to navigate.[6] In contrast, hunter-gatherers, nomads or those with less hierarchical structures are more likely to experience non-possession trance, including out-of-body experiences.[7] This doesn't mean that they don't happen within various social structures; it's just that they may not be an established part of life, utilized by the community to meet their needs.

For Bourguignon, possession not only raised the question of 'Who am I?' but also 'Who am I in relation to, or in comparison with, these others?'[8] If possession trance has a function in complex social worlds,

---

* They lacked adequate information for the other 10 per cent.

what might the function of OBEs be? I think the answer lies in what features of daily life are most critical to survival; in nomadic or less hierarchical societies, route-retrieval and spatial navigation would be particularly important. Thus, for OBEs, the question might be, 'Where am I in relation to my surroundings?'

OPENING AND CLOSING THE THIRD EYE

While the prevalence of trance practices across diverse cultures underscores their integral role in human societies, the persistence of these practices is not guaranteed, especially in the face of cultural and political upheaval. Some anthropologists suggest that shamanic practices in Siberia, in particular shamanic flight, were lost due to cultural oppression during the Soviet period, when the previously nomadic population was encouraged to adopt urban and agricultural lifestyles.[9] During this time, shamans in this part of the world suffered from state persecution and were either exiled or executed. As anthropologist Piers Vitebsky reports in his book *The Shaman* (1995), some people were even thrown out of moving helicopters while challenging them to 'fly', a reference to their shamanic flight.[10] The Tuvan shaman Ainara tells us that shamans even performed a ritual during the Soviet era to remotely close the 'third eye' of everyone in the country; psychic abilities are generally associated with an open 'third eye' (the invisible eye in the middle of the forehead that represents insight and intuition) – a concept derived from the region's Buddhist roots. This ritual was thought to protect anyone with psychic abilities, like shamans, from persecution.

Once this oppression was lifted, what emerged was different from the practices of the original nomadic societies – now 'possession trance' and other abilities were more common than shamanic flight.[11]

These days, the specialisms of Tuvan *kham* (shamans) range from healing, visions, the ability to read minds or feel others' emotions, and see the future, as well as travel to other realms. Although some shamans work alone, there are a number of shaman associations that can be comprised of people with different skill sets, ensuring that clients have a one-stop shop for all their spiritual needs. In general, although modern-day Tuvans follow Buddhist holidays and moral values, it is not uncommon for them to also visit shamans to troubleshoot life's challenges or to help with supernatural experiences and abilities. 'Visiting shamans is a regular thing for us,' says Saryuna, a Buryat woman living in Tuva, 'like visiting doctors or psychologists.'

Tuvan shamans believe that the world is composed of three main realms: *ustuu oran* (upper world), where good people go when they die; *aldiy oran* (lower world), where bad people go when they die; and *ortaa oran* (middle world), inhabited by the living. Svetlana, a Tuvan shaman who we will meet later, told us that white shamans (*ak kham*) journey to the upper world and heal others, while black shamans (*kara kham*) travel to the lower world and communicate with the deceased. As multiple shamans told me, it is not only they who can journey to these worlds; regular people can as well, usually in dreams. The difference seems to be that shamans can go there not just in dreams, but also during waking trance – including at will.

During our time in Tuva, we repeatedly heard that regular people had experienced a spike in psychic abilities in the past couple of years. 'Astrologers say that there is something special about this year,' one woman says. With this in mind, I asked Ainara whether anyone had ever 'unclosed' the third eye of everyone in the country. It turns out that this wasn't necessary. 'There is a date of expiry on rituals,' Ainara explains. It is interesting to me that the effect of rituals are only believed to last for a certain period of time, as this suggests a need for periodic maintenance, according to the times.

Given that psychic abilities are associated with an open third eye, it is advised, once psychic abilities arise, to visit a shaman to either close the third eye, as mentioned earlier (usually when the person is too young to handle their abilities) or to open it, which can lead to shamanic apprenticeship. Choosing to ignore psychic abilities, on the other hand, can lead to illness ('shamanic sickness') or bad luck for the individual or their loved ones. We also hear, however, that people need to be careful about which shaman they choose to visit, as some can steal their abilities without their knowledge. In one case, a boy had been seeing ghosts interfering with drunk people on the street. First, his family took him to a psychiatrist, believing him to be mentally ill. When the prescribed medicine failed to work, they took him to see a shaman who offered to close his third eye. However, after this ritual, the child's behaviour changed drastically, and he started to lash out. His family then took him to see a different shaman, who told them that instead of closing the boy's third eye, the first shaman had stolen his abilities for herself. He is now studying under the new shaman.

I have been repeatedly warned to be careful which shamans I meet as part of my research, as there is apparently an increasing number of 'black shamans' who are only interested in money and power. We hear an example of this over breakfast one morning with a novice shaman. During lessons with the head shaman, he and another novice said they saw a group of naked men fly through the window into their room and try to frighten the group. The others didn't see anything, but suddenly felt disturbed. The head shaman recognized their faces; they were from another shaman association, one which reputedly asks for 300,000 roubles (about 2,600 British pounds) plus sex in exchange for opening a student's third eye. 'They thought they looked cool during the attack,' the novice said as she sipped her latte, 'but actually they were just naked and ugly.'

Perhaps due to stories like these, although the belief in shamans is widespread in Tuva, not everyone will understand when their loved one decides to go down this path themselves. A local woman whose two friends had recently become shamans tells us, 'I wondered if they had joined a cult, or had maybe watched too many movies, or were having problems at home. But if they're happy, then, okay.'

I also had a chance to join one of these groups. Two years ago, my friend Sayana asked the head of a local shaman association a few of my questions about OBEs, and asked what I should do about my experiences. 'She can come and study with us,' he replied. I was surprised at this, having never met them. At the time of my travels in Tuva, they were opening a school where anyone could learn to become a shaman. Not all local shamans are happy with this, believing it to be nothing more than the commodification of their traditions. There are also concerns about screening and aftercare. 'It's nothing to open someone's third eye,' the novice shaman explains. '[But] most shamans won't teach you how to handle what can come next.'

I experience my own third eye opening on what is probably the most eventful day of our time in Tuva. An old family friend of Sayana's who runs a tour company drives us to a yurt on the outskirts of the town of Kyzyl one morning, where we meet a young shaman named Aisa and her father. They offer us a seat and ask us to take a moment to say hello to the space. Aisa's shamanic dress is hanging up on the wall with her drum, and atop her desk sits a wolf skull, *ereng* (staff) and incense. On a table against the wall are Buddhist images and sweets, which they share with us while we speak. Aisa, who describes herself as a white shaman (see definition earlier, on page 212), had been working as a surgeon in a remote region of Tuva when her abilities became recognized and requested by visitors at the hospital. Since then, she has been working as both a surgeon and a shaman. In addition to performing a range of rituals, she can also speak to ghosts and exorcize *doora*, 'devilish creatures' that can attach to a person or place and bring illness. She also pays close attention to her dreams, which, as a staunch Buddhist, often feature Buddhist themes, such as encounters with a Buddhist lama.

When we ask if she has experienced shamanic journeys, she describes visions that she sees like a film behind her eyes, unlike the immersive, 360-degree journeys that define an OBE. An hour into the interview, I tell her about my experiences, which I had decided to suppress, and she offers to open my third eye there and then. As she peers at me intently, she reveals that I hadn't actually ever closed it; it was still there, but I'd just been ignoring the signs. She explains that she can nevertheless make my third eye stronger, not as part of a shamanic initiation (these are more elaborate rituals, typically held at shamanic locations in nature), but simply to help me with my daily life. Aisa takes my hands and leads me through a guided meditation, instructing me to imagine that I'm a tree, blossoming as I receive her energy. Afterwards, it feels like fresh blood is coursing through my veins.

* * *

Although I felt safer in Kyzyl than in most large Western cities, I began to question my decision to go there after a nerve-wracking interview where *I* was the one being interviewed, and not by choice. After the interview with Aisa, we were in the car on our way to lunch when Sayana received a phone call. A couple of minutes later, she held the phone to her chest and turned to face me. 'Samantha, do you have your passport?' she asked.

I answered no and waited for her to explain. 'We've been asked to be interviewed...' she said, as she finally hung up. As she used to work as a journalist there, I expected the interview to be a journalist or blogger wanting to know about our travels. Instead, she continued with '...by the secret service.' The Federal Security Service (FSS/FSB), the successor to the KGB, had just requested that we meet with them immediately at a restaurant in the city.

'WHAT!?' I felt beads of sweat protrude through my palms.

Sayana replied with a shrug, 'It's not surprising, actually. I've been expecting them to call. I'm only surprised that they took so long.' (It had been a week since we entered the country.) 'Don't worry,' she said, 'they just have to check that you're not a spy.' This clarification didn't help my nerves.

After we picked up my passport, our driver dropped us off at the designated restaurant, where we waited for about ten minutes. Finally, two men walked in and approached our table. Sayana translated. 'I'm sorry to bother you,' the officer in charge said. 'It's a difficult time for our country, so we have to interview all foreigners these days.' They then led us outside and into the hotel lobby next door, where we sat on the sofa while they remained standing. It occurred to me that nobody – not our driver who thought we were at the restaurant, or anyone else, now knew where we were. I tried not to think about this, and instead focused on the beautiful wall-sized mural of a mountain landscape in front of us, and the limbs of a large tree awkwardly spreading across the ceiling. The officer asked for several details about my life in South Korea, before turning to Sayana with a confession. 'I'm actually one of your Instagram followers,' he said. Surprised, Sayana translated this to me and, despite trying to maintain my composure, I couldn't help but let out a snort. I hadn't been aware that she was somewhat of a local celebrity until we'd arrived in Siberia, and several people had stopped her in the street and airport. But then I realized that the officer was alluding to a *different* kind of following.

'Oh really?' she replied, immediately understanding what he meant. 'What's your profile name? I'll follow you back.' To this, he smiled and returned to his notes. 'I tried looking at Samantha's profile, but it was set to private,' he said. The games continued after explaining that I was in the country to interview shamans. The officer helpfully recommended the name of a shaman in a town in western Tuva, before adding, 'I'm surprised your driver didn't take you there; he knows the place well.' With this, he let us go. As we headed back to the restaurant for lunch, Sayana looked at me wide-eyed as it dawned on her. 'How did they know who our driver was?'

'They're following me,' the driver revealed, when he joined us later. 'I meet a lot of foreigners through my job. It's okay though – if anything, it makes me feel safer.'

SHAMANIC FLIGHT

Out of the nine shamans we spoke to in Tuva (six while I was there, and three that Sayana had interviewed using my questions before the trip), five described having experienced their soul leaving the body during the phenomenon of shamanic flight. 'Usually, people don't believe it themselves when [the soul journey] happens,' said the Tuvan shaman Ainara who we were interviewing. She went on to describe her own journeys as 'sometimes like a dream, sometimes like a fairytale'.

As anthropologist Michael Winkelman notes, shamanic flight is often conflated with out-of-body experiences or astral projection, as understood in Western cultures.[12] However, in the West, the term 'out-of-body experience' is usually limited to when one's perception is subjectively separated from the body, while Tuvan shamans also include experiences in which another part of their soul travels without their conscious awareness. In descriptions of the *sunezin* leaving the body, it is sometimes hard to discern if they mean that this occurs while their mind remains anchored to the body, or whether their point of view and mind itself is experienced as though outside of the body. In fact, Sayana had to ask another Tuvan *kham* named Yuri, who she interviewed on my behalf, several times about his journeys before he answered directly. He would first 'answer' by describing the meaning of the mirror around his neck or the tools placed around him. Sayana continued to repeat the question patiently, until he realized what we wanted to know, and apologized, explaining that past interviewers had only asked about his material possessions – nobody had asked about his personal experiences.

The shamans we spoke with did not have a specific term for their soul travel experience. Instead, they simply said, 'I went to —.' However, Sayana noticed that there were two words that had no exact equivalent in English but were similar to the word 'soul' and were used in different contexts. 'Normally "soul" is translated into the Tuvan word *setkil*,' she says. 'This is the Western understanding of the soul, which is about the mind and feelings – something from the brain. But when we discuss the soul journey, we all start using the word *sunezin*, which translates as "ghost". In our opinion, the *sunezin* can travel and be lost, but not the *setkil*. The *sunezin* is part of your magical body, [or] astral body.' This reminded me of Sylvan

Muldoon's descriptions of the subconscious will that could wander around with or without the conscious mind accompanying it (see Chapter 8). It is also along the lines of the Scientologist concept of exteriorization, in which the thetan can be outside of the body 'with or without full perception', even while controlling the physical body.

In order to learn more about these journeys of the *sunezin*, I visited a shaman festival on the outskirts of Kyzyl where several shamanic associations had set up in yurts or wooden cabins. Electronic dance music played from a central cabin, and people milled about at the small café, jewellery stand and fire pit, where several shamans were preparing for the opening ritual. In one of the yurts, we met Tuvan *kham* Svetlana and five of her shaman colleagues. On one side of the desk was a large bear claw, and, on the other, a bowl of biscuits

Tuvan kham *Svetlana sits in front of a desk of shamanic tools and offerings.*

– offerings to the spirits. Svetlana explained that *sunezin* journeys to other worlds can come on suddenly, without warning, happen during sleep or dreams, or be induced through concentration or drumming. In terms of the voluntary induction of this trance state, Svetlana does this by closing her eyes and using a drum (*dungur*), which she described as the 'horse' that transports the shaman to the other world. Interestingly, drumming has been shown to synchronize brain waves, in particular enhancing theta-wave production, which, as discussed in Chapter 5, is conducive to OBEs.[13]

Svetlana's description of the drum as a 'horse' that carries the shaman to other worlds illuminates the profound symbolic and functional role of this instrument in the *sunezin* journey, and the imagery of movement and crossing boundaries echoed strongly in her explanation of the experience. 'You can move in a straight line,' she said, 'and you know that you're not yourself; everything is different. You are no longer in this world. You can follow the fire to any place, you can see from above, climb mountains and cross rivers. It depends on how strong your horse is. If you see an obstacle, you can cross it.' Yuri described it happening during a ceremony that is usually performed once every summer to honour and connect with the ancestors. During this ceremony (called a *dagylga*), which can be performed alone or with other shamans, ancestors are fed traditional Tuvan food, milk tea and sometimes milk alcohol by a fire.

The role of physical items like the feathered headdress and staff is crucial for these journeys. 'Shamans can go to the upper world with their head,' Yuri explained, 'That's why I need feathers in my headdress, so I can fly to the upper worlds.' Yuri and others also described spirit helpers who can reside within their shamanic tools

Tuvan kham *Yuri wears his traditional ceremonial headdress.*
Photo credit: Denis Gavrilov

such as the *ereng* (traditional staff). Aisa had already told us that she used her *ereng* in dreams to set boundaries with negative aspects of herself. There were many examples of how the meaning and function of these belongings can change depending on the practitioner. Svetlana mentioned that bird feathers and *ereng* were used in *sunezin* travel to disguise the shaman from spirits, who would then instead see them as a bird flying or a snake slithering on the ground. The idea of concealment from spirits in this way also extends to the protection of children in daily life, as parents in Tuva will sometimes wipe a bit of soot on a child's nose or forehead so that spirits either won't be interested in them, or will see something else entirely, like a household object.

SHAMANIC TRAVEL FOR HEALING

Although *sunezin* journeys might take different forms, using these experiences to heal and help others seems to be the most consistent theme across the interviews I conducted in Tuva. In most of Yuri's experiences, he is visited by his oldest ancestor, who assists his travels to the spirit realm. 'When I realized that my soul can go out of the body,' he says, 'it went to my ancestors and I had to ask them to help the people who came to me for help, to protect them and send them happiness.' He also explained that the energy stored during the *dagylga* ceremony can also be shared with others over the following year.

The shamanic journey can start with an accident, illness or symptoms that doctors can't explain. While the symptoms sometimes abate after shamanic initiation, often there can still be sickness or discomfort that accompanies their work. Ainara's experiences started from childhood, which she credits to 'the spirits, so that we get used to it early on'. If it starts later, she explains, people can find it difficult to handle, although it can sometimes begin later in life, after an accident or illness. Ainara's experiences are often accompanied by intense vibrations – similar to those accompanying the OBE onset, as discussed in Chapter 6 – which she feels all over her body at once, even in her bones. 'It's the worst,' she says. 'The more energy you have, the more vibrations, and you might not even be able to stand. You should help others, and then you'll have less energy and feel better.' Sayana's mother, Marina, doesn't agree with this sentiment about helping others in order to feel better, as sometimes she can feel sick after healing others. However, this didn't stop her from healing as many people as possible – like the other shamans we spoke to, this was more than an occupation; it was a calling.

Although retired now, Marina had once worked as both a nurse and a shaman. Like Yuri and Svetlana, her journeys usually happen while drumming, but they can also happen during sleep. She differentiates them from dreams, explaining that her journeys are weird and sometimes unclear, and can involve meetings with other souls, including her granddaughter. 'While my granddaughter was sleeping, her soul ran to me and asked me to help [with her hearing problems],' she said. (She now has only minor hearing problems.) She described her first out-of-body experience, which had happened ten years before in Kyiv. 'I was treating a girl for fibrodysplasia ossificans progressiva [a disease that makes muscle tendons turn to bone], working with the *dungur* (drum) – maybe I sound like a crazy woman, but I was flying with the *dungur*.' The girl was physically sitting in the room with her at the same time as she could see the girl's soul in a 'parallel world', and flew with her soul over a river to bring her back to her body.

'Maybe it's not the point,' she continued, 'but some diseases that are considered untreatable can be treated in "another world". For physical diseases, sometimes the doctor can just treat the body, but sometimes the source of the illness is not in the body, so shamans can go to another world and treat the soul.' After this, Marina went back to Russia and wasn't aware of whether the girl recovered or not, but as a nurse, she thinks that this is unlikely, since it's such a difficult disease to treat with any healing modality. However, later, while she was still living in Kyiv, she also treated the close relative of the former president of the USSR. This patient had come to her with issues in the thyroid gland, which an ultrasound later showed had been cured after treatment with Marina. Following this, another member of the family came to her with the same issue, and this was also healed. The doctor was surprised and wondered whether there had been a mistake during the first check-up – not an uncommon conclusion after shamanic healing, according to Marina. Despite retiring from her work as a shaman several years ago, Marina did not have any further conscious journeys, but old clients will occasionally get in touch to say that she has helped them in their dreams during difficult periods, so perhaps her *sunezin* hasn't followed her into retirement.

Earlier, I suggested that, in contrast to possession, which anthropologist Erika Bourguignon suggested is linked to the question 'Who am I in relation to others?', the OBE might relate to the question 'Where am I in relation to my surroundings?' In speaking with these shamans, the *social* significance of place became clear. This was about questions like 'Where is the *sunezin*?' and 'Where can I find the spirits and ancestors that can help my community?' The answer to both questions was the upper and lower worlds accessible via shamanic travel. In these spaces, they can heal a patient by retrieving their wandering *sunezin* or gain energy or information from spirits to share with their community. However, as I was to soon learn, these journeys weren't without their risks...

THE RISKS OF *SUNEZIN* TRAVEL

During our chat, my friend Sayana mentioned the growing popularity of astral projection in the West to her mum (Marina), who repeated '*Nyet, nyet*' ('No, no'), with wide, panicked eyes. 'Her voice changed,' Sayana remarked, 'I've never seen that before. ... It wasn't her.' Marina explained that there are things that practitioners might not know how to handle. There are risks even for trained shamans, who sometimes have trouble returning to their body, or encounter difficult or hostile figures. Marina then described a spontaneous experience during sleep, when she awoke to feel an entity pulling her soul out of her body and through the window. She was able to stop it by holding onto the windowsill until it let go. (During my stay, I slept rather unsoundly in that room.) And the shaman Yuri described having been to the Moon twice, and having difficulty coming back to his body.

'I could feel the minds of spacemen or others who were there,' he said. 'Only talented shamans with a calling can come back from *space*.'

As he was coming back to his body, Yuri could see that the fire below (on the Earthly plane) was nearly extinguished, and he watched as the other shamans prayed and waited for him to reanimate his body. He is sometimes able to follow the sound of the drum from the upper world to navigate his way back to his body. However, on one occasion, he said that there were some 'things' (which he didn't describe) that prevented him from coming back, and he began to cry. 'I have my drum and know that I can come back with it though,' he said, as if reassuring himself. 'I know it's my horse and it can do it.' However, after travelling to the upper world, Yuri is often tired for several days. He explained that sometimes he comes back to his body and finds that it is beating his drum so hard that he can't open his fingers unless he pries them open with the other hand.

When we explained to Ainara about how astral projection is being practised in the West and asked whether she had any advice for people wanting to learn, she said that the average person shouldn't do this; only those who are gifted should learn.

I asked, 'How can these people know if they are gifted and should have the experience or not?'

She thought for a moment, before suggesting that those who say they can do this are either imagining it, lying or shamans.

When I asked Svetlana if there are any risks involved in this practice, she said that there is the issue of entering certain otherworldly realms without permission, explaining that while some shamans can work in all realms, others are limited to only the spaces that their ancestors had worked in. 'The risks are huge,' she continued. 'Working with the *dungur* (drum) and working with other worlds are difficult and often prohibited. You have to strengthen your *sunezin* to keep it in your body. Tuvans get into a trance state different than other shamans; there are beautiful ancestral secrets that we've kept all this time. And you are asking to know our secrets. .... These worlds are very thin and dangerous. It's not to be played with.'

SOUL LOSS

In Ainara's office (just after our interview with the secret service), I wanted to ask her opinion on my own personal out-of-body experiences, in particular why I was being pulled to certain places. As a popular shaman who comes highly recommended by Sayana's family friend, I was eager to hear her opinion. 'I often feel pulled from my back,' I explained to her. 'Have you ever experienced being pulled in your journeys? Or do you actively direct your movements?'

'Lots of people experience this,' she replied. 'In Tuva, it's very normal. When you get out, how do you come back to your body?'

'Sometimes I get pulled back again,' I replied, 'or I sometimes black out, or just find myself back in my body.'

'Is it out of your control?' she asked.

'Yes. Or sometimes it feels like my time is running out, or I might feel tired, like I'm falling asleep [within the experience].'

'What is your physical body doing at the time?' she asked.

'Lying down or sitting up.'

'So you're sleeping or unconscious?'

'It would normally happen as soon as my back hit the bed,' I replied, 'vibrations and floating out; or in the middle of the night, and sometimes during waking meditation.'

'Does it happen when you're walking?'

'No, but I was worried that it would start happening. It was happening almost every night at one stage, and then it happened one day as soon as I leaned against the sofa during the day. That's one reason I stopped.'

She asked me to take a seat in front of her and started shaking divination stones and dropping them onto the desk. She then took my hands, closed her eyes and let out a low whistle that conjured the sound of wind howling over fields. 'When your mental body leaves your physical body,' she continued, 'where does it go?'

'Usually I'm in my immediate environment, or my mum's place, or somewhere else that I know, but often I seemingly go into the future.'

'What do you do there?'

'Usually exploring, sometimes interacting with people there. In the future, I seem to be in the body of another woman.'

'Did you ever play with magic?'

'A little – white magic – when I was a teenager,' I replied.

She dropped my hands onto the desk, as though she now knew the answer. 'So maybe you lost your soul,' she said, finally. In her opinion, a spirit had probably latched onto me as a child, and was showing me the places I see, while, little by little, taking my soul. 'When your *sunezin* goes on a journey, it's easy to lose it,' she warned. 'Here in Tuva, it's okay because shamans can call it back, but in Western countries, it's easy to lose.'

'Okay.' I exhaled slowly, not really sure what to say. 'So, if I wanted to get my soul back in Tuva, what would I do?'

She ripped off a piece of paper and wrote down a small list of ingredients (milk and other things), and said that she could meet me the next day at 11 a.m. for a 'soul retrieval' ritual. It was on a donation-only basis; Sayana told me that about 20 British pounds would be enough.

'You shouldn't practise [out-of-body experiences],' she continued, handing me the paper. 'It's not normal to have out-of-body experiences.' This felt confusing to me, as earlier she had said that it was normal, no? 'It's dangerous and means that your soul left your body. It's possible to learn how to do it, but only for gifted people – it's not for everyone. ... Each time your *sunezin* leaves the body, it touches the grave. There are beings in the spirit realm that can take your *sunezin*.'

Afterwards, Sayana must have read the look on my face as we stopped for refreshments. 'Don't feel too bad,' she said as we walked back to the car. 'I was also told that I lost my soul – two years ago when I was depressed. And a shaman said that to my son years ago, too, as well as to my grandma whenever she was ill.' In these cases, the soul retrieval rituals helped them feel better. 'Soul loss' is seen as a spiritual illness; rather than signifying the complete loss of one's soul, it may mean that fragments of it have been lost or taken by entities such as *doora* ('devilish creatures' that can bring illness) while awake in the body, or while the *sunezin* travels. Sayana's mum Marina later explained that her *sunezin* can sometimes wander somewhere, but because she is a shaman, she is able to call it back by calling her own name. She emphasized that this is one of the main differences between shamans and non-shamans, the latter of whom might not be able to retrieve their soul.

The day after having my third eye opened, being interviewed by the FSB (the successor to the KGB) and being told that I'd lost my soul from having OBEs, I was tempted to go to Ainara's suggested soul retrieval session, if only in a participant–observer capacity. However, I decided against it in the end when I remembered that changes to techniques, frameworks and initiations can stop or change the nature of certain spiritual experiences (which will be discussed in the next chapter). Instead, an hour before the appointed time, I was on my way to a café to do some writing, when I crossed paths with a wolf-like dog, which suddenly ran at me and snapped at my leg. Luckily, a scream and a swing of my backpack stopped the attack before the dog could bite me, but I spent the next ten minutes shaking and looking over my shoulder as I walked in the other direction.

Twenty minutes after the incident, I was safely writing in a hotel lobby when a man walked in and looked at me intensely, before sitting at the next table. He was wearing dark, traditional clothes, covered in dust, as if he had just come from the countryside, and had amulets and animal claws draped around his neck (Sayana later said that he was probably a shaman). This man stared at me for the next ten minutes or so before leaving without ordering anything, still staring as he exited the door. I tried to tell myself that all of this was just a coincidence – and it probably was. But I couldn't help but think about what Sayana had told me before arriving in Tuva: that the land here has a special energy that affects the people on it in powerful ways, to extremes of good, bad and weird. And I couldn't help but wonder if this was connected to the previous day's events. Did the shaman send the dog? Did the FSB send the man? Or, as my dad jokingly suggested over the phone after my trip, were the dog and the man one and the same?

Perhaps it would have been wise to spend the money and go back for my soul, after all!

CHANGES OVER TIME

The nature and timing of OBEs can evolve over time, influenced by factors such as new induction techniques, a new approach to meditation, or changes in how the experiences are framed. There may be changes as part of the 'kindling' process, as explained on page 61, which can seem like different stages or levels of out-of-body experiences. We have seen this with some Eckists whose Soul Travel experiences can become more subtle over time, and with Jane's OBE entities which were invisible in childhood but visible once she became an adult. Transition signs like the vibration sensations can become gentler over time; the International Academy of Consciousness says that this is due to the experiencer's energetic body becoming less viscous with practice, like honey becoming less sticky as it warms up.

Sensory experiences during the OBE can also transform over time. German author and OBEr Jurgen Ziewe notes that the sounds in his OBEs have changed, each change heralding a new 'stage of awakening', which he likens to a spiritual initiation. According to Jurgen, there is no final stage; consciousness continues to evolve. Visual clarity can also change over time, like in the case of Korean astral projector Natam, who initially experienced blurry vision during her OBEs, but later 'saw' more clearly.[1] OBEs can also progress in clarity and colour as the experience continues, usually the further one is from the body's location. My own early experiences were frustrating due to the darkness, and I often had to feel around with my 'hands'. However, after a conversation with my friend Eve, who described her clear, technicolour OBEs, I had an OBE that night and had the idea to wait in place instead of struggling to move around like usual. Slowly, the environment brightened, becoming as vivid as a waking or dream scene, as if it needed time (or patience) to render.

Sometimes these changes can be temporary. My friend Caz, a DJ and admin of the Facebook group 'Conscious Explorers', shared a voice note while staying at the Monroe Institute, which she has trained at on multiple occasions:

'What happened when I started to do the Gateway [an OBE program] was that I started having a different kind of OBE, where, instead of leaving my body, it felt like a clearing opened up in my consciousness, as if my mind was looking into a place. And it was still kind of flying over, but it felt like I was watching it from my bed, rather than moving myself.' The residential OBE trainer, Luigi Sciambarella, told Caz that this had also happened to Robert Monroe later in life.

'It's almost like you've got this drone flying around,' she continued, 'and you're seeing it on the screen in front of you. ... It was like, yeah, I'm in bed and boom! – this clearing has appeared in my consciousness, and I'm now spying in the building next door, kind of thing.' Caz suggested that it might have been triggered from the conditions at the Monroe Institute. 'They give you a 30-minute exercise, and I've never been good with exercises,' she said. 'I always get into a panic that they're going to be over soon.' She also felt distracted by the talking on the tapes they play as part of the induction practice, as she prefers to do things in her own time. But as she was there to do the Gateway course, she wanted to respect their way of doing things. In the end, she found it to be more relaxing than her usual method, and it led to her experiencing this different type of journey.

Caz later mentioned that her OBEs have since gone back to the other 'regular floaty style', but that she feels that she can still draw from the new astral observation skill when she wants to.

In contrast, some transformations appear more permanent. While in Busan in 2022, I spoke via Zoom with Jenn Kim, a Korean–American *mudang* (shaman) raised in a Christian household in New York. Her shamanic vocation began with spontaneous 'visions' or 'underworld journeys' (she wasn't sure what to call them).

'I was just sitting in [my friend's] living room in Brooklyn,' she said, 'and, out of nowhere, I was not in the living room anymore. It was like watching a movie that I had no control of – and also being part of the movie. I wasn't aware that I was sitting in my friend's living room; I felt like whatever was happening was really happening to me.'

These recurring and intrusive visions, featuring spirits, ancestors and living people, left Jenn terrified. She did not seem to have a choice of whether to go or not – she was simply taken, feeling the sensations of 'going through spaces': 'My grandmother took me up into the sky and then somehow, we were in Korea, and she led me into a forest or a mountain, but in that vision, it was like leading me to the underworld, because it was a very dark place. I couldn't see anything... I don't know if Korean shamans actually journey or go into the underworld per se. I don't know if they do. But I've had visions of it.'

'It's because of these experiences that I felt a need to figure out why this was happening, and do whatever I could to stop it.

I was living in fear,' she explained. Jenn feared that her intrusive underworld journeys would occur while she was driving with her children, potentially causing an accident, and sought answers from a variety of sources. Initially, these experiences led her to believe that she was haunted, but her understanding shifted when she learned about *shinbyeong* or 'spirit sickness' in Korean shamanism. Her visions, interpreted through the indigenous Korean religion *mugyo*, were seen not as hauntings but as ancestral guidance leading her to become a *mudang*. The spirits do not necessarily intend to cause distress resulting from 'spirit sickness', she added. Jenn's 'spirit mom', the head *mudang* who initiated her told her that spirits have 'thorny hands' (*ggashi son*), meaning that, even if they don't mean to hurt the living, the nature of the material and spiritual worlds colliding can in itself cause harm, unless mitigated by initiation or ritual supervision.

Jenn likened her shamanic initiation to an 'electrical upgrade', which addressed the spirit energy that was influencing her, increasing her capacity to process it. It even changed the nature of her subsequent out-of-body journeys. 'I think, pre-initiation, the visions were intrusive and felt violent, because spirits didn't want me to deny anymore,' she said. 'It was the breaking down so I could wake up and accept. Now, in prayers or ritual settings, the visions are more controlled and gentler.' The visions also now only occur during pilgrimage, prayer or ritual. The change that the initiation brought on confirmed for both Jenn and her husband (previously a sceptic) that her visions were spiritual in nature. What once terrified her became a means of engaging with her ancestors, deepening her connection to her heritage despite living far from Korea. Jenn's journey illustrates how initiation can bring clarity and peace to what were once overwhelming experiences.

MEDITATION SICKNESS

A change that can occur as a result of mental cultivation practices such as meditation, whether intended for astral projection practice or not, is the onset of 'meditation sickness' symptoms. According to *The Oxford Handbook of Meditation* (2021), 'meditation sickness' is a Buddhist term that can refer to a range of issues, including deluded insights during meditation, hallucinations, pain, excessive heat or cold, depression, lethargy and dizziness.[2] Symptoms can last just for one day or one retreat, they can recur (e.g. each time one meditates or attends a retreat), or they can endure, in some cases for as long as 12 years in what can be seen as a 'Kundalini process'.[3] It's important to remember that, just as with the positive effects of meditation, Kundalini and OBEs, there is always the question of whether the negative effects are related to the practice or experience itself, or other factors such as lifestyle or illness. In any case, just as in *mudang* Jenn's experience, there are frameworks and practices that can help ease such symptoms, or the effects can be mitigated by figuring out the trigger and avoiding it.

Some participants in the energy-like somatic experience (ELSE) study mentioned in Chapter 6 (see page 88) reported negative effects from meditation, such as anxiety from not understanding what was happening, not sleeping, feeling 'wired, like having drunk 50 cups of coffee,' becoming flighty or emotionally volatile, having weird dreams or hallucinations, involuntary movements, having too much sexual energy which could negatively impact relationships, experiencing physical discomfort or feeling one's energy drained, and interestingly, having technological devices freeze after touching them.[4] Other studies specifically on Kundalini also list potential negative side effects including indecisiveness, boundary issues, grandiosity, mood swings,[5] neurosis and insanity.[6]

I experienced 'meditation sickness' symptoms firsthand in the form of hallucinations, but it was only later that I came to realize that this had been triggered by my own induction practice. In the movie *Flatliners* (2017), a group of medical students sneak into a laboratory at night to induce heart failure and have near-death experiences. Although the students initially feel more alive afterwards, one by one they start to see the apparitions of people they have wronged. Perhaps, after reading about the overlap between OBEs and apparition cases earlier (see pages 40–1), this is easier to believe. It took a few personal experiences for me to believe that this really was possible...

I was on the platform at Notting Hill Gate station, in London, UK, one afternoon when I noticed a man leaning against the wall at the far-left end of the platform. He seemed to be daydreaming, with one leg bent, his foot placed flat against the brick wall. I couldn't stop glancing at him, because he looked so effortlessly cool in his loose, rust-coloured three-piece suit. I had been studying costume, and it looked like a very expensive checked wool, and I thought how strange it was that he would use it for an outfit that looked like an ordinary clerk's attire from the 1910s or 20s, instead of for a fancy-dress party or something. As the train began to approach, I looked away as my eyes followed the carriage for a split second, and, when I looked back, he was gone. The only exit was to my far right; even if he had been on a skateboard, he couldn't have covered that distance in the time he had. I also noticed a yellow box jutting out of the wall where he had been leaning. I walked up to it and tried leaning against it and bending my leg like he had, and realized that there was no way he could have placed his foot on the wall with the box there.

The next time this happened, I was walking on a quiet street (heading east on Brewer Street, towards Lexington Street, I think – also in London) when I saw a woman in Victorian clothing walking towards me on the footpath. Her hair was a mess; she looked like she was wearing a petticoat with no overskirt; and she was looking around in a daze, as if amazed by what she was seeing around her. I laughed, assuming that this was a candid-camera-style time-traveller prank. I continued chuckling as I passed her, but when I looked back (she should have been no more than two steps behind me), she was gone. I looked in nearby shops and behind the parked car across the street, but she was nowhere in sight.

The third time this happened, I was on my way to a charity dinner at the UK Parliament for work. The first two apparitions just mentioned didn't seem to notice my presence, but this one looked right at me. In my diary, I described the encounter, which happened in the spring of 2012:

Me and my boss were walking along, and I looked up to see a man with dark brown hair in a tuxedo, about my height and age, just standing there staring at me, as if he was waiting to talk to me or something. He looked straight at me and didn't look away. It was as if he knew me, he looked excited, happy and, more than anything, amazed to see me. I didn't want to make a big scene by keeping on looking at him, I looked at him as long as he was in my sight, and he didn't take his eyes off me. He looked dressed to go in for dinner as well, as everyone ahead of us were in their tuxedos and dresses in the queue to go in. I looked back after walking a couple of steps past him, but he wasn't there – not in the queue or the street in either direction.

My first reaction to these encounters had been *Wow, I guess it's true what they say, London really is haunted!* I hadn't been ill or taking any medications, alcohol or recreational drugs, and I couldn't think of why else I would see something like this. Later, I noticed that this only happened when I had been regularly meditating specifically in order to have out-of-body experiences. I lived in London for another decade, during which my out-of-body experiences and associated meditation practice slowed as I focused on my work and studies, and, alongside this, these waking experiences stopped, too. I noticed that if I took up an OBE induction practice again for a few days or more, bizarre things would start to happen again, such as sensing a presence, feeling vibrations at night, or hearing sounds that nobody else would hear, like a cat's meow in an empty room. This might be seen as meditation-induced psychosis by some, or the cultivation of spiritual abilities that allowed me to peek into other worlds. In any case, it shows that when aiming for one type of phenomenon, we can easily end up landing on another at times; I intended to kindle OBEs, *not* apparition sightings!

There is still a long way to go before we understand which types of techniques and conditions lead to which types of experiences, but I find it a fascinating topic to explore. Learning about this has made me reflect on my experiences in childhood, and wonder if my astral projection practice may have kindled my experiences of things like cement- or worm-like skin or my bizarre 'out-of-arm experience' (see page 23), which could be classed as hallucinations, one of the symptoms of meditation sickness. The closest I have come to finding descriptions similar to those of my own experiences like this is with what is known as 'Alice in Wonderland syndrome', or cenesthopathy, which is defined as 'abnormal and strange bodily sensations', which can include 'the feeling that a hand has turned to jelly'[7] (or in my case, cement or worm skin). My Blue Ghost sighting (see page 23) may also have been brought on by meditation, or the 'blankie forcefield' that I created may have been to blame. I had reasoned that if the ghosts of the house couldn't see me under the blanket, they would leave me alone. But this might actually have caused a lack of oxygen, which can cause hallucinations. Of course, there's also the reason that I had the blankie forcefield to begin with – others had already seen apparitions in the house. It's just that mine didn't seem connected to the property in the ways that the sightings of others had. In any case, my out-of-body experiences during adulthood happened *long* after I'd retired my magic duvet barrier at the childhood farmhouse, but the one common denominator I could find for my personal experiences was astral projection meditations.

When 'meditation sickness' occurs, some people will pin the blame back on the individual, hinting that they are not ready or not evolved enough for the practice. While this might be reported by some experiencers themselves, there can be a whole host of causes, as well as prescribed treatments. Factors that seem to cause or worsen energy-like somatic experiences, according to the study mentioned earlier, are intensive spiritual or meditation practice, having life stressors or a history of trauma, sleep deprivation, not eating enough or eating a vegetarian diet, not being sufficiently 'wired' for the energy, or even being at certain locations or around certain teachers. Participants shared that the following helped with disturbing or enduring ELSEs: changing the type of meditation they practised (e.g. chanting, or switching the object of focus), using embodiment therapies or grounding activities, such as acupuncture, massage, tai chi, yoga, bending over to let the energy drain out, or saltwater bathing, and anti-anxiety medication, or generally 'having a less tense brain.'[8] Dietary changes were also said to help, such as cutting down on meat, sugar and caffeine, although some Tibetan Buddhists recommend *more* meat and alcohol, or eating more root vegetables or foods that help the digestive system.[9] According to the 2016 findings of clinical psychologist Phillip Ross Buttner's PhD thesis, 26 per cent of meditators reported 'disruptive anomalous energetic or kinaesthetic experiences', but the majority of subjects were able to manage their ELSEs by reframing their experiences as 'a sign of psycho-spiritual release or healing', or by engaging in self-regulation strategies such as resourcing and body-oriented exercises.[10]

MITIGATING NEGATIVE OBEs

Avoiding unwanted OBEs can be straightforward when the cause is clearly known, like with fainting due to nutritional deficiency, or exhaustion due to overwork. However, experiences that are unavoidable, uncontrolled or intrusive require more consideration. Both research and popular depictions of OBEs tends to either focus on the negative effects in pathological cases or the positive effects in healthy populations without due attention to the nuances in between. I cast my net wider for my 2022 master's thesis and found that whether the experience was forced, spontaneous or deliberate, and whether any entities present were viewed as part of oneself or not, the most important factor in attaining a positive experience was the ability to set boundaries. This could be done either by opening the boundaries, embracing even the frightening aspects of the out-of-body environment or entity within a supportive and empowering framework, or by setting firm boundaries through avoidance or fighting.[11] When unable to direct one's own movements during the experience, the solution can come in the form of directing energy mentally using focus and attention while in this state, or a new empowering practice during wakefulness.

Eugene, an entrepreneur in the Seoul area, is not sure what had caused his experiences, but he did not want to discuss them with anybody until now. As a child, he had suffered from night-time crying fits and sleepwalking, and became afraid of death around age 13 or 14, although he couldn't recall why. To cope, he sought answers in philosophy and the teachings of Indian gurus, and taught himself to meditate. It was around this time that he started to have out-of-body experiences. Eugene speculated that these OBEs may have been connected to his sleepwalking, fear of death and his desire to seek answers, or may have been caused by the spirits. His experiences involved spirit intruders 'in energy form' (with no face), who he sensed or saw approach him and try to hold him as he floated around his room. He also sometimes viewed his body from above, but this did not seem as impactful as the presence of the spirit intruders. Although Eugene was not sure whether these 'intruders' had positive or negative intentions (he suspected the latter), he did not want anything touching him and preferred to assert his boundaries. Although Eugene's first reaction was to ask for spiritual help when a spirit was trying to grab him, this did not work, and he next improvised by mentally directing his energy. 'I can move my energy to, you know, defeat the spirit,' he says. 'I don't know if it's real but I have like energy coming from my third eye, and I can use that third eye energy to defeat the other spirit. ... a few times I did it.' In time, this would work, and the spirit intruders would leave him alone now that he had greater control.

When Eugene was 20 years old, he was studying in the United States and was introduced to a South Korean guru who had created his own meditation technique for connecting with the 'energy of the universe'. Eugene became his disciple and learned this technique, which involves holding certain postures while visualizing the movement of energy throughout and beyond the body. This was pleasant and allowed him to become aware of new areas of his body while also merging with the universe, adopting its power and making him stronger than the spirits that had harassed him. At the same time, he knew that his body already holds and creates energy, he explained, because he feels his cells vibrating and his bodily heat, and can feel energy 'sparkling' on his fingers, which are like antennae receiving the energy. For Eugene, this energy, while being objectively real, is not coming from outside but is already a part of him, while in the experiences in which his soul, or perception, was out of his body, he was confident that the spiritual beings he met were real and not a part of him, although he was not sure how he knew this.

He called these new experiences 'energy OBEs', in contrast to the ones floating around his room, which he called 'dream OBEs'. Eugene suggested that, in these new experiences, his energy, rather than his soul or perception, was extending outside. He induced these energy OBEs at various times, both around sleep and during the daytime. While at first, he could only feel the sensation of energy during this meditation, his skill developed to the point that he could now feel it whenever he wanted, suggesting the 'expectation, practice, attention and bodily responsiveness' that anthropologists Cassaniti and Luhrmann described as being involved in the process of cultural kindling.[12] Since experiencing this energy, Eugene no longer experiences his 'dream-OBEs' or frightening spirit encounters, which he credits to his alliance with the universe that the 'energy OBEs' facilitate. This radical shift in his experiences, which were apparently catalyzed by his guru's meditation, also raises the question of power dynamics and the lack of informed consent, due to the lack of knowledge around how certain practices can halt or transform mental or spiritual experiences. Eugene did not speak about his past to his guru, so his guru was not made aware of the experiences he had had, nor did his guru ask about them. In his case, thankfully, this was a positive change.

As seen in the accounts presented, OBEs are dynamic and transformative experiences shaped by individual practices and cultural or spiritual frameworks, which often provide entirely new perspectives on the self and the cosmos. While some transformations, like Jenn Kim's post-initiation journeys or Eugene's energy OBEs, appear lasting, others, like Caz's drone-like experiences, are temporary or situational. Many of these changes arise unexpectedly, prompting meaningful interpretations on various aspects of the experience. For example, changes in the quality of the senses, like hearing or vision, can serve as indicators of the level or realm being experienced. In the next chapter, we will explore experiences that hint at an underlying telepathic or psi-related dimension to this phenomenon, including how sensory perceptions can be clues to its authenticity.

VERIDICAL EXPERIENCES

'The sceptic says, "I want the proof, the objective proof, then I will believe it!" And the projector replies, "You cannot have objective proof. You must experience it, then you will have the proof."'
– Sylvan Muldoon, *The Projection of the Astral Body* (1929)

Despite what some may think, the tendency of OBEs to inspire beliefs in the soul and afterlife is not merely due to naïve realism or a simple assumption that what is seen is objectively real. In Chapter 3, we discussed that at least some OBEs can be explained by encoded spatial memories. However, there is also the question of why some experiencers visit locations or see events that they couldn't have possibly stored information for – but that turn out to be real. For instance, how did my brother see our neighbour *and* the type of cheesecake she was holding?

Over the years, I've noticed that, more often than not, people are *sceptical* of their OBEs, interrogating them before they let these experiences change their views on reality. The features that are the most convincing are not always the subjective exit of the self from the body, but elements that seem to prove the existence of phenomena like telepathy, clairvoyance or precognition. Veridical phenomena – experiences verified by external events – frequently reinforce beliefs in the 'Akashic Records' or collective consciousness, envisioned as a vast reservoir of memories and information accessible to all.

The case of the astral projecting adoptee Saroo Brierley and his nocturnal journeys to his home village might be explained by the ability to access old encoded spatial memories, but other cases are not so easy to understand. American abolitionist Harriet Tubman (1822–1913), who escaped slavery and went on to rescue dozens of others from the same fate, had experienced journeys of the soul after suffering head trauma as a child. In 1869, Tubman's biographer Sarah Bradford writes:

[Tubman] imagines that her 'spirit' leaves her body, and visits other scenes and places, not only in this world, but in the world of spirits. And her ideas of these scenes show, to say the least of it, a vividness of imagination seldom equalled in the soarings of the most cultivated minds.[1]

These visions could strike Tubman without warning as she was working, and were accompanied by loud noises such as rushing water, music or screaming. Although to others it looked like she had been sleeping or unconscious during these episodes, she was adamant that this was not the case. Historian Kate Clifford Larson notes that Tubman's inability to speak during these episodes, her hyper-religiosity and her OBEs are also symptoms of temporal lobe epilepsy[2] (which can be caused by childhood head injury). This, coupled with a desire to escape enslavement, may have led to her experiences, which some speculate helped her to escape without detection, due to their seeming precognitive nature. Bradford notes that these journeys could predict the places and people that she would meet on her way to freedom:

She declares that before her escape from slavery, she used to dream of flying over fields and towns, and rivers and mountains, looking down upon them 'like a bird', and reaching at last a great fence, or sometimes a river, over which she would try to fly, 'but it 'peared like I wouldn't hab de strength, and jes as I was sinkin' down, dare would be ladies all drest in white ober dere, and dey would put out dere arms and pull me 'cross.' There is nothing strange in this, perhaps, but she declares that when she came forth she remembered these very places as those she had seen in her dreams, and many of the ladies who befriende'd her were those she had been helped by in her visions.[3]

I have come across several cases like this over the years, some of which seem immediately meaningful, while others can seem random and leave the experiencer wondering why they ended up in these places.

ROCHESTER CATHEDRAL

Hedge witch Jane has also had veridical experiences. 'Like in my childhood experiences, I just became aware – or woke up – as I was flying over this town, that I now know is Rochester. And then I flew towards a cathedral, I landed somewhere, I wanted to go in, and then there was a young teenage boy who was a guide. There wasn't just me, there was a small group of people. And that boy led me to the main entrance, because I tried to go through the side, and he told me, "No, not there," and then he led me towards the crypt downstairs. And he kept repeating, like, "This is Rochester Cathedral, you need to remember." He kept saying it so many times, which suggests that he knew that remembering details after an OBE can be fuzzy.'

'He was definitely, like, his own being,' she insists. 'I don't feel like it was something that my subconscious created. When he led me down to the crypt, he showed me some weird tunnels down there.' Jane later looked up Rochester Cathedral (she had never been to the town), and it was the same as she had seen in her experience. And, at a later date, she saw on the news that tunnels had been found under the cathedral, just like in her experience.

THE BUMBLEBEE

During an astral projection retreat I attended in the early 2010s, we were each told to think of a password and keep it to ourselves; we would then try to meet each other out of body and see if we could exchange the passwords. The first word that popped into my mind was *snowdrop*, because of my obsession with galantamine at the time (see pages 82–3). Then, thinking that this might be difficult for the non-native English speakers present, I changed it to *orange*. One of the attendees was a fruitarian called Theodora*, who was quiet and down-to-earth, but sometimes she would share the most extraordinary experiences.

Although I shared the room with another attendee, one night I decided to sleep in the large room downstairs, squishing into a space among the sleeping bags beside a new friend that I had made called Alison. Early the next morning, we trod into the lounge for our daily sharing circle. Theodora shared that she had gone out of body and went downstairs to the large room to see Alison and I sitting up chatting. (I'm not sure whether she was aware that we were actually sleeping beside each other in the room that night.) Theodora said that she had approached us and asked for our passwords.

'You said something like snow drrrr?', she said to me.

My eyes widened. 'My original password was snowdrop!', I said.

Then she turned to Alison, 'You said navel.'

'My password was abdominals,' Alison replied.

Now it was Alison's turn to share her experience. 'I saw you too,' she said to Theodora. 'There was a cartoon bee buzzing right next to your head.'

'My password was bumblebee!' Theodora exclaimed.

I didn't have any recollection of an OBE or dream that night, but even so, it seemed that Theodora had extracted my password without my knowledge (which was a little unnerving). It was interesting that she heard me say my initial password rather than 'orange', and that 'abdominals' had been replaced with 'navel', while Alison had seen a visual representation of Theodora's password, instead of the actual word. This made me rethink the nature of OBE content and how it's presented to us. I thought about the shamans and flying witches who used this state to try to get information, similar to remote viewing. Although in the popular imagination, an out-of-body experience is thought to reveal an exact physical replica of the space or information we seek, in reality, the mechanisms underlying these environments seem much more complex and mysterious.

OBE EXPERIMENTS IN SOMERSET

In 2017, I had the opportunity to conduct OBE experiments at a reportedly haunted location in Somerset, UK. It was an amateur, preliminary set-up, with motion detectors and CCTV both outside the door and inside the target room, which was next to the one I was sleeping in. An object was placed on a chair in the middle of the closed room, and it was my mission to find out what it was during an OBE. In the middle of the night, I had an OBE and went into the target room. The light was on and one of the team, Craig, was sitting up in bed. My first thought was that I must be awake and had ruined the experiment by barging in. But then I realized that there was no way that he would be in this room, as he was on call for search-and-rescue and had insisted on having the room closest to the exit, on the other side of the wing. I turned my attention to the chair where, to my frustration, I found not one but several objects. I muttered that there was only supposed to be one object there at the time. My colleague said that I was in the wrong room, and that I needed to go to the target room. I knew that I was definitely in the right room, having arrived just as I would in my normal waking body.

I noticed that Craig seemed to have an almost fuzzy technicolour quality to him. There was something 'off' and artificial about him that reminded me of the clones from the 2018 film *Annihilation*, as if he wasn't entirely present. A few of the objects on the chair also had a strange, almost cartoon-like quality to them. The most prominent object was a walkie-talkie, which seemed more realistic. Then I noticed a small object next to it that I had never seen before, and I picked it up to get a closer look. It was a flat, plastic hook-like tool. As I held it, I suddenly felt tired, and was back in bed, going out of body again. I wasn't able to go back into the target room, as the air seemed to be warped, and it felt like I was moving in slow motion through treacle if I tried going anywhere to the left of my bedroom.

The next morning, I made my way into the common area, where a video camera and chair had been set up for me to be interviewed. When I got to the part about the objects on the chair, I was told that there had only been a harmonica and a motion sensor on it at that time. However, there *had* been a walkie-talkie on the chair for several hours before this, while they were setting up the room. When I described the mysterious plastic object I held in my hand, I was given a pen and paper to sketch it. Craig perked up and googled an image.

'Is this what you saw?' he asked.

'Yes, that is exactly what I saw. What is it?'

'It's a line cutter. I think I have one in my van.' Craig was a climber, and line cutters were an important part of his equipment. As many climbers also visited this location, it was likely that there was also a line cutter in storage somewhere on the property, or in the room at some point. To many people, this would be a failed experiment, but for me, it was an intriguing peek into how this state of consciousness might work.

THE BLUE HOUR

I spoke with Graham Nicholls, author of *Navigating the Out-of-Body Experience* (2024), who has been a participant in a number of scientific studies on OBEs. In one experiment led by parapsychologist Dean Radin at the Institute of Noetic Sciences in California, Graham was placed in a Faraday cage and asked to use his mind to try to remotely influence the way in which photons (light) travelled in the double-slit experiment set up in their lab. As this study showed significant results suggesting that it was possible to influence the double slit experiment remotely, he was also asked, off the record, to try to affect the experiment from the out-of-body state. Graham knew that his best shot of transporting his consciousness to Radin's lab was to wait until he had a 'Peak Experience' – an ecstatic, elevated feeling – during an OBE. In his experience, this would be signalled by either deep 'cerulean' blue or 'crystalline' golden lighting, which were often the most accurate and even clairvoyant. Once he identified his next Peak Experience, he therefore willed himself to the lab and did everything he could to affect the interferometer, including punching it. Disappointingly, although the experiment was online and recording 24/7, 365 days a year, the lab never got back to him with their results. However, I was curious about his association of colour with the veridical nature of the experience.

My conversation with Graham led me to reflect on my own encounters with the colour blue. My experiences, which spanned years, were striking in their vividness and felt profoundly different from ordinary dreams. My first childhood and adult OBEs were both monochrome blue (see page 23 for my Blue Ghost experience and page 25 for my Three Intruders experience), a shade I've only ever seen during predawn on certain mornings. At age 18, four years after having seen the Blue Ghost and eight years before the Three Intruders, I had one more 'blue experience'. This time, after a period of sleep, I found myself 'awake' and floating horizontally, like a slow-moving Superman, through a courtyard of townhouses. There was one door open and one boarded up, and I explored a little before waking up. The experience felt different from my other dreams. One year later, I visited Rome, Georgia, where I felt a strong sense of déjà vu and felt drawn down one particular street. I was surprised when I came across an area of townhouses and was hit with a spark of familiarity. I ran between two houses to find myself in the same courtyard I had dreamt of the year before during my second blue experience. I couldn't believe what I was seeing. Like my dream, there was one door boarded up and another open (both abandoned), with a walkway in between. The difference was that they were switched – a mirror image of what I had seen.

Curious, I read as many papers as I could about the perception of colour, both in hallucinations and normal sight, looking out for any mention of blue in particular. In my quest to understand the unique colour perception during OBEs, I came across the concept of 'blue cone monochromacy' – seeing everything in blue – which can be caused when the only cones and rods working are those responsible for night vision. This made me wonder whether a different type of perception was in use during OBEs, or whether the mind creates a 'snapshot' of the environment to store in spatial memory at certain times (like at night), which is then retrieved during the experience. When I asked Graham why he thought he saw blue and gold during his experiences, he had already come to the idea that it had something to do with the 'blue hour' which takes place before sunrise and after sunset, and the 'golden hour' which occurs after sunrise and before sunset, imbuing the environment with these colours.

In terms of the mirror-image feature I saw in my second blue experience, I have not yet been able to find any clues about a similar phenomenon in scientific papers. However, interestingly, my mirror-image experience isn't unique; I have come across a couple of similar cases, like from Jane, who says she saw a church in an OBE that she later encountered in waking life, in a part of London that she hadn't visited before. The church and grounds were a complete mirror image of what she had seen in the OBE. I also spoke with Myron Dyal, an American artist with epilepsy who sometimes has OBEs triggered by his seizures. In some of these OBEs, he is in a replica of the actual room he's in, but this, too, is a mirror image. When I asked Graham about mirror-image OBEs, he said that he hasn't come across anything like this, although he added that this might be because he hasn't asked. However, he's of the opinion that in order to understand the OBE, we have to understand perception, and so features like these might provide clues about where to look.

A VISIT TO DR FORCATO'S LAB?

Earlier, you heard about me interviewing Dr Cecilia Forcato about her work and experiences with OBEs (see page 48). The strange thing is how I came to find about her in the first place. In December 2023, I was sleeping when I suddenly found myself 'awake' as I walked up a staircase, with no conscious recollection of how I got there. The next floor opened onto a laboratory with a few people in white coats, and a woman with a red bob who seemed like the leader. None of them could see me. The woman opened a door and I peeked into the room to see her check on four participants lying on what were either recliners or cots, with electrodes splayed out on their pillows. I decided to wander further down the hall, which opened onto a bigger room. There, a man was sitting next to somebody sleeping on a cot. He looked up and met my eyes.

'You can see me!' I said, surprised.

'Yes, because I'm having an out-of-body experience, too,' he replied.

'Let's exchange names,' I suggested, 'and then wake up and see if we can contact each other.' I told him my name. I'd tried this a few times before, and although it had never come to anything, it didn't stop me from trying.

'I'm Alejandro (something),' he said. I didn't catch his surname.

'Okay, wake up and try to find me online!'

When I woke up, I picked up my phone and opened Instagram, wondering if there was anyone named Alejandro already on my contacts list. There were two, one in the United States who didn't look like the man I saw, and then one in Argentina who *did*. I clicked on his profile and saw the words *astral projector* under his name. Not so strange, as most people follow my account because of an interest in this subject. I later found out that he heard about me through an Argentinian medium that I had done an Instagram live talk on OBEs with. However, Alejandro and I had never interacted before.

I sent him a message telling him about this experience, ending with 'I don't know if it's a coincidence or not, but if you had an OBE, let me know!' His reply came within the next day. 'I don't remember having an OBE this morning,' he replied, 'but that doesn't mean that I didn't!'

Alejandro asked for more details about what I saw, and when I described the lab, he responded, 'You know what, months ago I was part of a scientific study on OBEs. I slept in a lab, wired and connected to electrodes, having OBEs. That's crazy, Samantha. I don't know what to think.'

I checked Alejandro's Instagram profile again. Maybe he had photos of the lab or a photo of him with electrodes on his head, and I had seen it on my feed? But he hadn't posted anything alluding to the experiment. Next, I asked him if there was a woman with a red bob working at the lab. In response, he sent two photos of a woman with a red bob: the person in charge of the experiment, Cecilia. A few weeks later, Alejandro and I video chatted, and he put me in touch with her.

I still don't know for sure whether this was an amazing imaginary coincidence or if I had somehow dropped into somebody's out-of-body experiment. If so, the strangest thing is that it wasn't at the same *time*. The experiment had taken place months earlier – although Alejandro told me that there would likely be future experiments, too. If I truly had made contact with the lab from the other side of the world, then, *why?* My best guess was that having taken part in a similar study the year before, we were on a similar 'wavelength' in terms of our thoughts or interests.

When I finally spoke with Cecilia, who suggested that OBE content draws from encoded and stored memories, she said: 'But this doesn't explain what happened to you and my lab! I saw the drawing you made – that's my lab.' I had sent a sketch of what I saw that night.

Cecilia told me that there was no way that I could have learned about the lab or OBE experiments, whether knowingly or unknowingly, as there was nothing about them online. She also pointed out that the lab had undergone construction work over the past year. The next day, she sent me a video tour of her lab. To my surprise, my OBE depiction hadn't been completely accurate. It was as if someone had taken snapshots of the location and then performed a cut-and-paste job on it, moving rooms around like squares on a board. The large room I remembered was actually on the other side of the floor and far more spacious. Similarly, while I'd seen a room with four cots in a row, there were actually four small rooms in a row, each containing one cot.

These discrepancies raised more questions than answers. Could these differences reflect memory encoding errors, dream-like distortions, or something else entirely? I wondered if I had perhaps entered Cecilia or Alejandro's dream, where features might be less precise. Or perhaps the construction work had messed with the collectively encoded map of the laboratory. Whatever the explanation,

I was grateful to have connected with both the researcher and participant, and learned more about their work.

In remote viewing (see page 77), errors like this are called 'analytical overlays'. For example, if the target is a flower, the remote viewer might get an impression of multiple sections radiating from a point. But before this impression fully forms, the logical mind interferes, labelling what it sees and distorting the image. Instead of a flower, the remote viewer might end up with an image of a bicycle wheel.

Curious about how this applied to OBEs, I spoke with Damon Abraham, a former volunteer researcher for the International Academy of Consciousness (IAC) and International Association for Near-Death Studies (IANDS). I asked whether he thinks the term 'analytical overlay' could also be applied to OBEs. In his opinion, it could. He referenced an example of this from author Robert Monroe, who once claimed to have visited a friend's home during an OBE. Monroe saw a group of people sitting around a table playing with jumbo playing cards. Later, when he verified the experience, his friend confirmed that there had been a group of people sitting around a table – but they had been sorting mail, not playing cards. This raises an intriguing question: which part of the OBE is accurate, and which are products of the mind's interpretative overlays?

THE 'ASTRAL INTERNET'

This naturally leads to another question: when we have OBEs, are we truly leaving our bodies, or are we accessing worlds stored or connected through the body? Are we leaving this world, or diving deeper into it – a layer that reveals our inherent drive for connection? Both author Graham Nicholls and I (and probably many others) had independently landed on the perfect analogy of how OBEs work: the

Internet. In 2015, I created a Facebook news group called *The Astral Internet*, dedicated to the latest OBE research and exploration. The name came about after some of my seemingly veridical experiences mentioned earlier, which hinted that we can connect with other minds during an out-of-body state of consciousness. Graham echoes this concept, suggesting that the out-of-body environment might function much like the Internet, with the brain acting as a computer connected to a vast network. This analogy might explain both telepathy and veridical OBEs, as the experiencer might be tapping into this 'astral Internet'.

Graham argues that future research on veridical OBEs should focus on what actually happens in OBEs. In the past, experiment protocols have been largely based on assumptions of what researchers think should happen, which often come from pop culture or sensationalist claims. For example, a study by psychologists Patrizio Tressoldi and Luciano Pederzoli (of which Graham was a participant) found that experiencers sometimes zoom in on 3D objects to see detail within OBEs. So Graham suggested that, instead of asking the participant to read something written on a flat surface during their OBE, as some experiments have done, a small 3D object would be a better target to test psychic perception.[4] It is unclear why experiencers seem to focus on certain features in the out-of-body environment over others, and whether this is due to the underlying mechanisms of the state of consciousness or due to individual preference.

We might also look to past studies and communities for clues about the methods that produce the most accurate results to 'connect' to this space. An experiment that Graham Nicholls participated in at the Rhine Research Centre revealed that he had more positive results seeing a remote target using out-of-body experiences followed by sensory deprivation, with remote viewing protocols least effective (remote viewing is generally reported as less immersive and vivid than OBEs). This suggests that the OBE is the best-known mode of consciousness for the tasks. But there are also several different ways of entering the OBE. In Chapter 4, we saw that Dean Shiels and Susan Blackmore associated deliberate OBEs with more imaginary content, or spirit and non-Earth planes than spontaneous ones, which are more realistic. But this might depend on when the OBE is induced. Graham told me that forced OBEs, as well as OBEs induced from wakefulness, seem to have the most accuracy (or less 'analytical overlays'). He questions whether some experiences that are labelled OBEs are really OBEs at all, especially when they start from sleep or dreams. In Papua New Guinea, 'dreaming OBEs' were similarly thought to be less real than 'magic-induced OBEs' (see Chapter 12). However, for me, some of my most veridical experiences have been induced from sleep and dreams. Perhaps these sleep- and dream-related OBEs are just taking us to another weirder corner of the astral Internet?

I discussed this analogy with my Tuvan friend Sayana, who agreed that, in her experience, this also seemed similar to how the OBE phenomenon works in Tuva. 'It's just that some people decide not to join Wi-Fi, or have a weak connection,' she said, thoughtfully. 'Plus, there's a saying in Buddhism, that we know everything, we just have to *remember*.'

'But it doesn't seem like it's only from our own memories,' I added. I wondered, if analytical overlays can surface during the OBE, then might we also encounter the analytical overlays of others? This might explain why I saw the walkie-talkie, line cutter and semi-accurate science lab, and why Alison saw a cartoon bumblebee instead of a word, while Theodora heard Alison's password as 'navel' instead of 'abdominals'. It also calls to mind what the researcher in Chapter 13 learned from an indigenous community in Western Australia: that one of the greatest risks of having an OBE is the inability to distinguish between what is real and what is imaginary. After all, as we have seen, these experiences can sometimes lead to accusations of cheating or claims of authority.

Whether through analytical overlays or encoded memories, OBEs hint at the complexity of how we perceive and interpret reality. In the next, and final, chapter, we will look at the phenomenon known as 'shifting' – and the 'shifters' who use practices similar to astral projection to move to their own curated alternate reality. The meaningfulness of these experiences calls into question whether veridicality should be the most valued or sought-after aspect of the OBE in the first place.

#SHIFTING REALITIES

'There's something about Harry Potter that makes life richer. Like,
when things get really dark and times are really hard, stories
give us places we can go where we can rest and feel held.'
– Emma Watson, who plays Hermione in the *Harry Potter* films

In an episode of *The Twilight Zone* entitled 'Miniature' (1963), our browbeaten protagonist visits a museum on his lunch break to get away from the stress of the office. He wanders away from the crowd into a quiet room and finds a dollhouse display in which a miniature doll is playing the piano. Amazed by its realistic movements and sound, he asks the guard about the mechanics behind it, and learns that the doll is just a block of wood, and that there is no movement or sound in the display. After getting fired from his job, the protagonist begins to visit the doll each day, and quickly falls in love with her. In the end, the man disappears, and during the search party, the guard sees a new miniature doll in the display that looks just like him.

Nowadays, most of us spend hours staring into the miniature worlds on-screen, which may not be quite real but move us nevertheless. Sometimes, when the bigger world seems cold or uninviting, the thought of disappearing into one of these scenes might be tempting. During the COVID-19 lockdown, a quasi-shamanic practice with just this aim took the online teen world by storm, fuelled by hashtags and powerful algorithms on platforms like TikTok and YouTube. Instead of ancestors and spirits, these practitioners were using altered states to visit their comfort characters. The experience – called 'shifting' – is said to be realistic like astral projection, but scripted like incubated dreams.

Naysayers argue that 'shifters' are just rediscovering lucid dreaming and slapping a new label on it, and no doubt the techniques will lead to lucid dreams for some people (like me when I tried it). As each practitioner will have their own cultural and physiological background, the results of shifting techniques will likely be different, even if they follow the same instructions.[1] For one month, I tried various shifting techniques, scripting that I would enter my favourite childhood television show. The first night that I successfully saw one of the characters, I was unable to talk to him. On the second night, I was able to interact with him but only as the actor, not the character, and there was a queue of other fans ahead of me. The night after, I finally found myself in the setting of the show, along with the character, but his hair was different. I recognized these as lucid dreams – they started as regular, non-lucid dreams, and they were bizarre and unrealistic.

On the other hand, many shifting accounts share features with OBE reports, such as vibrations, the sense of going through a tunnel, often beginning in a waiting room akin to Backrooms locations, or sometimes being in a bedroom from the fictional world, seemingly without any dream-like or symbolic imagery. Successful shifters also emphasize how real and non-dream-like it is, to the point that they might freak out, which will usually end the experience. I would argue that shifting is a new hybrid state of consciousness that is especially curated for Gen Z, and possibly an example of the intermediate state between lucid dreams and out-of-body experiences posited by Green and McCreery[2], mentioned on page 23.

Astral projection and shifting both involve altered states of consciousness, yet they serve different purposes and appeal to different motivations, which I find refreshing. While astral projectors generally tend to defer to the lesson of the experience, seeing it as an exploration of the spirit world or greater reality, shifters tend to take the reins and steer themselves to fictional worlds or better versions of their current lives. I had initially been planning on researching shifters for my master's dissertation, but I fell ill with COVID and took a sabbatical while I recovered. While doing preliminary research before getting sick, my supervisor told me that she thinks shifting was less about an obsession with media, and more about an escape from disappointments in personal relationships. This made sense; the younger generation was going through a critical stage in their social development during the social isolation of COVID-19 lockdown. In place of in-person interaction, there was an increase in personal media consumption and parasocial relationships, which involve a one-sided, intimate sense of knowing celebrities, influencers and fictional characters. The realistic setting of an altered state could make these parasocial relationships less *para*, thus fulfilling both emotional and social needs during quarantine.

After having lucid dreams as a result of shifting techniques, Canadian YouTuber Rachelle Au had an experience that seemed different, which started with her body going numb:

> When I woke up, I was actually confused because I was in my bedroom, in the house I used to live in. At this moment I didn't realize that I had shifted. ... I was like why am I here? ... I decided to go downstairs and I stopped at the living room, because that's where I saw [the *Harry Potter* character] Cho Chang, and [she]

was like 'Hi, cous'!' ... I actually scripted that she was my cousin. ... Then we were on the Hogwarts Express, we were sitting in a compartment with Cho, and then Cedric came in and kissed Cho on the cheek ... we were all just talking on the train for a while ... When we arrived at Hogwarts, I met up with Ron, Harry and Hermione at the feast, but instead of eating the food at the feast, we decided to play a prank on Crabbe.[3]

Rachelle's experience ended when she fell asleep at Hogwarts and woke up in her physical reality. Below, another shifter describes shifting directly into a room at Hogwarts:

I felt my consciousness leave my body. My eyes were still shut but I was somewhere else. The room/bed/atmosphere and even the smell changed. I opened my eyes and I was standing in my room at Hogwarts! I stared into a mirror, not believing it had worked, and really studying myself to make sure it was real (staring into a mirror in a dream always ALWAYS gives weird results, but this didn't...). Then I noticed a house elf – he was scurrying around making the bed. I asked him to leave the bed alone (I was so excited it had worked and kinda wanted to be alone to take it all in). The elf apologized (and I felt bad about it, lol), left, and then Severus was at the door before I could continue freaking out (shifting for him, I scripted I'm a teacher and we're dating – that's all you need to know for this). He looked at me kinda strange and asked if I was okay (it must've been obvious I was freaking out a bit).[4]

Netizens on the 'realityshifting' subreddit try to work out why Hogwarts is such a popular shifting location. One said that they hadn't even seen the films, but thought that the Hogwarts setting could provide them with the school life that they didn't have. Another comments that Hogwarts is popular because it's what their generation grew up with. Others are motivated by the thought of meeting their comfort characters – a well-known aim is to date *Harry Potter* character Draco Malfoy. For many, Hogwarts is a sanctuary in which they can feel accepted and loved. Fit_Currency121 writes, 'It's a chance to get a redo of a childhood that may have been filled with trauma. I come from a poor, uber-religious family. I went to high school for two years in south Texas, and I'm black and queer. I couldn't find peace at home and I couldn't find peace at school. Hogwarts is an opportunity to go somewhere I can learn things that will help carry me through my life (like magic) and maybe find better people.'[5]

In some cases, shifting has been associated with maladaptive dreaming, and some former shifters have said that they became obsessed with shifting or suffered an emotional crash after the high of the experience.[6] I have also seen a worrying trend whereby the desired reality is one in which the shifter has their ideal body type (instead of healthier weight management or body acceptance), or beliefs that death will shift the person to their desired reality. On the other hand, some shifters describe it as a cheap and accessible alternative to therapy. In addition to hanging out with their fictional crush, shifting is sometimes used to deal with the pain of being in a sick body, and to deal with issues from anxiety to a bad economy, climate change and war. A teenage girl in Ukraine shared that shifting helped her deal with the current war, while a shifter in Turkey told me that it improved her mental health without burdening those around her, who she said had their own problems to focus on. The experiences could also be a private way to explore different parts of themselves in scenarios different from the norm, without any digital footprint or judgement from others.

SHIFTING TECHNIQUES

The vast majority of videos and posts about shifting are about the techniques, with only a minority of content recounting successful attempts. However, in principle, the practice ticks all three boxes in Blackmore's list of skills required for deliberate OBEs (as also listed on page 78): the ability to let go of the external world, the ability to mentally construct an alternate world, and the ability to shift one's attention to it.[7] In order to get into this state, shifters practise scripting, affirmations, meditation, visualization and subliminal videos for hypnosis. They write scripts according to what they want to experience in as much detail as possible, sometimes with images and dialogue in a scrapbook format. This practice has been likened to Carl Jung's active imagination, which utilizes the acting out of scenarios with toys or writing. Once the scenario has been decided and visualized, the next step is to lie down and use the chosen shifting method.

Visualizing a scripted scenario is also similar to the Golden Dawn technique mentioned earlier, in which the practitioner focuses on an image in their mind until they can spring into it (see page 79). A common affirmation is 'I am at Hogwarts'. As we have already explored, meditation and visualization can increase absorption and kindle the ability to switch into another 'Story of Experience'. With what is called the Julia Method, the shifter repeats affirmations such as 'I am, I am', while the Raven Method mixes affirmations with lying down in the starfish position and counting to one hundred. Some of the techniques will be familiar to astral projectors, such as imagining a rope extending upwards and then mentally climbing it, which is known in shifting as the Rope Technique, or the use of binaural beats (as mentioned on page 84).

SHIFTING COSMOLOGIES

In just a few short years, shifters have developed their own lingo to refer to certain characteristics and environments that they experience:

- Current reality (CR): original reality;
- Desired reality (DR): target destination;
- Waiting room: The place between CR and DR;
- Mini-shift: A very short, usually seconds-long shift, which usually ends due to excitement or fear;
- Perma-shift: A permanent shift to another world; this implicates beliefs about the multiverse and the law of attraction;
- Clone: Another self that one can shift into in the DR, while the CR body continues as normal (usually sleeping). Some shifters believe that *this* (our current physical world) is the 'core' world, with others branching out of it that we can travel to; others see all worlds as equal, which means that clones from other worlds can also visit this one (implying that it might also be able to inhabit the CR body – which resembles Robert Monroe's '"I" There' and perhaps possession).

The way that shifters talk about their experiences differs from astral projectors in several ways. While astral projectors will often say, 'I came back to my body', shifters usually use the expression, 'I came back to my CR'.

As discussed throughout this book, the realism of the experience can lead to beliefs based on what one encounters. Although some use shifting merely as a kind of astral tourism to fictional or inner worlds, some believe that these experiences are objectively real. Disparities in familiar environments often suggest thoughtforms or dream content to astral projectors, while shifters will likely see this as evidence that they are in a parallel world. Some will script a meeting with a real person, in which case the experience is thought to take place in a parallel world that most aligns with the shifter's desires.[8]

Some even believe that fictional worlds like Hogwarts are real, and when experiences go off-script, this can feed into the perception. It can become a kind of mystical fan fiction when shared with other shifters. For example, if someone sees Draco Malfoy eat ice cream during their experience, other shifters might see this as confirmation that Draco likes ice cream and then script in a date to an ice-cream parlour.

In a conversation I had in 2023 with Haitian–American film director Michelange Quay, he described the Bwiti rituals he's participated in as 'Rocky Horror Picture Shows', explaining the importance of complicit fantasy and shared performance in the healing effects of this ancient central African iboga tradition. When I tell him about shifters, he suggests that they may be facilitating their own healing through story. As anthropologist Joey Rositano demonstrates in his documentary about Jeju Island shamanism, storytelling itself is an important healing modality as it reframes emotions.[9] Anthropologist Michael Winkelman argues that mythical stories can help us to both model our behaviours and provide a buffer against personal loss. 'Storytelling creates connectedness that provides understanding through linking the sufferer's past and social context,' he writes, 'giving an acceptable explanation within the patient's worldview that provides a sense of confidence of eventual mastery over illness … [providing] psychological integration by linking the individual's suffering to broader contexts of positive expectations or endurance.'[10] At the beginning of this chapter, I quoted Emma Watson who says that 'stories give us places we can go where we can rest and feel held.' For many of Gen Z, that place isn't the upper world or an astral city – it's Hogwarts.

As psychological anthropologist Tanya Luhrmann argues, how our minds act upon impressions (or not) depends on how we have learned to organize and construct information.[11] Gen Z are digital natives who have grown up with multi-platform lives, switching between on- and off-screen, or on- and offline worlds, both of which are socially meaningful. The accessibility and ease for them of switching between such worlds contributes to the way that they approach altered states – taking the reins much like they can take the remote. It also occurs to me that, through repetition and absorption with emotionally driven films, the fictional places we watch can become coded into our spatial memory, just like our sleeping environment, perhaps allowing these places to be more easily retrieved in an OBE. Earlier (in Chapter 3 on page 51), biologist Cecilia Forcato had suggested that we might jump to worlds beyond the immediate environment (or OBE waiting room) as a way to regulate our emotions or avoid fear. In contrast to this, shifters are not leaving anything to chance and are curating scripted realities in which to heal, explore and even date.

EPILOGUE

I began this journey after my brother's 'X-ray superpower' experience in which he 'went outside' during a nap and accurately saw our neighbour approaching the house with a cherry cheesecake. This led to an astral projection practice from age eight, hundreds of personal experiences, and meetings with hundreds of other experiencers from various backgrounds. In attempting to find out exactly what the out-of-body experience is, I learned that it is a human capacity shaped by biocultural features and spiritual frameworks, and utilized or customized to meet distinct personal or cultural needs. It is used to get information, to protect family and the community from afar, to meet with deceased loved ones or to learn about the future, among other things. But there is a 'wildcard' element to this phenomenon – it can lead to unexpected experiences and changes, ensuring that it can both reinforce and shape beliefs.

After taking a break from my regular practice to research this subject and write this book, I had always intended to dive back into the practice again, hopefully more prepared. There was still the question of whether these experiences will snowball again (triggered from sitting on the sofa), but at least I now had friends I could reach out to who could understand. But there was one question that concerned me more: what if I start having the hyper-realistic 'Future Tokyo' experiences again and start to believe that we're living in a simulation?

To prepare myself for this possibility, in the spring of 2024, I took a train to Cambridge (England) to meet up with Rizwan Virk, an MIT-trained computer scientist, video game pioneer and lecturer at Arizona State University, who has written two books on what is called the 'simulation hypothesis'. This hypothesis was popularized by films such as *The Matrix* (1999) and *The Thirteenth Floor* (1999), and the work of academics like Nick Bostrom, Director of the Future of Humanity Institute at Oxford University. Rizwan isn't sure that our reality is computer-generated per se, but argues in his books that we are in some type of simulation, and that this idea is compatible with some religious beliefs.

On the wall next to the table where we sat for our interview was a framed photo with the words, 'Wayne Sleep OBE' – a neat synchronicity given the subject of our conversation. Meeting Rizwan felt like a natural progression in my journey to understand the unexplainable, allowing me to finally voice a theory I had long hesitated to share – that the strange, recurring nature of my OBEs seemed to align with the concept of a simulated reality. I had spent years interviewing others about their strangest, most baffling and meaningful experiences, and now I prepared myself mentally to risk either being seen as a nutcase or being believed, and recounted some of my recurring 'Future Tokyo' experiences to him.

'When was your last experience?' he asked.

'About three years ago,' I replied. 'I used to have them more frequently, but strangely, it stopped.' Since then, I've continued to have OBEs, but not of the 'Future Tokyo' kind.

'What was your last experience like?' he asked, setting his cup of London fog on the coffee table.

I explained that my last experience of this kind began with a regular non-lucid dream. I was in a courtyard when a woman who somehow felt real, rather than part of the dream, began staring at me in a way that made me lucid. I decided to use this opportunity to induce an OBE, closing my eyes and focusing until I felt a vague buzzing course through my dream body. I suddenly found myself in bed, but now the room had a greyish tint, and there was less furniture than usual. I started to float upwards automatically, watching as the room became smaller and smaller below. The ceiling seemed endless as I approached it backwards, and I could barely make out a shadowy figure hovering next to my bed below. It seemed to follow me up a small distance, but I was going too fast, and it seemed to give up. Finally, I was pulled to the side, and it now seemed as though I was looking into other ceilings, in other rooms with patterned concrete.

I pivoted again and saw that I was being pulled through the basement corridor of a shopping mall – not the usual one, but one that I had seen nevertheless. The pulling stopped and I was 'placed' standing at a counter where several teenagers in uniforms were working, almost like a fast-food restaurant but without the food. As I stood there, I noticed that this time felt different from before – I couldn't seem to access all of my brain or memories, and I wondered if I was in an android body (I had experienced this once before). I eyed the exit. What would happen if I just ran?, I thought. For some reason, I wondered whether I could stay in this world for longer, without going back to my body, if I ran.

In front of me was a device that reminded me of a barcode scanner, but it had writing on its screen. An employee casually indicated towards the device as if it was obvious what to do with it. As I tried to work out what it was, I looked further down the counter and saw the same woman from my dream earlier. She caught my eye and nodded, but seemed too busy to help. I knew that this was some sort of review, and worried that this meant that I was on the wrong path in life. On the other hand, this was a new experience for me, and I was excited to perhaps get some answers.

This experience was unlike any I'd had before, and it felt like a big deal. The writing on the device (I couldn't see it clearly) went red; there had apparently been some error. I got the attention of one of the staff, who tried to fix it. In the meantime, the sound became jumbled and loud, which felt out of place with the environment. I went to the counter and tried to explain this to somebody else, when I started to feel my connection with the place disintegrate. With no sense of travel, I suddenly found myself back in my bedroom, but I was still out of body. I panicked. I yelled up at the ceiling that I wanted to go back, but this didn't change anything.

After this experience, I reconsidered my previous simulation theory. I wondered whether this is where I would 'wake up' once I die. I also wondered if, instead of being a real human in a simulation, I was a character originating in the simulation (perhaps to someday be uploaded into a real android body in the year 2545). Wouldn't that be a twist on the OBE narrative?!

Rizwan seemed to agree that this is possible. 'A lot of companies are looking at using virtual training grounds, like self-driving cars,' he said. 'It's a lot easier and quicker before you send it out into the real world, because if it crashes in there, it's okay. But this idea of training AI within the simulation to interact with other AI – that's part of the research I'm doing here [at Cambridge].' He explained that this is different from something like ChatGPT, which is a disembodied AI. I didn't know this before meeting Rizwan, and the fact that we were both thinking of this common idea was itself synchronistic enough for me to think that we could well be currently living in some strange, video game-like reality.

I can't really say that I fully believe in the simulation hypothesis, but the way this series of experiences ended was awfully simulation-like. 'Sometimes I wonder if it's because there was a malfunction,' I suggested. 'They're probably like, she's not that important anyway, let's just leave it.'

'She's on a long queue of support maintenance we need to get to,' Rizwan added.

'Probably.'

As I boarded the train back from Cambridge, I couldn't help but wonder if this entire journey – starting from my brother's cheesecake vision to this moment of existential questioning – had itself been part of some grand, orchestrated simulation, either generated from my brain or something far greater. Whether we are players, observers or creations within this reality, one thing is certain: the out-of-body phenomenon continually reminds us of the vast, uncharted territories of consciousness. Regardless of the framework we use to interpret OBEs – spiritual, scientific or simulated – they hold a mirror to our deepest curiosities about existence. For now, I'm content to live in the mystery, with one eye open for the next unexpected adventure.

REFERENCE NOTES

Introduction

1. Wilde (2011), pp. 27–28, 37; Levitan *et al.* (1999).
2. Blackmore (1993), p. 175.
3. cf. Green (1968); Levitan *et al.* (1999).
4. Boas (1989).

Chapter 1. Beginnings

N/A

Chapter 2. Apparitions

1. Lang, Andrew (1897) *The Book of Dreams and Ghosts.* London, New York and Bombay: Longmans, Green, and Co., pp. x–xii.
2. Guénon, René (2004) [2003] *Theosophy: History of a Pseudo-Religion* [trans. Alvin Moore, Jr.]. Hillsdale, NY: Sophia Perennis, pp. 82–9; Lachman, Gary (2012) *Madame Blavatsky: The Mother of Modern Spirituality.* New York: Jeremy P. Tarcher/Penguin.
3. Blavatsky, Helena P. (1966) [1888–1889] *Collected Writings, Vol. X.* Wheaton, IL: The Theosophical Publishing House. pp. 220–1.
4. Tyrrell, G.N.M. (1961) [1953] *Apparitions.* New York: University Books, pp. 149–150.
5. Ibid.
6. Bruce, Henry Addington (1914) *Adventurings in the Psychical.* Boston: Little, Brown, and Company, pp. 721, 841.
7. Dyer, T.F. Thiselton (1893) *The Ghost World.* London: Ward and Downey, pp. 867–871.

8. Lukianowicz, N. (1958) Autoscopic phenomena. *A.M.A. Archives of Neurology and Psychiatry* 80: 199–220.
9. Muldoon and Carrington (1929), p. 67.
10. Hart, Hornell (1953) *The Evidential Status of ESP Projection.*
11. Bruce, pp. 711–712.
12. Tanous, Alex D.D. and Cooper, Callum E. (2013) *Conversations with Ghosts.* Guildford: White Crow Books, p. xxi.
13. Ibid., p. 89.
14. Green, Celia and McCreery, Charles (1975) *Apparitions.* London: Hamish Hamilton, pp. 33–34.
15. Ibid.
16. Green and McCreery. (1975) pp. 2-4
17. Poynton, John (2017) President's Letter. The SPR's Philosopher-Presidents: Henry Sidgwick, Part II. Paranormal Review, 81.

Chapter 3. OBEs as 'Isolation Zones'

1. The Twilight Zone (1959) 'Where Is Everybody?'
2. Fisher, M. (2016) *The Weird and the Eerie.* London: Repeater Books, p. 15.
3. Parsons, Kane (2022) 'Backrooms.' *YouTube.* Available from: https://www.youtube.com
4. Lloyd, Andrew (2022) 'The backrooms: how a creepy office photo became an Internet bogeyman.' *Vice* [online]. Available from: https://www.vice.com
5. Treasure, Samantha Lee (2023) 'Out-of-body experiences in the screen age.' In *Deep Weird*, Jack Hunter (ed.), August Night Press.

6. Rothman, Joshua (2018) 'Are we already living in virtual reality?' *The New Yorker* [online]. Available from: https://www.newyorker.com

7. Seth, Anil. (2017) 'Your brain hallucinates your conscious reality.' TED Talk. Available from: https://www.youtube.com

8. Blanke, Olaf (2005) The out-of-body experience: disturbed self-processing at the temporo-parietal junction. *Neuroscientist* 11(1): 16–24.

9. Pitron, V. and de Vignemont, F. (2017) Beyond differences between the body schema and the body image: insights from body hallucinations. *Consciousness and Cognition* 53: 115–121.

10. Palmer, J. (1978) 'The out-of-body experience: A psychological theory.' *Parapsychology Review* 9: 19–22; Blackmore, Susan (1984) 'A psychological theory of the out-of-body experience.' *Journal of Parapsychology* 4893, 201–218; Blackmore, Susan J. (1986) 'Spontaneous and deliberate OBEs: A questionnaire survey.' *Journal of the Society for Psychical Research* 53(802): 218–224; Blackmore, Susan (1993) *Dying to Live: Science and the Near-Death Experience.* London: Grafton, p. 175; Irwin, Harvey J. and Watt, Caroline (2007) *An Introduction to Parapsychology.* Jefferson, NC and London: McFarland and Company, pp. 175–191.

11. Peterson, Robert (2019) *Hacking the Out-of-Body Experience.*

12. Green and McCreery (1975), pp. 35, 38.

13. cf. Hurd, Ryan (2016) 'Towards an evolutionary psychology of out-of-body experiences.' In *Consciousness Beyond the Body: Evidence and Reflections,* Alexander De Foe (ed.), Melbourne: Melbourne Centre for Exceptional Human

Potential, pp. 62–69; McClenon, James (1997) 'Shamanic healing, human evolution, and the origin of religion.' *Journal for the Scientific Study of Religion* 36(3): 345–354.

14. Treasure, Samantha Lee (2023) 'Out-of-body experiences in the screen age.' In *Deep Weird*, Jack Hunter (ed.), August Night Press.

15. Fisher, M. (2016) *The Weird and the Eerie*. London: Repeater Books, p. 15.

16. Hurd, Ryan. (2016) 'Towards an Evolutionary Psychology of Out-of-Body Experiences.' In *Consciousness Beyond the Body: Evidence and Reflections,* Alexander De Foe (ed.), Melbourne: Melbourne Centre for Exceptional Human Potential, pp. 62–69; McClenon, James (1997) 'Shamanic healing, human evolution, and the origin of religion.' *Journal for the Scientific Study of Religion* 36(3): 345–354.

Chapter 4. The Cross-cultural Occurrence of OBEs

1. See Wilde, David J. (2011) *Finding Meaning in Out-of-Body Experiences: An Interpretative Phenomenological Analysis* [PhD thesis], University of Manchester, for a review.

2. Kohr, R.L. (1980) A survey of psi experiences among members of a special population. *Journal of the American Society for Psychical Research* 74: 395–411.

3. Tylor, Edward B. (1871) *Primitive Culture: Researches into the Development of Mythology, Philosophy, Religion, Art, and Custom*. London: John Murray [Kindle version], location 6532.

4. Metzinger, Thomas (2005) Out-of-body experiences as the origin of the concept of a 'soul'. *Mind and Matter* 3(1): 57–84.

5. Tylor (1871) *Primitive Culture: Researches into the Development of Mythology, Philosophy, Religion, Art, and Custom.* London: John Murray, pp. 384–387.
6. Metzinger (2005).
7. Shiels, D. (1978) A cross-cultural study of beliefs in the out-of-the-body experiences, Waking and Sleeping. *Journal of the Society for Psychical Research* 49, 697–741.
8. Nguyen, Vinh-Kim and Lock, Margaret M. (2011) *An Anthropology of Biomedicine*, Chapter 3.
9. Malinowski (1951) [1927] *Sex and Repression in Savage Society.* London: Kegan Paul, Trench, Trubner and Co., pp. 92–93, cited in Lohmann, R.I. 'Dream Travels and Anthropology', in *Dream Travelers: Sleep Experiences and Culture in the Western Pacific* (2003), Roger Ivar Lohmann (ed.), New York: Palgrave Macmillan, pp. 1–18.
10. Lohmann (2003).
11. Shiels (1978).
12. Ibid.
13. Blackmore (1986)
14. Natam (2019) 'How I finally achieved my first astral projection' [online]. Available from: https://www.youtube.com
15. Murray, C.D., Fox, J. and Wilde, D. (2006) Poster presentation: 'Investigating the Multidimensional Nature of Body Image, Sensorial Representation and Phenomenology in Relation to Different Forms of Out-of-Body Experience', 6th Bial symposium: Behind and Beyond the Brain. Porto, Portugal, cited in Wilde (2011).
16. Cassaniti and Luhrmann (2014).
17. Braithwaite, Jason J., Broglia, Emma and Watson, Derrick (2014) 'Autonomic emotional responses to the induction of the rubber-hand illusion in those that report anomalous

bodily experiences: evidence for specific psychophysiological components associated with illusory body representations.' *Journal of Experimental Psychology: Human Perception and Performance* 3(40): 1131–1145.

18. Kessler, Klaus and Braithwaite, Jason J. (2016) 'Deliberate and spontaneous sensations of disembodiment: capacity or flaw?' *Cognitive Neuropsychiatry* 21(5): 412–428.

19. Milne, Elizabeth, Dickinson, Abigail, and Smith, Richard (2017) 'Adults with autism spectrum conditions experience increased levels of anomalous perception.' *PLoS One* 12, 5: e0177804

20. Carr, Michelle and Solomonova, Elizaveta (2018) 'Dream recall and content in different sleep stages.' In *Dreams: Biology, Psychology and Culture*, K. Valli and R. Hoss (eds.), Greenwood Publishing Group.

21. LaBerge, Stephen, Levitan, Lynne and Dement, William C. (1986) Lucid dreaming: physiological correlates of consciousness during REM sleep. *Journal of Mind and Behavior* 7: 251–58.

22. McCreery (2019), p. 6.

23. McCreery, C. (2019) *Out-of-the-Body Experiences: Implications for a Theory of Psychosis.* Oxford Forum, p. 22.

24. 'Narcolepsy'. National Institute of Neurological Disorders and Stroke [online]. Available from: https://www.ninds.nih.gov

25. Steiger, A. and Pawlowski, M. (2019) Depression and sleep. *International Journal of Molecular Sciences* 20, 3.

26. St-Onge, Marie-Pierre, Mikic, Anja and Pietrolungo, Cara E. (2016) 'Effects of diet on sleep quality.' *Advances in Nutrition* 7(5): 938–949.

27. Benton, David, Bloxham, Anthony, Gaylor, Chantelle, Brennan, Anthony and Young, Hayley A. (2022) 'Carbohydrate and sleep: an evaluation of putative mechanisms.' *Frontiers in Nutrition* 9.

28. Tanaka, Eizaburo, Yatsuya, Hiroshi, Uemura, Mayu, Murata, Chiyoe, Otsuka, Rei, Toyoshima, Hideaki, Tamakoshi, Koji, Sasaki, Satoshi, Kawaguchi, Leo and Aoyama, Atsuko (2013) Associations of protein, fat, and carbohydrate intakes with insomnia symptoms among middle-aged Japanese workers. *Journal of Epidemiology* 23: 132–138.

29. Peterson, Robert (2023) 'Inner Ear Muscle Technique.' *The OBE Outlook On Life* [online blog]. Available from: https://obeoutlook.blogspot.com

30. Fox, Oliver (1962) [1939] *Astral Projection: A Record of Out-of-the-Body Experiences*. Secaucus, NJ: The Citadel Press.

Chapter 5. Practitioners and their Induction Techniques

1. Urban, Hugh B. (2011) *The Church of Scientology: A History of a New Religion*. Princeton and Oxford: Princeton University Press, pp. 37–39.

2. Ibid., 42.

3. Church of Scientology of Tampa (no date). 'What is the difference between Scientology and Dianetics?' Available from: https://www.scientology-tampa.org

4. Urban, p. 3.

5. Church of Scientology of Pretoria (no date). 'Religious Principles, Creed, Symbols and The Human Spirit', Official Church of Scientology Video, Church of Scientology of Pretoria (scientology-pretoria.org.za).

6. Church of Scientology of Tampa (no date). 'What is the difference between Scientology and Dianetics?' Available from: https://www.scientology-tampa.org

7. Urban, p. 78–81.
8. Hubbard, L. Ron. (1954) [2007] *The Creation of Human Ability: A Handbook for Scientologists*. Los Angeles: Bridge Publications, pp. 382–385.
9. Ibid., pp. 63–65.
10. Urban, pp. 77, 113–115.
11. Blackmore (1986).
12. Wang, H., Callaghan, E., Gooding-Williams, G., McAllister, C. and Kessler, K. (2016) 'Rhythm makes the world go round: an MEG-TMS study on the role of right TPJ theta oscillations in embodied perspective taking. *Cortex* 75, 68–81.
13. Greer, Mary K. (1995) *Women of the Golden Dawn: Rebels and Priestesses*. Rochester, Vermont: Park Street Press, pp. 109–111.
14. Crowley, Aleister (2012) *Magick: Liber ABA*, 2nd revised edition. San Francisco: Weiser Books, p. 625, cited in Rinde, Adrian Johansen (2015) [PhD thesis], Norwegian University of Science and Technology.
15. Muldoon, Sylvan and Carrington, Hereward (1929) *The Projection of the Astral Body*. London: Rider and Co., pp. 5–7.
16. Muldoon and Carrington (1929), pp. 99–103, 124.
17. Irwin, Harvey J. (1988) 'Out-of-the-Body Experiences and Dream Lucidity: Empirical Perspectives.' In *Conscious Mind, Sleeping Brain: Perspectives on Lucid Dreaming*, Jayne Gackenbach and Stephen LaBerge (eds.), New York and London, Plenum Press, pp. 353–368.
18. Homer (1880) *The Odyssey* [trans. Alexander Pope]. New York: John Wurtele Lovell, p. 114.

19. Schwarcz, Joe (2022) 'Odysseus' Snowdrop Odyssey.' Office for Science and Society, McGill University. Available from: https://www.mcgill.ca

20. Solcà M., Mottaz A. and Guggisberg A.G. (2016) 'Binaural beats increase interhemispheric alpha-band coherence between auditory cortices.' *Hearing Research* 332: 233–237; Jirakittayakorn N., Wongsawat Y. (2017) Brain responses to a 6-Hz binaural beat: effects on general theta rhythm and frontal midline theta activity. *Frontiers in Neuroscience* 11: 365, both cited in Perez, Hector D. Orozco, Dumas, Guillaume and Lehmann, Alexandre (2020) Binaural Beats through the Auditory Pathway: From Brainstem to Connectivity Patterns. *eNeuro* 7, 2.

21. Herrmann, C.S., Strüber, D., Helfrich, R.F. and Engel, A.K. (2016) 'EEG oscillations: from correlation to causality.' *International Journal of Psychophysiology* 103, 12–21, cited in Lopez (2020).

22. Winkelman, Michael (2013) 'The Integrative Mode of Consciousness: Evolutionary Origins of Ecstasy.' In *Ekstasen: Kontexte – Formen – Wirkungen.* Ergon-VerlagEditors: Torsten Passie, Wilfried Belschner, Elisabeth Petrow, pp. 67–83.

23. Nicholls, Graham (2024) 'Infra-liminal sound' [online] Available from: https://www.grahamnicholls.com/infra-liminal-sound

Chapter 6. Transitions: Vibrations, Kundalini and Sound

1. Woollacott, Marjorie H., Kason, Yvonne and Park, Russell D. (2021) Investigation of the phenomenology, physiology and impact of spiritually transformative experiences – kundalini awakening. *Explore* 17(6): 525–534.

2. Cooper, David J., Lindahl, Jared R., Palitsky, Roman and Britton, Willoughby B. (2021) Like a vibration cascading through the body: Energy-Like Somatic Experiences reported by Western Buddhist meditators. *Religions* 12(12): 1042.
3. Graux J., Lemoine M., Gaillard P. and Camus V (2011) Les cénesthopathies: un trouble des émotions d'arrière plan. Regards croisés des sciences cognitives et de la phénoménologie. *Encéphale* 37: 361–370. In Jimeno, Natalia and Vargas, Martin L. (2017) Cenesthopathy and subjective cognitive complaints: an exploratory study in schizophrenia. *Psychopathology* 51(1): 47–56.
4. Cooper, David J., Lindahl, Jared R., Palitsky, Roman and Britton, Willoughby B. (2021) Like a vibration cascading through the body: energy-like somatic experiences reported by Western Buddhist meditators. *Religions* 12(12): 1042.
5. Muldoon and Carrington.
6. Peake, Anthony (2011) *The Out-of-Body Experience: The History and Science of Astral Travel.* London: Watkins Publishing, pp. xiii–xvi.
7. Strassman, Rick (2001) *DMT: The Spirit Molecule.* Rochester, Vermont: Park Street Press; Muldoon and Carrington, p. 85.
8. McDonnell, Wayne M. (1983) 'Analysis and Assessment of Gateway Process.' U.S. Department of Defense. Available from: https://www.cia.gov/readingroom/docs/CIA-RDP96-00788R001700210016-5.pdf
9. McCreery, Charles (no date) 'Out-of-the-body experiences: implications for a theory of psychosis', Chapter 5, p. 20 [online]. Available from: https://www.celiagreen.com/charlesmccreery.html

10. Jourdan, Jean Pierre (1994) Near death experiences and transcendental experiences: neurophysiological correlates of mystical traditions. *Journal of Near-Death Studies* 12, 3.
11. Peake, Anthony (2024) *Near-Death Experiences.*
12. Kieffer, Gene (1994) The near-death experience and kundalini. *Journal of Near-Death Studies* 12(3): 159–176.
13. Greyson, Bruce (1993) Near-death experiences and the physio-Kundalini syndrome. *Journal of Religion and Health* 32, 4 (Winter).
14. Irwin, Harvey J. and Watt, Caroline (2007) 'Out-of-body experiences.' In *An Introduction to Parapsychology, 5th revised edition*, H.J. Irwin and C. Watt (eds.), Jefferson, NC: McFarland and Co. Inc., pp. 179–196.
15. Stefanov, Miroslav, Potroz, Michael, Kim, Jungdae, Lim, Jake, Cha, Richard and Nam, Min-ho (2013) The primo vascular system as a new anatomical system. *Journal of Acupuncture and Meridian Studies* 6(6): 331–338.
16. Lockley, Martin (2019) Kundalini Awakening, Kundalini Awareness. *Journal for the Study of Religious Experience* 5, 1.
17. Singh, Kirpal (1974) *The Teachings of Kirpal Singh*. Blaine, WA: Ruhani Satsang, p. 193.
18. Natam (2019) 'How I finally achieved my first astral projection' [online]. Available from: https://www.youtube.com
19. Blanke, O., Landis, T., Spinelli, L. and Seeck, M. (2004) Out-of-body experience and autoscopy of neurological origin. *Brain*, 127(2): 243–258.

Chapter 7. 'Stealth Mode'

1. Fox, Oliver (1962) [1939] *Astral Projection. A Record of Out-of-the-Body Experiences*. Secaucus, NJ: The Citadel Press, p. 72.

2. Green, Celia E. and McCreery, Charles (1994) *Lucid Dreaming: The Paradox of Consciousness During Sleep*. London: Routledge, p. 115.
3. Treasure, Samantha Lee (2018) [questionnaire]. Available from: www.zombiesinpjs.com
4. Treasure, Samantha Lee (2019) *Encountering Figures in Out-of-Body Experiences: A Qualitative UK Study* [unpublished bachelor's thesis], Birkbeck, University of London.
5. Leadbeater, Charles W. (1933) *The Astral Plane*. Aydar, India: The Theosophical Publishing House, pp. 35–45.
6. Treasure (2018).
7. Treasure (2019).
8. Fox (1962), p. 40.
9. Treasure, Samantha Lee (2023) 'Out-of-body experiences in the screen age'. In *Deep Weird*, Jack Hunter (ed.), August Night Press.

Chapter 8. Navigation

1. Muldoon, Sylvan, and Carrington, Hereward (1929) *The Projection of the Astral Body*. London: Rider and Co., p. 10.
2. Treasure, Samantha L. (2018) [questionnaire]. Available from: www.zombiesinpjs.com
3. Goldney, K.M. 16/2/53 [Society for Psychical Research archives, Cambridge University Library].
4. Muldoon and Carrington (1929), pp. 5–7.
5. Crookall, Robert (1964) *The Techniques of Astral Projection*. Whitstable, UK: Whitstable Litho Limited.
6. McCreery, Charles (2019) *Out-of-the-Body Experiences: Implications for a Theory of Psychosis*. Oxford: Oxford Forum.

7. Alvarado, Carlos S. (2012) 'Explorations of the features of out-of-body experience: an overview and critique of the work of Robert Crookall.' *Journal of the Society for Psychical Research* 76.2(907): 65–82.

8. Green, Celia E. (1968) *Out-of-the-Body Experiences.* London: Hamish Hamilton, p. 100.

9. Treasure (2018).

10. McIntosh, Alastair I. (1980) 'Beliefs about out-of-the-body experiences among the Elema, Gulf Kamea and Rigo peoples of Papua New Guinea.' *Journal for the Society for Psychical Research* 50(785): 460–478.

11. Monroe, Robert (1971) *Journeys Out of the Body.* New York: Doubleday, p. 129.

12. Johnson, Jerry Alan (2002) *Chinese Medical Qigong Therapy, Volume 3.* Pacific Grove, CA: The International Institute of Medical Qigong, pp. 195–196.

13. Jefferson, R.B. (1982) 'Chapter 4: The archaic anatomy of individual organs', in *The Doctrine of the Elixir*, Coombe Springs Press; Pregadio, Fabrizio (2023) Golden Elixir Press; Pregadio, Fabrizio (2006) 'Early Daoist meditation and the origins of inner alchemy', in *Daoism in History: Essays in Honour of Liu Ts'un-yan*, Benjamin Penny (ed.), London: Routledge, pp. 139–40.

14. Muldoon and Carrington, p. xvii.

15. Ibid., p. 18.

16. Ibid., p. 44.

17. Ibid., pp. 29–30.

18. Ibid., p. 100.

19. Ibid., pp. 19–24.

20. Ibid., pp. 11–12.

21. Ibid., p. 75.

22. Wilde, David, p. 309.

23. 'The real-life subject of "Lion": Saroo Brierley', 12 July 2017. *Talks at Google* [online]. Available from: https://www.youtube.com

Chapter 9. My 'Future Tokyo' Experiences

1. Sheriff, Robin (2017) Dreaming of the Kardashians: media content in the dreams of US college students, *Ethos* 45(4): 532–554.
2. Monroe, Robert (1971) *Journeys Out of the Body,* pp. 72–75.
3. Peake, Anthony (2011) *The Out-of-Body Experience*, pp. 180–185.
4. Monroe, Robert (1994) *The Ultimate Journey*, pp. 198–199.
5. Laughlin, Charles and Rock, Adam J. (2014) What can we learn from shamans' dreaming? A cross-cultural exploration. *Dreaming* 24(4): 233–252.

Chapter 10. Alien Contactees

1. Mack, John E. (2007) *Abduction*, p. 44.
2. Hilbert, Janet (2020) 'Ask the expert: managing sleep attacks with narcolepsy.' *Healthline* [online]. Available from: https://www.healthline.com/health/narcolepsy/ask-the-expert-narcolepsy [Accessed 18 May 2024.]
3. McCready, David (2016) *Real Alien Worlds: A Brief Encyclopaedia*. London: McCready Publishing.
4. Badmington, Neil (2004) *Alien Chic: Posthumanism and the Other Within*. New York: Routledge, p. 90.
5. Devereux, Paul (1992) *Shamanism and the Mystery Lines*. London: Quantum, p. 215–216.
6. Ibid.
7. Harvey-Wilson, Simon Brian (2000) *Shamanism and Alien Abductions: A Comparative Study* [master's thesis], Edith Cowan University.
8. Ibid.

Chapter 11. Eckankar and Soul Travel™

1. Lane, David C. (2017) [1977] *The Making of a Spiritual Movement*, Walnut, CA: MSAC Philosophy Group, p. 36.
2. Twitchell, Paul (1970) *The Far Country*, pp. 12–13.
3. Lane, *The Making of a Spiritual Movement*, p. 10; Lane, 'Eckankar,' p. 115.
4. Lane, *The Making of a Spiritual Movement*, p. 45.
5. Twitchell, 'Eckankar: The bilocation philosophy,' quoted in Lane, *The Making of a Spiritual Movement*, p. 42.
6. Eckankar, *Frequently Asked Questions*. [online] Available from: https://www.eckankar.org
7. Eckankar, 'Glossary of ECK Terms' *Soul Adventure Magazine*, Vol 1, No.2, p.34
8. Bellamy, Dodie. 'Eckankar: a former member revisits the movement'.
9. Eckankar, *A Gateway to Soul Travel*.
10. Eckankar, *Frequently Asked Questions*.
11. Lane (2017), pp. 79, 97; Lane, 'Eckankar', p. 117.
12. Lane (2017), pp. 55
13. Eckankar Online Book Store, *The Art of Spiritual Dreaming*.
14. Twitchell, 'Outsight,' quoted in Lane, *The Making of a Spiritual Movement*, p. 136.
15. Lane, *The Making of a Spiritual Movement*, pp. 34–40; Lane, *Gakko Came From Venus*, p. 83.
16. Diem-Lane, *The Guru in America*, Chapter 3; Lane, *Gakko Came From Venus*, p. 83.
17. Klemp, *Spiritual Experiences Guidebook*, pp. 28–30.
18. Peake, Anthony (2011) *The Out-of-Body Experience: The History and Science of Astral Travel*. London: Watkins Publishing, pp. 21–22.

19. Klemp, *Spiritual Experiences Guidebook*, pp. 28–30.
20. Ibid., p. 32.
21. Eckankar, 'Soul travel'. Available from: https://www. eckankar.org/experience/soul-travel/
22. Klemp, *Past Lives, Dreams, and Soul Travel*, pp. 190–191.
23. Bellamy, Dodie. 'Eckankar: a former member revisits the movement'.
24. Lane, David C. (2015) *The Skeptical Text*. Lulu.com, p. 18.

Chapter 12. Astral Projection and Witchcraft

1. Schrock, Marilyn (2009) *Wake Up, Church! The Enemy Is Within Your Gates*, p. 38.
2. Ibid., p. viii.
3. Ibid., pp. 5, 17–18.
4. Ibid., pp. 2–7.
5. Ibid., p. 10.
6. Ibid., pp. 39–46.
7. Koopan, Gobal (2019) *Astral Projection and the Abuse of Women: A Pastoral Challenge* [PhD thesis], University of Pretoria, p. 181.
8. Ibid., p. 126.
9. Schrock (2009), p. 51.
10. Koopan, pp. 139–177.
11. Molendijk, M.L., Bouachmir, O., Montagne, H., Bouwman, L. and Blom, J.D. (2022). The incubus phenomenon: prevalence, frequency and risk factors in psychiatric inpatients and university undergraduates. *Frontiers in Psychiatry* 14(13): 1040769.
12. Baland, Jalal and Ramachandran, Vilayanur, S. Sleep paralysis and the 'bedroom intruder': the role of the right superior parietal, phantom pain and body image projection. *Medical Hypothesis* 83(6): 755–757.

13. Molendijk *et al.* (2002).
14. Klemp, Harold (1987) 'Methods of the black magician.' *The Mystic World* (Winter), in Lane, David (2017) [1977] *The Making of a Spiritual Movement*. Walnut, California: MSAC Philosophy Group, pp. 114–115.
15. McIntosh, Alastair I. (1980) Beliefs about out-of-the-body experiences among the Elema, Gulf Kamea and Rigo peoples of Papua New Guinea. *Journal for the Society for Psychical Research* 50(785): 460–478.
16. Jenness, D. and Ballantyne, A. (1920) *The Northern d'Entrecasteaux*. UK: Clarendon Press.
17. McIntosh (1980).
18. Malinowski, B. (1922) *Argonauts of the West Pacific*. UK: Routledge and Kegan Paul, p. 249, in McIntosh (1980).
19. McIntosh (1980).
20. Ginzburg, Carlo (1983) [1966]. *The Night Battles: Witchcraft and Agrarian Cults in the Sixteenth and Seventeenth Centuries*. Translated by Tedeschi, John and Tedeschi, Anne. Baltimore: Johns Hopkins University Press.
21. Stewart, Charles (2023) Untitled lecture. LAByrinth Dream Lab, London. Italy witches who have OBEs.
22. Wilby, Emma (2013) [2005] *Cunning Folk and Familiar Spirits: Shamanic Visionary Traditions in Early Modern British Witchcraft and Magic*. Brighton, Chicago and Toronto: Sussex Academic Press, p. 146.
23. Ibid., p. 147.
24. Ibid., p. 88.

Chapter 13. The Astral Marketplace in the 21st Century

1. Urban (2011), p. 39.
2. 'Who we are' (no date). *International Academy of Consciousness* [online]. Available from: https://www.

iacworld.org; 'The organization' (no date). *International Academy of Consciousness* [online]. Available from: https://www.iacworld.org

3. Melton, Gordon (1990) *New Age Encyclopedia*. Detroit: Gale Research, p. xiii.
4. Ellwood, Robert and Partin, Harry (1988) Religious and Spiritual Groups in Modern America. Englewoods, NJ: Prentice Hall, pp. 14–15.
5. Heelas, Paul (1996) *The New Age Movement: The Celebration of the Self and the Sacralization of Modernity*. Oxford: Blackwell, p. 169, cited in Urban, Hugh, B. (2000) The cult of ecstasy: tantrism, the New Age, and the spiritual logic of late capitalism, *History of Religions* 39(3): 268–304.
6. Weiler, Marina, Acunzo, David, J., Cozzolino, Philip, J. and Greyson, Bruce (2024) Exploring the transformative potential of out-of-body experiences: a pathway to enhanced empathy. *Neuroscience and Biobehavioral Reviews* 163: 105764.
7. Greyson, Bruce (1993) The physio-kundalini syndrome and mental illness. *The Journal of Transpersonal Psychology* 25, 1.
8. Weiler, Marina, Acunzo, David, J., Cozzolino, Philip, J. and Greyson, Bruce (2024) Exploring the transformative potential of out-of-body experiences: a pathway to enhanced empathy. *Neuroscience and Biobehavioral Reviews* 163: 105764.
9. Bourguignon, Erika (1968) 'A cross-cultural study of dissociational states.' [Report for National Institute of Mental Health, Bethesda, Maryland.]
10. White, Rhea, A. (1997) 'My EHE odyssey: an ongoing process of formulation.' In *Exceptional Human Experience: Background Papers II*, R.A. White (ed.), New Bern, NC: EHE Network, pp. 137–138.
11. Davis, Erik (2020) 'High weirdness: drugs, esoterica,

and visionary experience in the seventies.' *Psychedelics Today* [online]. Available from: https://www.everand.com/podcast/492964980/Erik-Davis-High-Weirdness-Drugs-Esoterica-and-Visionary-Experience-in-the-Seventies-Erik-Davis-High-Weirdness-Drugs-Esoterica-and-Visionary

12. Blackmore, Susan, J. (2017) *Seeing Myself: The New Science of Out-of-Body Experiences*. London: Robinson.

13. Crowley, Aleister (2012), p. 68.

14. Crowley, Aleister (1954) *Magic Without Tears*. New York: Ordo Templi Orientis, Chapter LXIII: 'Fear, a bad astral vision.'

15. Crowley, Aleister (2012) p. 68.

16. Metzinger (2009); Carruthers (2015).

17. Treasure, Samantha Lee (2019) *Encountering Figures in Out-of-Body Experiences: A Qualitative UK Study* [unpublished bachelor's thesis], Birkbeck, University of London.

18. cf. Leadbeater, C.W., *The Theosophist*, May 1906, pp. 568–576 and June, pp. 649–659.

Chapter 14. *Sunezin* Travel in the Republic of Tuva

1. Kehoe, Alice Beck (2000) *Shamans and Religion*. Prospect Heights, Illinois: Waveland Press, Inc., pp. 2, 8, 82.

2. Bourguignon, Erika (1968) 'A cross-cultural study of dissociational states.' [Report for National Institute of Mental Health, Bethesda, Maryland.]

3. Bahrami-Rad, Duman, Becker, Anke and Henrich, Joseph (2021) Tabulated nonsense? Testing the validity of the ethnographic atlas. *Economics Letters* 204.

4. Bourguignon, Erika (1968).

5. Peters, Larry G., and Price-Williams, Douglass (1980) Towards an experiential analysis of shamanism. *American Ethnologist* 7(3): 397–418.

6. Bourguignon, Erika (1968) 'A cross-cultural study of dissociational states.' [Report for National Institute of Mental Health, Bethesda, Maryland]; Bourguignon, Erika and Evascu, Thomas, L. (1977) Altered states of consciousness within a general evolutionary perspective: a holocultural analysis. *Behavior Science Research* 12(3): 197–216; Greenbaum, L. (1973) 'Societal correlates of possession trance in Sub-Saharan Africa', in *Religion, Altered States of Consciousness and Social Change*, Erika Bourguignon (ed.), The Ohio State University Press, pp. 39–57; Winkelman, M. (1986) Trance states: a theoretical model and cross-cultural analysis. *Ethos* 14(2): 174–203.

7. Bourguignon, Erika and Evascu, Thomas, L. (1977) Altered states of consciousness within a general evolutionary perspective: a holocultural analysis. *Behavior Science Research* 12(3): 197–216.

8. Bourguignon, Erika (2004) *Suffering and healing, subordination and power: women and possession trance. Ethos* 32(4): 557–574.

9. See Zeljko, Jokic (2008) The wrath of the forgotten ongons: shamanic sickness, spirit embodiment, and fragmentary trancescape in contemporary Buryat shamanism. *Sibirica* 7(1): 23 – 50.

10. Vitebsky, Piers (1995) *The Shaman.* London: Duncan Baird Publishers, p. 136.

11. cf. Winkelman, M. (2003) Shamanism and survival. *Cultural Survival Quarterly Magazine* 27(2).

12. cf. Winkelman, Michael (2009) *Culture and Health: Applying Medical Anthropology.* San Francisco: Jossey-Bass, p. 406.

Chapter 15. Changes over Time

1. Natam (2019).
2. Ahn, Juhn, Y. (2020) 'Meditation Sickness.' In *The Oxford Handbook of Meditation*, Miguel Farias, David Brazier and Mansur Lalljee (eds.), Oxford: Oxford University Press.
3. Cooper *et al.*
4. Woollacott *et al.*
5. Greenwell, B. (1990) *Energies of Transformation: A Guide to the Kundalini Process*. Cupertino, CA: Shakti River Press.
6. Krishna, Gopi (1974), p 149.
7. Jenkins G., and Röhricht, F. (2007) From cenesthesias to cenesthopathic schizophrenia: a historical and phenomenological review. *Psychopathology* 40: 361–368.
8. Cooper, David, J., Lindahl, Jared, R., Palitsky, Roman and Britton, Willoughby, B. (2021) Like a vibration cascading through the body: energy-like somatic experiences reported by Western Buddhist meditators. *Religions* 12(12): 1042.
9. Ibid.
10. See Buttner, Phillip Ross (2016) *A Precarious Path: An Inquiry into the Travails Faced by Westerners Practicing Theravadin Buddhism* [PhD thesis], Institute of Transpersonal Psychology, Palo Alto, CA, USA.
11. Treasure, Samantha Lee (2022) *Out-of-Body Experiences in the South Korean Populace: Navigating Spontaneous and Deliberate Soul Journeys* [master's thesis], SOAS University of London.
12. Cassaniti and Luhrmann (2014).

Chapter 16. Verdical Experiences

1. Bradford, Sarah H. (1869) *Scenes in the Life of Harriet Tubman*. Auburn, NY: W.J. Moses, p. 56.

2. Larson, Kate Clifford (2004) *Bound for the Promised Land: Harriet Tubman, Portrait of an American Hero*. New York: Ballantine, p. 44.
3. Bradford, Sarah H. (1869) *Scenes in the Life of Harriet Tubman*. Auburn, NY: W.J. Moses, p. 79.
4. Tressoldi, Patrizio and Pederzoli, Luciano (2022) What is it like to be out-of-body? Phenomenal accounts of experiencers. *Qeios*.

Chapter 17. #Shifting Realities

1. Luhrmann, Tanya (2011).
2. Green, Celia and McCreery, Charles (1994), p. 75.
3. Au, Rachelle (2021) 'I shifted to Hogwarts' [online]. Available from: https://www.youtube.com/watch?v=foAf-vOLs_4 [Accessed 26 July 2024.]
4. *Reddit r/shiftingrealities* (2020). 'I just shifted successfully again!' by LearnStalkBeInformed. Available from: https://www.reddit.com/r/shiftingrealities/comments/kdbve5/i_just_shifted_successfully_again_i_was_in_my_dr/ [Accessed 25 July 2024.]
5. *Reddit r/realityshifting* (2024). 'Why Hogwarts?' by Purity_Insanity. Available from: https://www.reddit.com/r/realityshifting/comments/17eb1cm/why_hogwarts/ [Accessed 25 July 2024.]
6. Colombo, Charlotte (2022) 'Reality shifting where users say they're transported to another life has exploded on TikTok, but former shifters say it harmed their mental health.' *Business Insider* [online]. Available from: https://www.businessinsider.com/shifttok-reality-shifting-respawn-amino-reddit-tumblr-instagram-twitter-tiktok-2021-12 [Accessed 3 May 2023.]

7. Blackmore, S.J. (1986) Spontaneous and deliberate OBEs: a questionnaire survey. *Journal of the Society for Psychical Research* 53(802): 218–224.
8. Treasure, Samantha Lee (2023) Shifting to Hogwarts: astral projection, the next generation. *Parapsychology Australia Online.* Available from: https://www.youtube.com/watch?v=3WQT77GzBmw [Accessed 25 July 2024.]
9. Rositano, Joey (2013) Spirits: The story of Jeju Island's shamanic shrines. Part One: 'Story Healing.' Documentary.
10. Winkelman, Michael (2009) *Culture and Health: Applying Medical Anthropology.* San Francisco: Jossey-Bass, p. 63.
11. Luhrmann, Tanya (2011).

ACKNOWLEDGEMENTS

I would firstly like to thank my family for supporting and inspiring me, and to the brilliant team at Arcturus, in particular Tania Ahsan, Vanessa Daubney, Kelly Thompson, Felicity Forster and Linda Storey.

To my friends Sayana Tsoi, Anthony Peake, Anita Miller and Priyal Chitale, who helped me make my vision of this book a reality, and went above and beyond what most friends would do.

To Minjun for being so understanding and encouraging as this book ate up the hours we could have spent playing video games or exploring the country together.

This book wouldn't be possible if it wasn't for the experiencers and scholars I was privileged to interview. Among the many people I am grateful to are Tree Carr, Eyob Derillo, Dr Cecilia Forcato, Alejandro Dajil, Rizwan Virk, Myron Dyal, Susan Leybourne, Ryan Sprague, Graham Nicholls, Mike Marable, Rex Yapi, Damon Abraham, Michelange Quay, Sayan Saaya, Saryuna Ayusheeva, Elena Tyan, Valentino Megale, Jennifer Cox, Jennifer Kim, Caz Coronel, Ewelina Klosinska, Rodrigo Montenegro, Anna Komitska, Mike Clelland, Ladrhyn Bex, Kim McCaul, Sam Gandy, Danielle Gerald, Ryan Hurd, Pascal Michael, Jazz Rasool, Yijia Tu and Joey Rositano.

And lastly, to the following cafés for providing excellent writing spaces while I was on the move: Why We Have a Pie and Marina Café on Geoje Island (South Korea), The Barbican in London (UK), Art Café in Kyzyl (Russia), and Gimi Café in Berat (Albania).

INDEX

ABOUT THE AUTHOR

Samantha Lee Treasure grew up on a farm in Ontario, Canada, where there were multiple reports of ghost sightings, and she became especially interested in out-of-body experiences (OBEs) after her brother's experiences of such phenomena. This led her to learn how to have them herself and to pursue a BSc in Social Sciences and an MA in Medical Anthropology in order to research them cross-culturally. During her studies in London, she conducted fieldwork with experiencers in both the UK and South Korea, and she also conducted a cross-cultural and cross-disciplinary study on sleep paralysis with a psychiatry professor in Russia. Her chapter *Out-of-body Experiences in the Screen Age* for the edited volume *Deep Weird* (2023) explored the ways in which OBEs are changing in the modern day, which her second book *Phantom Media* (2026) will expand upon by covering *various* altered states. Samantha divides her time between London, UK, and Geoje Island, South Korea.